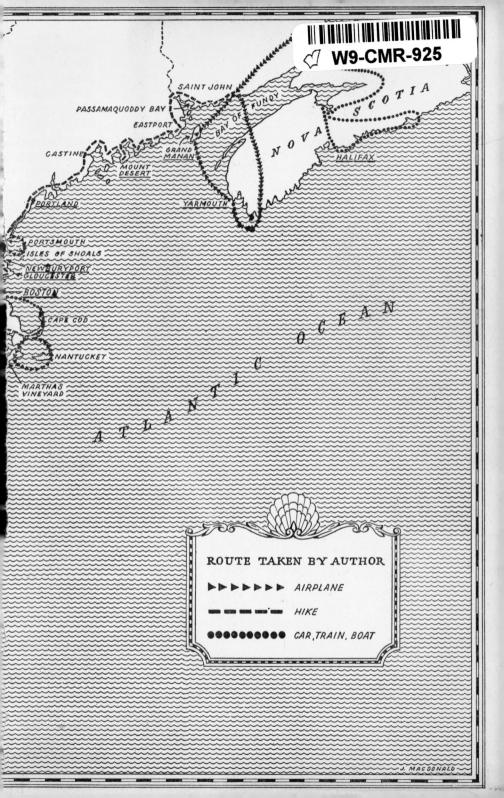

W9-CMR-925

SAINT JOHN

PASSAMAQUODDY BAY

EASTPORT

NOVA SCOTIA

BAY OF FUNDY

CASTINE

GRAND MANAN

MOUNT DESERT

HALIFAX

PORTLAND

YARMOUTH

PORTSMOUTH
ISLES OF SHOALS
NEWBURYPORT
GLOUCESTER
BOSTON

CAPE COD

NANTUCKET

MARTHAS VINEYARD

ATLANTIC OCEAN

ROUTE TAKEN BY AUTHOR

▶▶▶▶▶▶▶ AIRPLANE

━ ━ ━ ━ ━ HIKE

●●●●●●●●●● CAR, TRAIN, BOAT

J. MAC DONALD

Strange Tales from Nova Scotia To Cape Hatteras

BOOKS BY EDWARD ROWE SNOW

A PILGRIM RETURNS TO CAPE COD

FAMOUS LIGHTHOUSES OF NEW ENGLAND

PIRATES AND BUCCANEERS OF THE NEW ENGLAND COAST

THE ROMANCE OF BOSTON BAY

STORMS AND SHIPWRECKS OF NEW ENGLAND

MYSTERIES AND ADVENTURES ALONG THE ATLANTIC COAST

Strange Tales from Nova Scotia To Cape Hatteras

EDWARD ROWE SNOW

Dodd, Mead & Company · New York

PRINTED IN THE UNITED STATES OF AMERICA
BY THE CORNWALL PRESS, INC., CORNWALL, N. Y.
DESIGNED BY STEFAN SALTER

IN MEMORY OF
CAROLINE ALDEN KEATING ROWE
MY GRANDMOTHER
WHO SAILED THE SEAS WITH HER HUSBAND
CAPTAIN JOSHUA NICKERSON ROWE

Introduction

*J*T ALL began one warm afternoon in the spring of 1949 during a routine check-up at the doctor's office.

"Say," he said, "you look as if you'd gained a little weight. Step up on the scales there and we'll see."

I walked hesitantly toward the scales, for I *had* noticed lately that my clothes were getting a little tight. When the indicator finally came to rest at an alarmingly high figure, the doctor peered at it and said, "Just as I thought—you're about forty pounds overweight." He added firmly, "If I were you, I'd do something about it."

I had planned to spend the summer collecting material for a new book by traveling up and down the Atlantic Coast, and I wondered how I could possibly make the trip and concentrate on a program of pound-reduction at the same time. My last book, which had necessitated over 27,000 miles of travel, had been possible only because of the airplane, and sitting for long stretches in either airplane or automobile is not conducive to loss of weight. This book, however, was not to take me so far afield, and when later a friend proposed that I "kill two birds" by traveling on foot, I knew he had the solution to my problem.

Immediately, I read all the books on weight and exercise that I could find. I was amazed to discover that the health experts claimed that it was necessary to walk fifty-six miles in order to lose a single pound! My scientific curiosity was aroused, and I was more than ever determined to make the hike and test the claim of the experts.

INTRODUCTION

I started out from Saint John, New Brunswick, after flying over to Nova Scotia, Cape Sable Island, Yarmouth and Grand Manan Island. Soon I was hiking at a steady clip of about forty miles a day. In my best day, I covered sixty-one miles and in my worst a mere twenty-four. Altogether, I traveled 1158 miles on foot in thirty-eight days, averaging better than thirty miles a day at speeds between three and five-and-a-half miles an hour.

My weight went down at more than twice the rate the health experts had claimed possible. At the end of the hike, I had lost forty-two pounds and regained the trim figure which was mine a quarter of a century ago.

Hiking brought other benefits. I got acquainted with people I would otherwise have missed altogether. One day in Damariscotta, Maine, I met Henry Beston, the well-known New England author, and he expressed pleasure that I was hiking instead of driving. "The hiker sees things in their true relationship to the earth," Henry Beston said. "In an auto everything is a travel movie in which the windshield becomes the screen. There is no sense of reality."

My sense of reality was certainly strengthened by the two hundred and seventy-odd dogs which challenged me in the course of the hike, a bear encountered in northern Maine, a friendly porcupine and several completely uninterested skunks. I was offered no less than thirty-eight rides, all of which I had to decline, and was nearly run down by eleven different automobiles.—All in all, it was an experience I shall never forget.

As to actual writing of the book, I was helped more than ever by my wife, Anna-Myrle, whose efforts enabled me to finish the volume in time for publication. Dr. Robert E. Moody of Boston University kindly consented to read most of the chapters of this book, and his historical knowledge aided me greatly.

Besides those mentioned in the text, there are many others who were kind enough to help me with one phase or another of this book:

INTRODUCTION

William Alcott, J. J. Alicki, William Ayoub, Nat Barrows, Henry Beston, Alice Powers Blackington, Grace Bixby, Dorothy Blanchard, Clarence S. Brigham, Helen Bain, Dorothy Carmichael, Buchanan Charles, Walter G. Davis, Edward Dunn, Dorothy Fearing, Gertrude Ford, Henry Gillen, Thomas Johnson, Jimmy Jones, Margaret Hackett, Francis Haskell, Marion Haskell, Vincent Holmes, Mrs. J. W. Hobbs, John Light, Dorothy McDevitt, Florence Madison, Thomas J. Manning, Robert I. Nesmith, Mary T. Quinn, Foster M. Palmer, Melville F. Rogers, Edith W. Rounds, Marion B. Rowe, Irwin Smith, Addie E. Snow, Alice Rowe Snow, Florence Snow, John G. Snow, Walter Muir Whitehill.

In addition to the institutions mentioned in the book itself, I am grateful for the help furnished by the following: Bostonian Society, Boston Public Library, New York Public Library, Harvard College Library, Boston Athenaeum, Peabody Museum, Essex Institute, American Antiquarian Society, Rhode Island Historical Society, Block Island Historical Society and Maine Historical Society.

EDWARD ROWE SNOW

Winthrop, Massachusetts
September 7, 1949

Contents

CONTENTS

Illustrations

ILLUSTRATIONS

Part One

CAPE SABLE TO SAINT JOHN

1. Grand Manan Island and the Miracle of the Cliff

COUNTLESS shipwrecks have taken place against the steep, rocky shores of Grand Manan Island, but one disaster in particular has always held great interest for me. The story, when I first heard it fifteen years ago, was that a ship had hit the northeastern cliffs at the height of a great storm and that all aboard were lost except one sailor who had survived and miraculously climbed the sheer face of the promontory. What interested me especially was that no one before or since has been able to climb the perpendicular face of this great headland at the same location.

During the past fifty years there have been several variations of this shipwreck story, each with its own special point of interest. All agreed, however, that a man had accomplished the miracle of climbing the three-hundred foot cliff. One variation was that there was not one surviving sailor but seven; another held that two sailors, one white and one Negro, were the only ones rescued; a third maintained that seven men were saved but that all except the cliff-climber died a few days after reaching the island. According to a fourth story, the climbing sailor left a mitten halfway up the cliff and, later, when the residents doubted the truth of his story, he cited the mitten as proof. His claim, the story continued, was verified when one of the scoffers was lowered down over the side and found the mitten.

3

Before we get on with our investigation of the sailor's miraculous climb, it might be well to know a few facts about the setting of the story.

The island of Grand Manan is twice as large as all of the Bermudas; its forty-six square miles are comparable to the area of Nantucket, and though it is only six miles out from West Quoddy Head, Maine, it belongs to Canada. The earliest known spelling of its name, recorded in 1585, is *Menan*. This changes to *Menane*, as used by Champlain, and finally to *Manan* in 1713. The French introduced the prefix *Grand*, and it has been adopted by the English.

I have been told by Buchanan Charles, Grand Manan's historian, that the rock formations on the eastern side of the island belong to the Paleozoic and Precambrian eras, from 330,000,000 to a billion and a half years ago, while the formations of the north, west and south sides date back to the Triassic periods and are from 160,000,000 to 185,000,000 years old. The island is a paradise of cliffs. Those of you who have marveled at Monhegan and Block Islands will be even more impressed by the miles and miles of Manan's towering ledges formed in all shapes and sizes.—Incidentally, the great tides of the Bay of Fundy do not affect the island. The rise of the tide at Grand Manan is only from nineteen to twenty-two feet.

On my way to Grand Manan I landed at Saint John Airport in Pennfield, New Brunswick. Unfortunately, as soon as we were on the ground it began to rain, and soon fog set in. It was several days before the fog moved on, and for a while I was afraid I wouldn't be able to fly to Grand Manan at all. But finally there was a break in the leaden skies, and I called up Jack Wade to let him know that the weather was clearing and that I was ready to go. Wade, hero of many thrilling air rescues in the north country, agreed to allow his pilot, Douglas Stults, to fly me to Grand Manan.

On several previous occasions I had flown over Grand Manan at heights of between one and five thousand feet and had been fascinated by its beautiful rocky cliffs, its lighthouses, and the long sweep of the island itself. But I had never landed there. I was, therefore, full of excitement when Doug Stults and I took off in his Stinson.

The moment we were airborne, we could see Grand Manan, long and high, out ahead of us. A snowstorm coming from nowhere played tag with us for twenty minutes or so. As we flew over the Wolves, two islands located between Pennfield and Grand Manan, Grand Manan had faded from view in a blur of whirling snowflakes. The snow rattled and stung on the plexiglas, then melted to form small rivulets which streaked across the glass and flipped off into the atmosphere.

We were now approaching Grand Manan, but the thick snow prevented our seeing what was below. Since the cliffs of the island rise to four hundred feet, we went up to a safe seven hundred and circled, watching for the first signs of the island through the snow. Then, of a sudden, the storm ended, and we flew out into an area of good visibility. Our destination lay below us a quarter of a mile away, a very welcome sight to two lonely sky voyagers. Doug banked the Stinson and then circled the area twice where the clearing indicated an air strip. We dropped down for a perfect three-point landing on the cleared field, and came to a stop four hundred feet later, at a point where the pine trees were massed on both sides of us.

Doug told me that Mr. Small, the owner of the field, would probably come to meet us. Soon we heard an ancient truck chugging its way up the steep road which leads to the air field. The truck wheezed to a stop, and a middle-aged Canadian climbed out. "I'm Oscar Small," he began, "and I suppose you're Snow. We were waiting for you all day yesterday, but you never did come. It was nice and sunny here in the morning —where were you?"

5

"If you'd been over on the mainland you'd have known why we didn't leave," I answered. "It was thick fog all day long, and not a plane flew in New Brunswick."

"Well, now that you're here, what is it that interests you?"

"I want to try to get the real story of the *Lord Ashburton* wreck," I said, "and I'm especially anxious to learn the truth about the man who is said to have climbed a three-hundred-foot cliff."

"Why, that was old Lawson, the shoemaker," answered Mr. Small. "I knew him before he died and he told me the story many times. Seems to me we've got something about it over at the house. Let's go down there and see what we find."

Later I examined Mr. Small's pictures of the island while he found the clippings he had saved concerning the wreck. These confused me more than ever, for the newspaper articles didn't agree with any of the previous stories I had heard. We spent half an hour discussing the various sources of information, and then Mr. Small drove me over to the graveyard where the victims of the *Ashburton* disaster were buried. After studying the inscription and photographing the monument in the rain, I wanted to visit the headland several miles away where the ship was wrecked in 1857.

Oscar Small had work to do, but he delegated Lowell Brown, a young friend, to hike out to the headland with me. After a long, tiring walk through the forest and across Eel Brook, we reached the top of the 350-foot rise at the northernmost point of the island. Then we started downhill toward the edge of the cliff, and soon stood at the top of a sheer three hundred-foot drop.

"Here it is," said Lowell, his voice rising in excitement, for there is something about a high promontory overlooking the ocean which always makes one feel adventurous and enthusiastic. "Here's where James Lawson climbed up from the wreck of the *Ashburton*. I still don't see how it was possible." Indeed it

6

did look like an impossibility, for there seemed to be no foothold anywhere along the vertical section of that precipitous cliff. And yet we know that he did climb the cliff and lived to tell about it!

Watching our footing very carefully, we climbed down thirty or forty feet until the cliff began to drop off in perpendicular fashion. Far below on the beach a thirty-foot log looked no bigger than a toothpick. A short distance from us, on a steep shoulder which jutted out at right angles toward the sea, stood a single pine tree about thirty feet high which had braved both winter snowstorms and the summer gales.

Finally we completed our survey of Ashburton Head. But I never did see one of our objectives. Three huge circles were supposed to have been painted on the cliff to indicate the exact position of the *Ashburton* disaster. Hunt as we would, we never found them, nor could they be seen later from the plane, though we flew less than eighty feet away from the cliff. Evidently they have faded out with the years.

Returning to Oscar Small's, I decided to talk over the various stories of the shipwreck with the islanders who had gathered in his house in the idea that perhaps from them I could discover what really happened during that terrible night when the *Ashburton* struck the cliffs of Grand Manan. Our discussion of the conflicting stories was an important contribution to the final account, and when we had finished an hour later I was able to arrange the facts in some semblance of order. But several of the many variations needed more research, and I thought that the local papers available in Saint John would be the best source for the information I needed. After I had interviewed everyone on the island who was willing to help, I was ready to return to the mainland.

Doug Stults flew back with me in half an hour, and when I landed at Saint John I hastened to examine the local papers. As I had hoped, they yielded further valuable information. A month later more facts came in from George H. Russell, and then I felt that I had a complete story of what happened. The following account is as detailed and accurate as it can be at this late date, ninety-two years after the disaster.

On November 17, 1856, the *Lord Ashburton*, a ship of one thousand tons, sailed in ballast from Toulon, France, with a ship's company of twenty-nine, bound for Saint John, New Brunswick. After an uneventful voyage across the North Atlantic, Captain Owen Creary of Pictou, Nova Scotia, drew abeam of Cape Sable Island on Christmas afternoon and soon entered the Bay of Fundy. When he sighted Grand Manan Island a little later, Captain Creary was confident of reaching port within a few days at the most. But terrific headwinds soon began to form and the violence of the gale drove the *Lord Ashburton* off her course. Captain Creary was forced to put out to sea for safety.

Again and again Captain Creary tried to reach the Bay of Fundy, but each time the wind forced him back. On no less than four occasions he sighted the high cliffs of the island which was to prove his doom, and each time the changing wind drove him out to sea again. The weather grew colder and colder, and ice started to form on the ship and rigging. The waves crashed against the *Ashburton*, sending icy spray forty feet high—spray which froze within a few moments.

On Saturday night, January 17, 1857, Captain Creary, sighting Partridge Island Light at the entrance to Saint John Harbor, hoped that his worries were over. But the threatening cliffs of Grand Manan Island remained a constant danger. When the wind changed again and came in strong from the northeast, he began to wonder if he would ever reach port. Then it started to snow in a heavy, smothering downfall which soon blotted out all seamarks and landmarks, and the waves began to build up in size and strength. Before midnight all the men on the doomed ship knew that a great northeast snowstorm had set in, and their thoughts turned to their families. A few hours before, they had been within easy distance of port and now they were shut off from all contact with home by the gale.

With the coming of dawn, a terrible sight presented itself. The ocean was a seething mass of foam and waves, tossed by a high shrieking wind, and the snow was thicker than ever. There was no way of determining the ship's location, although every one of the twenty-nine sailors knew that the northeast gale was pushing them inevitably in the general direction of the cliffs of Grand Manan. That Sunday passed without any appreciable let-up in the terrible storm, and all hands waited with fear and anxiety for the darkness which soon came. Midnight passed, and still the storm continued.

Toward one o'clock in the morning, the lookout aboard the *Lord Ashburton* heard the distant sound of breakers and warned the captain of what lay ahead. But there was nothing that could be done, and the ship rushed on through the gale toward certain destruction. The booming of the distant surf grew louder and louder above the roar of the wind and the sea. Then with a final lunge the proud ship struck the rocks at the foot of the cliff, hitting the boulders at a point abreast of her forechain, as Captain Creary shouted out: "My God, my God, we are all gone!"

The chief officers ordered the boats lowered away, but the commands were futile, for no small boat could survive in that maelstrom of surf, rocks, wind and shattering timbers. The *Lord Ashburton* went over on her beam ends; the foremast and mainmast went by the board and the mizzenmast soon followed. The captain and crew gathered together on the starboard quarter had no idea in the blackness of that January night what part of the island they had struck. Each man prayed that somehow he might get ashore alive.

The seas swept in across the deck, and almost every successive wave claimed its human victim. Soon there were only ten men aboard the ship. Those ten survivors, watching their chances, decided to let themselves down into the surf in the partial lee created by the ship's quarter. One by one they leaped into the surging waves. Some attached themselves to broken fragments from the *Ashburton*, while others struck out boldly for shore.

James Lawson, a young native of Bronholm, Denmark, was among those who attempted to swim to land. After a terrific struggle against the waves and debris, he found himself nearing the shore, only to be caught in the powerful undertow. Fighting desperately, he attempted to free himself but was drawn inexorably beneath the waves. When he rose to the surface again, he could hear his drowning shipmates shouting all around him, but he was powerless to help either himself or the others nearby.

A wave pushed him high on the rocky beach, and he managed to struggle to his feet, but the next wave tore him away and drew him far out into the deep water again. Time after time, he was tossed ashore by one wave and pulled out to sea by another. At moments he believed himself safe, and then he would lose his footing and find he was out over his head. If the tide had been going out, he might have had an easier time, but now the water, dead low at the time of the wreck, began to rise again.

Finally, a wave mightier than all its predecessors overwhelmed Lawson in its terrible grasp and rushed on with him toward the rocky cliff. A moment later he was dashed against the base of the cliff. Although stunned, he clung desperately to a rocky abutment there. Before the next wave could catch him, Lawson struggled away from its grasp and collapsed just above the reach of the oncoming tide. After resting awhile, he tried to stand, but the effort was too great. He needed to collect his strength, but before he could do so, the tide came in and caught him at the base of the great cliff. Finding a projecting pinnacle, Lawson grasped it with both hands.

Now every wave surged against him. He was soon waist-deep

in the water, but he still clung tenaciously to the pinnacle. Realizing that he was fighting a losing battle with the oncoming tide, Lawson cried aloud in his desperation. To his amazement, his cry was answered by a shipmate who had managed to get ashore from the wreck. The sailor grasped Lawson and helped him to climb onto a projecting shelf just above the high tide mark. There Lawson rested until dawn.

When the sun came up, he saw that his friend had disappeared. Though Lawson did not know it, the man had gone just around the bend of the cliff where five others from the wreck were huddled on the narrow shore.

The cliff towered three hundred feet above Lawson, and he knew that unless he climbed to the top to get aid, he would freeze before night fell. He had lost his shoes and socks in his fight to gain the shore, and he realized that his feet were freezing even as he began the climb which made his name famous through the years on Grand Manan Island.

The northeast storm was bringing ever-increasing winds, but in their terrific surge up the cliff they actually helped Lawson as they swirled around him. The winds of sixty and seventy miles an hour which hit the Grand Manan cliff that January day were to figure prominently in the remarkable feat which Lawson accomplished.

Lawson stopped to rest when he had reached the more difficult part of the cliff. Then he glanced again above him at the towering precipice. Determined to reach the top, he stood up, and the force of the wind seemed to brace him against the rock. As he began to work his way up the sheer face of the promontory, he found that the wind was so strong that he could support his weight by grasping tiny crevices and ledges which ordinarily would not be sufficient to help a climber. Inch by inch he ascended, leaving behind a trail of blood from his torn feet.

Three-quarters of the way up he reached a sheer fifteen-foot wall, smooth as the side of a ship, with no hand-holds at all. He knew that he could not scale it. Clinging to a crevice 225 feet in the air with the unbroken surface of the cliff above him, he felt that his last hope was gone and that his life was about to end.

But James Lawson was a stubborn Dane. After thinking the situation over carefully, he retraced his tracks twenty-five feet down, inched his aching body across to a ledge some distance away, and finally discovered a fresh trail of minute crevices which led upwards. The wind was now blowing about eighty miles an hour and seemed literally to push him up the cliff. Foot by foot he neared the summit. At last, the top of the cliff was just ahead. The last few feet were much easier to scale and finally he achieved his goal. Collapsing helplessly at the top of the three-hundred-foot cliff, he fell into unconsciousness.

Half an hour later he awoke. Rested considerably, he was able to get to his feet. Ahead of him were deep snowdrifts, and he doggedly struggled through them. Then in the distance he saw a barn. Dragging his bleeding feet step by step he eventually reached the building, pulled open the door and collapsed on a pile of hay. Now that he had accomplished his purpose, Lawson fell into a deep sleep of exhaustion.

An hour later the snow stopped falling and the wind swung around to the north. This was the customary signal for Mr. James Tatton, who lived nearby, to hike out to the headland and scan the ocean. Many of us enjoy doing that very thing today. But it was fortunate for Lawson that Tatton took his usual after-storm walk that January 19th, for he came across the bloody footsteps in the snow and followed them to the barn. There he discovered the shivering, unconscious form of James Lawson. After reviving him, Tatton half-led and half-carried Lawson to the nearest residence, the home of Mr. and Mrs. Bennett. Here Lawson was given treatment.

Others were sent to discover if anyone else from the wreck might still be alive, and after several hours they found six men clustered at the foot of the towering cliff. The tide had gone down, and the men were carried along the base of the cliff to safety.

After rescuing these six survivors, the island volunteers returned to look for more victims of the shipwreck. Rounding another headland as they made their way along the rocky beach, they came across a long row of men evidently sitting down to rest. The leader of the rescuers stepped up to the first man and spoke to him. There was no answer—every man in that long row was dead, either by freezing or by drowning. Later that day the twenty-two lifeless bodies were carried up to the graveyard, where they were buried together in a single plot. The brother of Owen Creary arrived from Pictou later that year to claim the captain's body, but the twenty-one sailors still lie in the cemetery on Grand Manan. Little is known about them, except that one sailor named Sweeney came from Portland, Maine, and that the chief mate was a native of Brighton, England.

Early the next month the seven survivors were taken ashore to the Marine Hospital at Saint John. As a result of his climb up the face of the cliff, James Lawson lost his toes and part of both feet. It is said that his stay in the Saint John hospital lasted more than five years. When he finally recovered, Lawson returned to Grand Manan Island and set himself up as a shoemaker there.

James Lawson was living on the island in 1872 when the *Sarah Sloane* was wrecked near the spot where he had been cast against the cliff in 1857. On this occasion only one man lived to tell the story, a young Baltimore Negro named Charles Turner. The other seven crew members were drowned. It is said that at the time of the *Sloane* shipwreck Lawson was extremely solicitous on Turner's behalf and assisted in getting him to Captain Eben Gaskill's residence. Turner's feet were badly frozen and later they had to be amputated.

The remains of the other members of the crew were eventually found on the shore, horribly mutilated by the pounding on the rocks, and were buried in the cemetery beside those lost from the *Ashburton*. Two of them were afterwards removed to the mainland.

In 1874 the Canadian Government erected a fog signal near Ashburton Head at Long Eddy Point, around the headland northwest of the location of the two shipwrecks. James Tatton, the man who found Lawson near death in the barn, was appointed as the new fog-signal keeper.

Lawson remained at his chosen vocation, shoemaker of Grand Manan Island, and eventually became a good workman. He was always troubled by his feet, of course, and walking was difficult for him. But he led a long and full life, during which he married and had two children. He died at a ripe old age on February 22, 1918.

My first contact with Lawson's story came one day when I was doing research work for my *Storm and Shipwreck* book. Captain Ernest Delesdernier Sproul was telling me of shipwrecks around Quoddy Head, and he mentioned James Lawson and the *Ashburton*. He said that the sailor dropped a mitten halfway up the cliff and that when the others later doubted his climbing the cliff, he challenged them to lower a man over the edge to verify the story. When the mitten was discovered, the doubting Thomases were forced to believe that Lawson had climbed the cliff.

Captain Sproul's story may be correct, for it does fit into the circumstances of the wreck. But the other accounts mentioned earlier can be altogether disregarded. We do know that there were seven men saved from the *Ashburton*, but obviously the story of the young Negro's survival has been confused with the *Sloane* disaster fifteen years later.

Scores of other wrecks have occurred on the island, including a French ship more than two centuries ago, the bark *Mavourneen* in 1866, the *Humber* in 1872, and the two-master *Nelson*

Y. McFarland, lost with all hands during the winter of 1936-7. But for sheer drama and spectacular bravery, none of them can approach the *Lord Ashburton* disaster when James Lawson climbed a three-hundred-foot cliff to save himself and six others from death.

2. Wrecks Off Cape Sable

C APE SABLE in Nova Scotia and Cape Cod in New England are the best known capes in their respective regions, and their contours make them recognizable to all. Cape Cod goes northward and then describes a counter-clockwise twist that just escapes being a 360-degree turn. Cape Sable and the Nova Scotian peninsula, however, firmly face southwest in the general direction of New England. Both capes, because of their exposed locations, have destroyed hundreds of vessels of all types through the years.

In my *New England Storms and Shipwrecks* I have described or listed more than 1100 shipwrecks which have occurred in the vicinity of Cape Cod. The list of Cape Sable wrecks I have made totals 334, covering vessels wrecked between Saint Mary's Bay and Lockeport, Nova Scotia. From that list I have chosen only the outstanding disasters for this chapter.

The strangest wreck of all was that of the schooner *Cod Seeker*, which capsized on May 9, 1877. I had first heard of the *Cod Seeker* from Mr. Frank Goudey of Brockton, Massachusetts. He was anxious to have me substantiate his story by the records themselves, but, unfortunately, he was so young at the time of the wreck that he wasn't sure of its date. He thought, however, that the disaster occurred in either 1880 or 1881. It was many days later and after one hundred hours of actual research that I found my first clue, an item in an 1877 issue of the *Boston Post*, to the capsizing of the schooner. From then on it was merely a matter of visiting Yarmouth and Port Maitland

and examining all available material pertaining to the unusual event.

In the middle of April, 1877, the two-masted schooner *Cod Seeker* went down the ways at Coffin's Yard, Clyde River, Nova Scotia. Later that month she proceeded to Halifax, where she was outfitted for a fishing trip. On Monday, May 7, she cleared from Halifax with a crew of thirteen. This was her first fishing voyage, and her master, Captain Philip Brown, was determined to return a good load of cod when he sailed back into port. The ship's chief owner was Mr. Reuben Stoddart of Bear Point, and Stoddart's adopted son sailed as part of the crew.

All went well until Wednesday night when the schooner was running under foresail and jib off Baccaro Light. Suddenly, at about ten o'clock, a terrific squall hit the *Cod Seeker*, and over she went, capsizing without the slightest warning in ten fathoms of water. Leaping for one of the dories which floated free, Captain Brown and two crew members scrambled to safety. By this time it was blowing a gale, and in the darkness Captain Brown was unable to see if anyone else was alive. He felt that all were not lost, but since his dory had no thole pins and drifted quickly away from the capsized schooner, he was helpless.

Actually, two men had drowned in the cabin and another sailor, Ziba Hunt, had been sucked into one of the hatchways to his death. But there were still five others clinging to the over-turned bilges. These men grabbed the lines which had been dangling over the sides at the time of the capsizing and, securing themselves to the keel as best they could, waited for rescue. Unknown to them, there were two uninjured men trapped in the forecastle with enough air to keep alive for days!

Early the next morning the dory carrying Captain Brown and the two fishermen was swept ashore at Cape Sable Island. Here there were thirty fishing boats in the harbor, but the men were afraid to go out on account of the high gale. Captain Brown told them all his story of the disaster and pleaded for someone to go in search of survivors. Only one ship's master volunteered, Captain John Crowell of the schooner *Matchless*. Leaving the harbor within an hour, Crowell encountered severe winds and almost capsized his own ship, but he lashed the men to the jib-boom so that they could take in sail. In this way, he managed to navigate his vessel until they reached the vicinity of the *Cod Seeker's* disaster.

After maneuvering in the area for over an hour, Captain Crowell decided to put back into port again, for he reasoned that no sailor exposed to such a gale could survive it. At about this time he sighted the bilges of the capsized schooner eight miles southwest of Cape Sable Island. Sailing closer, Crowell spotted five men lashed to the windward side of the vessel. With skill and daring he brought his ship in to the lee of the wreck, and one by one, began to remove the exhausted sailors to safety aboard the *Matchless*. He managed to rescue four of them but when he returned for the fifth the unfortunate man slipped into the sea. No one could save him because of the gale.

Captain Brown sailed into Barrington that afternoon with the four rescued men, and they returned to their homes in Bear Point that night.

Unknown to either Captain Brown or the men he saved, there were still two men alive aboard the *Cod Seeker*—Samuel Atwood and James E. Smith, adopted son of Reuben Stoddart, the ship's chief owner. These two had been in the forecastle when the schooner capsized and, to their amazement, no water poured in to drown them. The hatchway was practically sealed off because of the storm, and at first the water leaked in only gradually. The schooner floated at an angle of about forty degrees to starboard, with her head higher than her stern. The salt bins had spilled out in the hold, and this prevented the schooner from righting herself later.

Samuel and James resigned themselves to death when the

water finally forced open the hatchway and started to pour in on them in the terrible confusion of the pitch black forecastle. But a short time later when the inundation stopped, the water was only about four and a half feet deep. The two began to wonder if they might not be saved after all. Perhaps they could live until rescue, for there were cookies and bread enough for several days. But their water supply was less than a quart! They'd have to go sparingly with that. Later the following day, when their four comrades were saved, they knew nothing about it because of the violent pitching and rolling of the schooner in the gale.

The next morning, the water in the forecastle began to rise, and soon it reached Smith's bunk. Still secured to the forecastle deck, the bunk was upside down and at the top of the over-turned forecastle. The two men crawled onto the bottom of the bunk to keep away from the rising water around them. Then, to their horror, they felt the schooner sinking. Down, down, down it went till it hit bottom with a dull thud, first at the mastheads and then at the hull. When the schooner had finally settled on the floor of the ocean, she was over on her beam ends more than before. The two men were now forced to adjust themselves to the new angle at which the vessel lay. They had to leave the under side of the bunk and brace themselves as best they could by clinging to the sides of the bunk under water up to their shoulders. It was much more difficult than before, and the realization of their unhappy lot was no encouragement. They were trapped alive in a sunken schooner at the bottom of the sea!

The hours went by, and every so often the schooner shifted to a new position on the ocean floor. It was a ghastly feeling to realize that they would probably never escape from their ocean prison. Both Samuel Atwood and James Smith prayed to God that they would be spared, but their prayers seemed hopeless.

Some time later—neither could ever tell exactly when—the

Cod Seeker gave a shiver, righted herself just a trifle, and then started to move, not along the ocean floor again, but up toward the surface. The men felt the schooner surge upward and clung as best they could to the increased slant of the bunk. A few minutes later they could tell that the ship had reached the surface of the sea, for not only did she settle down to a steady, swaying movement but she went over to her original position with her bilges out of water. The men crawled back atop the bottom of the bunk. The *Cod Seeker* was drifting along on the ocean, her course guided by the wind and tide. But she was still bottom up, and it appeared that she would stay that way.

Talking it over shortly afterwards in their old place on the bunk, James and Samuel decided correctly that the schooner had gone down because of the heavy bins of salt but that when the salt had finally dissolved into the water, the specific gravity of the schooner was affected and she was able to rise to the surface.*

Though their return to the surface was a stroke of luck, the men were still in a terrible predicament, and during the next twenty-four hours it was a constant struggle to keep alive. They were still able to munch the bread and cookies, but their drinking water was completely exhausted by now. Added to their troubles was a fresh gale which set the schooner tossing and twisting. At one time it seemed that the storm would send the *Cod Seeker* to the bottom again, but finally the gale subsided.

The morning of the next day arrived. It was Sunday and both men prayed that the Sabbath might bring them help. They were able to recognize the sun's reflection in the water as it came up through the open hatchway. But by this time the air in the forecastle was growing stale, and the two developed violent headaches and nausea.

Noon came, and the men found themselves suffering terribly

---

* Captain Frank H. Peterson of the Boston Marine Society remembers a four-masted salt schooner which did the same thing off Cape Hatteras.

from thirst. They realized that they had been entombed in the forecastle for over eighty hours and knew that help would have to come soon or it would be too late. So cramped and uncomfortable were they in their perch in the forecastle that on one occasion they almost decided to dive down through the hatchway and swim out into the sunshine where they might be seen and rescued. But in their weakened condition they realized that they might not reach the surface and that if they did, they might later wash off the bilges to their death. So they remained in their cramped quarters in the forecastle and prayed all day for rescue.

Toward evening an American schooner, the *Ohio*, commanded by Captain Dorr, was sailing through the waters west of Seal Island. Hailing from Vinalhaven, Maine, the fifty-nine foot schooner was homeward bound. Suddenly the lookout sighted what he believed was a whale and called Captain Dorr's attention to it. The schooner was brought in close, and all hands saw that they had come upon a derelict. Captain Dorr sent two men over in a dory to see if they could discover the name of the vessel. When they began to walk along the bilges, they heard a tapping sound coming from under their feet. The two fishermen, of French descent, believed that they were hearing the ghosts of drowned men and hurried back to the *Ohio*, where they told their story to Captain Dorr. The master laughed at them.

"Nonsense," he cried, "there are no ghosts. I'll go back myself." Calling two other hands, he rowed across to the derelict and went aboard the bilges. He could hear definite knocks and bumps coming from under his feet. Dorr struck the planking with his boots and then roared at his men, "There's someone alive down there! Go back aboard and get two axes—and be quick about it." While the men were gone he banged reassuringly to let the trapped men know they were going to be saved.

Meanwhile, Samuel Atwood and James Smith had been passing through various stages of ecstasy and despair. First they heard the heavy boots of the Frenchmen over their heads. They had responded by ripping a two-by-four piece of board from the bunk and pounding with it against the bilges. But there was no answer at all, and for the next ten minutes there was absolute silence. Perhaps they would not be rescued after all! Then when Captain Dorr landed on the *Cod Seeker*, they heard his steps and rapped frantically again. A few minutes later they were intensely relieved when an answering thump sounded directly above them, followed by another and then another. They pounded back in frenzied fashion, and the next sound they heard was that of Captain Dorr's axe crashing into the bottom of the *Cod Seeker*. The men in the forecastle realized that they had been discovered and both sent up silent prayers to God.

But there was still danger ahead. Two heavy axes now descended on the new planking of the bilges in an effort to cut a hole through and release the men. The wood began to crunch, and then the tip of an axe pierced the forecastle bulkhead. The result of the next blow was a fearful whistling sound as the air in the schooner, greatly compressed by the tons of water in the forecastle, rushed through the tiny opening. Again and again the axes descended, and with each blow, the hole in the planking widened. But suddenly Atwood noticed to his alarm that the water was rising higher in the forecastle. The release of the compressed air had once more affected the stability of the schooner, and she was sinking lower and lower into the sea.

Now desperate, James and Samuel tried to force themselves through the hole, but it was not large enough for either man. James worked his head and shoulder out into the sunlight, but he could get no further.

"Get in there before it's too late," cried Captain Dorr, and he pushed James back into the forecastle. The axes began again, and a few minutes later the opening was large enough to allow the two survivors, imprisoned for more than ninety hours, to leave their schooner.

Within half an hour they were resting in bunks aboard the *Ohio*. They were taken into Shag Harbor, and two hours later Samuel Atwood and James Smith returned to their homes at Bear Point, where they were greeted as if returned from the dead.

The derelict was found at sea and towed into Port Maitland. Here it was brought up on the shore at high tide. Frank B. Goudey, who gave me the first account of this story, was a boy of about thirteen, living in Port Maitland at the time, and he assisted in the pumping out of the schooner. The three dead members of the crew were found in the craft as she was being emptied of water. When the hole chopped in the bilges was repaired with fresh lumber, the schooner was ready for fishing again.

One day as the final planking was being placed over the hole, two men were seen standing nearby watching the proceedings. No one recognized that they were James Smith and Samuel Atwood. Finally they made themselves known, and told their incredible story. When they had finished and walked away, every man on the beach was silent. Smith and Atwood had not been recognized because both had visibly aged from twenty to twenty-five years during their awful experience in the overturned forecastle of the *Cod Seeker*.

THE PETRIFIED WOMAN

IN DECEMBER, 1837, the brig *Amaranth* sailed from Shelburne, Nova Scotia, bound for New York, with a load of granite. On December 18, she reached a point near the east side of Mud Island in Lobster Bay, almost due west from Cape Sable. There were eight persons aboard the brig: Captain George Card of

Windsor; Mr. Boyce of Halifax; David Cary of Bath, Maine; the cook and his wife; two sailors; and Margaret Flynn, a beautiful young girl from Waterford, Ireland. Margaret was a charming passenger and attracted the attention of everyone aboard.

When the wind died down, Captain Card anchored off Mud Island, but a violent storm hit the granite brig that midnight, and the *Amaranth* began to drag anchor. Suddenly the cable snapped, and the helpless vessel was soon driven ashore, where it went to pieces almost at once. The captain and two sailors were able to swim to the beach safely, but all the others perished. Later that week the bodies of the five victims came up on the shore, and they were carried across to the headland to be buried.

Thirty years later, a visitor with an overwhelming curiosity heard of the graves, learned where the beautiful Margaret Flynn had been buried, and for some unexplained reason decided to dig down and view her body.

The intruder was amazed by what he discovered. As he scraped away the final fragments of dirt from her remains, he found that her body had petrified into what looked like gray marble—except for the head which had withered away! Shocked by what he had uncovered, the visitor quickly buried the body again and fled from the scene.

That night, however, while in his cups, the island visitor told others of his unusual discovery. Within the next few years, after the discovery became common knowledge, several groups visited the headland at different times and opened the grave. Each party confirmed the terrible disclosure. Finally, during the period when Captain George Kinney lived at Mud Island, he became so disturbed by the repeated exhumations of the girl's body that he decided to put an end to it for all time.

Choosing a dark, moonless night, he went to the headland. Setting his lantern down close to the gravestone, he dug for two hours. Finally the body of Margaret Flynn was uncovered for the last time. Captain Kinney clumsily wrapped the remains of the young Irish girl in a sheet he had brought with him. Climbing out of the grave with the petrified remains, he set them down carefully, filled up the hole, and smoothed over the ground. An hour later he had taken the body to another part of the island, where he dug a new grave and re-buried the body. To this day no one has been able to discover the location of the girl's grave, so perhaps it is now safe for all time from the visits of the curious. In that secret location the body of Margaret Flynn, the petrified woman, still lies buried.

THE "HUNGARIAN"

ONE of the most heart-rending disasters in Cape Sable history was the loss of the steamship *Hungarian*, which sailed from Liverpool, England, on February 8, 1860. At three o'clock in the morning of February 20, she struck on the Horse Race, Cape Sable, at the height of a great storm. Thomas Nickerson, standing on the nearby shore at that very moment, saw the lights from the steamer. With the coming of dawn the *Hungarian* was visible on the Great Rip. Her mainmast and mizzenmast were still standing, with scores of desperate people clinging for their lives to the spars and masts as the waves swept across her decks. Her foremast had already gone by the board, and she appeared to be breaking up. By ten o'clock that morning both masts with their swaying human cargoes had crashed into the sea, and shortly afterwards the funnel of the ship also sunk below the surface.

The shores had been crowded with observers since an early hour, and at the fall of each mast there was an involuntary cry of anguish up and down the beach. But there was nothing that could be done, for the giant waves lashing the shore prevented the launching of a single lifeboat or whaleboat, and the stunned watchers on land gazed with sadness at the disintegration of the great steamer. There were 205 persons aboard the *Hungarian*, and although she was almost ashore when she was wrecked, the seas were so savage that every passenger and crew member perished. Not a single soul was able to swim ashore, and those who attempted to do so were literally smothered by the force of the waves.

. THE "PARAGON"

ON SUNDAY morning, December 20, 1868, the brig *Paragon* from Saint John, New Brunswick, anchored off Hilton's Head, Nova Scotia. She was dismasted and in distress, and several boats went out to her aid. There they discovered a story of horror.

The *Paragon* had left Saint John the previous Friday at noon, and struck a heavy gale from the northwest which started the vessel leaking badly. Even with the pumps going constantly, the water continued to gain, and by eleven that night there was six feet of water in the hold. The vessel became practically unmanageable. The fore and aft sails slatted off, and the seas broke completely over the brig. In the very cold weather, the spray froze to solid ice, and the vessel sank lower and lower in the ocean.

At quarter of two the following morning, the vessel lurched heavily and went over on her beam ends. At this time the steward was drowned in the cabin and the cabin-boy, George, disappeared over the side. An hour later the masts broke off at the deck, and the brig slowly righted, full of water. Eight o'clock came, and seaman Joseph Harris from Cornwall, Wales, was found frozen to death. The others were slowly freezing, and they allowed the brig to drift by itself where ever it might go.

The following day and night were horrible to recall. Second Mate McGee died while lashed to the poop, and the others felt that they would soon follow him. The bodies of the dead sailors were becoming badly mangled, and the survivors threw them into the sea. At four the next morning the brig had drifted to within four hundred yards of Yarmouth Light itself. An hour later the frost-bitten survivors managed to heave the anchor overboard before they collapsed on the icy deck.

Within three hours the *Paragon* was seen from shore, and the surviving crew members were rescued by men who came out to them in boats. They were taken to the local hospital and treated for frostbite and exposure. Fortunately, all the survivors recovered from their experience and left for home within a week.

THE SHIPWRECK WITH A HAPPY ENDING

A PERIOD of extreme poverty befell the Lower Nova Scotian peninsula shortly before Christmas in the year 1881. The people suffered acutely, and many died of malnutrition. However, there were several who predicted that the Lord would find a way to alleviate the sufferings of the poor Canadians. But Christmas came and went, and it was not until a few days later that help presented itself in a strange manner.

On December 30, 1881, at nine-thirty in the morning, the steamer *Moravian* of the Allan Line struck on Mud Island and was totally wrecked. Her cargo consisted of 701,241 pounds of cheese, 109,340 pounds of lard, 1108 fresh quarters of beef, 1672 bushels of peas, 500 sacks of flour, 116 barrels of pork, 448 barrels of apples, 546 cases of canned meats, 169 cases of mutton, and 29,285 bushels of wheat.

These supplies were a godsend to the local inhabitants, and by the time they had finished their salvage operations, the food shortage in Nova Scotia was at an end. Men, starving the week before, hardly noticed the loss of a quarter of beef or a sack of flour if it fell from an overloaded cart in being transported from the scene of the shipwreck.

Luckily, the wreck proved a loss only in money and supplies, for every person aboard the *Moravian* was saved. The hull of the vessel, originally valued at $400,000, was sold at auction on June 12, 1883, for $4,000.

BLONDE ROCK

THROUGHOUT the oceans of the world are many rocks and ledges which have proven an exceptional hazard to ships and steamers. A rock of this ominous type is located off the southern shores of Cape Sable, about sixteen miles southwest of Cape Sable Island and three miles south of Seal Island. Its name, Blonde Rock, is known to many mariners. All of them fear it, for hundreds of people have lost their lives there. At normal low tides it protrudes about two feet above the surface, but it extends under water for quite a distance both north and south of the area.

There is a conical warning buoy a short distance from the rock itself, and two miles to the southwest lies Blonde Rock Buoy, flashing its white light at night and warning the unwary mariner with its whistle by day and night. In the daytime one may also read the words *Blonde Rock* painted in large white letters on the red cylindrical buoy.

Many ships have met their fate at Blonde Rock. Some say that a French ship, the *Blonde,* was the first to meet disaster here, but this is merely a tradition. The first important disaster was the wreck of the famous clipper ship *Staffordshire,* which hit the rock at midnight, December 29, 1853. After floating free, she sank a few hours later, carrying 178 persons to their death. Forty-four were later rescued. This was one of the

greatest clipper ship disasters on record and took the life of a
well-known Cape Cod shipmaster, Captain Josiah Richardson.

Thirty-eight years later, on November 1, 1891, the new Fur-
ness liner *Ottawa*, commanded by Captain Dixon, crashed
against Blonde Rock at dead low tide, piercing a jagged hole in
her bottom. As the tide turned and came in, the seas increased
in fury, breaking over the decks of the *Ottawa*, which had
swung around and listed to starboard. The waves swept the
entire length of the steamer, and as the tide came in the steamer
filled with water. At low tide that night, the *Ottawa* was submerged at the stern and dry at the bow.

The captain now decided that he would have to abandon the
Ottawa. The port lifeboat was launched and the only woman
aboard, Stewardess Annie Lindsey, was put aboard with four
men. But before they were ready to row away the painter
snapped and the lifeboat was carried two ship's lengths from the
steamer when a giant wave capsized it. Annie Lindsay was
never seen again, but two men soon crawled on top of the over-
turned lifeboat. The boat drifted toward shore, and everyone
on the *Ottawa* believed that the others had also drowned. But
a second mighty breaker seized the lifeboat and righted it, revealing the two others clinging to the thwarts. They had kept
alive by breathing the air trapped under the lifeboat when it
capsized. All four men soon reached the shores of Seal Island,
where the residents helped them from the high surf.

Out on the *Ottawa*, the port jollyboat was made ready and
launched, and, in her, the pilot and four men reached Seal Island
safely. Shortly afterwards the storm increased, and Captain
Dixon ordered buckets of oil to be poured on the sea to windward. When the oil had calmed the troubled waters, another
lifeboat was put over, and every remaining man but the captain
jumped aboard. When it came Captain Dixon's turn, he leapt
over the side just as a severe squall hit the lifeboat, pushing it

away from the *Ottawa*. It was more than ten minutes before he could be rescued from his perilous position clinging to a line from the side of his ship, but seven hours later Captain Dixon and his crew landed safely at Seal Island.

On April 5, 1897, the steamer *Assaye* was wrecked at Blonde Rock. All sixty-three men aboard were saved, but the *Assaye's* wrecked hull remained to menace other ships.

On January 1, 1898, the steamer *Gerona* struck the wreck of the *Assaye* at Blonde Rock, but pulled off and altered her course in an effort to reach land. Leaking badly, the *Gerona* foundered twenty minutes later, just as four lifeboats were pulling away. One of them was smashed against the ship, but the sailors from the smashed craft were picked up by the other boats. Two of the lifeboats landed at Seal Island. The captain's boat headed for Mud Island, and here he found a solid white line of breakers ahead. Watching his chance, he steered the lifeboat into the beach successfully and all were saved.

Blonde Rock, which has cost the lives of several hundred persons within the last century, still stands sixteen miles off Cape Sable, but Blonde Rock Buoy with its blinker and whistle is now there to ward off future disaster to the unwary ship at sea.

THE "CITY OF MONTICELLO"

THE loss of the Yarmouth-bound paddle-wheeler *Monticello* on November 10, 1900, not two years after the steamer *Portland* sank off Cape Cod, caused great excitement and consternation in the Maritime Provinces. I have always been anxious to learn the story of a side-wheeler wreck which might shed further light on the fate of the steamer *Portland* which sank November 27, 1898, with the loss of all 176 persons aboard. Scores of theories concerning her sinking have been advanced; each new theory wins its adherents.* It seemed to me that a careful study of the wreck of the *Monticello* would be of great value in explaining the mystery of the *Portland's* loss. So it was in Yarmouth that I found my answer to that mystery in the disaster which befell the *Monticello*.

Built in 1866 in Wilmington, Delaware, and originally known as the *City of Norfolk*, the *Monticello* was almost sixty feet shorter than the *Portland* and had one stack instead of the two the *Portland* carried.

On Friday morning, November 9, 1900, the *City of Monticello* left her pier at Saint John, New Brunswick, bound across the Bay of Fundy to Nova Scotia. Proceeding on her regular course, she was aided at first by a strong northwest wind, but when she reached a point off the Petit Passage, the wind was increasing in intensity and making it difficult to keep the *Monticello* on an even keel. The Petit Passage is located between Long Island and Digby Neck, and even under good conditions it requires skillful navigation. But when Captain Thomas M. Harding, master of the *Monticello*, reached the passage, it was a wild, heaving mass of surf and foam.

Exerting all his skill, Captain Harding brought the sidewheeler safely through the passage, but when he reached Saint Mary's Bay he found that conditions were even worse. The wind had increased to gale force, and almost every other wave was hitting high against the vessel. His course from Petit Passage was almost southwest, leaving his starboard beam exposed to the sea.

Before long the starboard paddle-wheel was nearly out of the water because of the strong list to port which the *Monticello* was developing. Then a tremendous sea boarded the steamer, sliding along her stern and beam to enter over the starboard bow, smash in the forward saloon and do other serious damage. Immediately, the list to port became more pronounced, and

---

* In 1945 I contracted with a diver to visit the wreck, and his findings are elsewhere in this book.

water began to pour into the hold through a seam in the hull itself. The pumps were put into service, and for many hours they held their own with the inrushing sea.

Captain Harding called a conference with his officers. They considered stranding the *Monticello* on the western Nova Scotia shore near Church Point but decided it would be a dangerous lee beach. They agreed that an attempt should be made to reach Yarmouth. But the storm grew steadily, and by the time Cape Saint Mary's was reached, a terrible hurricane was lashing the coast. The water continued to rush into the hold, and by eight o'clock the next morning the sea came in faster than the pumps could force it out. By now the starboard paddle-wheel was out of water completely, and the *Monticello* had a list of about forty-five degrees. Soon afterwards the steamer swung around into the wind and became completely unmanageable.

The water in the hold crept higher and higher. At about nine o'clock that morning a plank must have given way, for the seas poured in and the pumps were rendered completely helpless. Captain Harding ordered the cargo thrown overboard through the port gangways, but this proved ineffectual. Although the jib was set, the steamer continued to head into the wind, which blew harder and harder from the northwest.

Finally the water reached the fires in the boilers and the engines stopped. Without power, the steamer rolled heavily, and Captain Harding ordered a drag put out to keep the steamer before the sea, with her stern to the wind. But everything failed, and the *Monticello* was soon in the trough of the sea, rolling fearfully with each successive wave. Shortly afterwards, at about eleven-thirty in the morning, she began to settle in the water, still at an angle of forty-five degrees, approximately four miles west of Chegoggin Point.

Cape Fourchu and Yarmouth were not far away, but Captain Harding knew that the *Monticello* could never reach her destination. She was a doomed ship, and the only thing he could do was to order the lifeboats put over. He stepped out on the bridge and gave the orders which sent the lifeboats over the side of the *Monticello* and down into the water.

Early that same morning passenger Albert S. Eldridge of Yarmouth had a talk with stewardess Katherine Smith. He sat down beside her at a table in the saloon, trembling visibly. Glancing across at Miss Smith, he said, "You know, Miss Smith, my people don't even know that I am aboard the *Monticello!* It'll be quite a shock when they find out."

"Don't talk like that!" she replied. "Everything will be all right—have no fear."

"I wish I could agree with you. Aren't you the least bit frightened?"

"Of course not," she replied. "Why, the *Monticello* has made this trip hundreds of times, and in worse weather, too. I'm not the least bit afraid. Don't you get worried, either—that's the worst thing you can do."

Eldridge rose from the table and stood looking down at her for a moment. "I'm really not scared. All I can say is that God will protect us no matter what happens." Eldridge disappeared for a minute or two and then returned to ask Miss Smith if he should not put on a lifebelt. She agreed that he should, and he went away again.

Then Purser Everett Hilton entered the saloon. "I'm afraid that I'm getting very dizzy," he confided. "Besides, I must admit that I'm worried and nervous."

In the women's quarters Miss Elsie MacDonald had stayed in bed until the last. At about nine in the morning Miss Smith, the stewardess, told her that she'd have to get up and dress, for all were warned that they might have to take to the lifeboats. Miss Ida Lawrence was the only other woman aboard, and the three went up on deck together. Although they had been nervous before, the knowledge that they might be abandoning the

Monticello in a bad storm made them realize fully that they were all in a very serious predicament.

When the time came to launch the lifeboats, every person aboard seemed to gain in courage and strength, and the boats were put over with determination and calmness. The first to jump in from the deck above was Captain A. Norman Smith, who was traveling as a passenger. He was quickly followed by Third Officer James E. Flemmings, and Quartermaster Wilson Cook. It was a long leap into the lifeboat, so when the time came for the three women to jump, the men braced themselves to catch them. Miss Smith leaped first and was safely caught. Then Ida Lawrence landed in the arms of the men, and was followed almost at once by the last woman aboard the *Monticello*, Elsie MacDonald of Yarmouth. Second Officer Murphy made a successful flying leap into the lifeboat, to take over the tiller, and then the craft was pushed away from the sinking side-wheeler.

Meanwhile, two other lifeboats which had been put over were in trouble. The second had gone under almost at once although still attached to the davit on the steamer, and the third had both davit-hooks on when the *Monticello* gave definite indications that she was going down.

Still listing at an angle of forty-five degrees, the *Monticello* suddenly gave an ominous pitch, and then slowly rolled over on her beam ends, carrying the last two lifeboats and their unfortunate occupants with her. A woman in the first lifeboat who was watching the terrible scene suddenly stood up and shouted at the top of her lungs: "Oh, my God, the steamer is breaking in two!"

The 232-foot side-wheeler was, indeed, slowly tearing apart amidships, and the screams and cries of the passengers still aboard were horrible to hear. The forward part sank bow first, and the after portion went down stern first. As the *Monticello* disappeared beneath the waves, the survivors in the one remaining lifeboat distinctly saw several persons standing on the ship. Captain Harding was among them.

Ten minutes after the *Monticello* sank there were only seven persons alive, all in the first lifeboat. Second officer Murphy took command, and his expert use of the tiller prevented the lifeboat's capsizing in the mighty combers which pushed it toward the distant shore. Murphy had to keep the craft before the sea or it would fill and sink. It seemed that he must collapse from the strain of holding the tiller, but he managed to stay at the rudder until they neared the shore.

The story can be most accurately continued from the account of Captain Smith:

When a short distance from land we tried to run the boat into a small beach between the rocks. I saw a tremendous comber coming after us and I shouted to all to hold on for their lives. I grasped both arms around the forward thwart with both hands locked by the fingers and waited for the result. In an instant the boat was lifted like an eggshell to the angle of 45 degrees, my grasp on the boat was broken, and I found myself thrown violently to the earth and grass on the beach. Sticking my fingers as deeply as I could in the bank I awaited the undertow. I was carried some distance, but on the next wave secured a strong hold and then crawled out of danger.

I observed Miss Smith and Mr. Flemmings crawling up on the beach, and afterwards was joined by Mr. Cook. I saw nothing of Mr. Murphy and the two girls after the comber struck us. They uttered no shout, and I do not know how they met their death. It seemed hard that after displaying so much courage and fortitude they should be lost when safety was so near. We walked up to Captain Vickery's house, where we found the family at dinner. They at once showed us every kindness, and after a hasty lunch Captain Vickery drove me to town.

During all the trying ordeal on board the steamer there was not the slightest confusion, but on the contrary everything was done in the most orderly manner. Captain Harding might have jumped into our boat, but paid no attention to it, keeping himself busy attending to the launching of the other boats, and serving life-belts to the passengers. . . . There can be no blame attached to Captain Harding. No more capable officer could be found. He was simply caught under conditions which looked favorable, but which turned out entirely different. I think it impossible that either of the men in the second boat could have survived long, as she appeared to sink almost immediately.

3. Evangeline and the Tragedy of Acadia

This is the forest primeval. The murmuring pines and the hemlocks,
Bearded with moss, and in garments green, indistinct in the twilight,
Stand like Druids of old, with voices sad and prophetic,
Stand like harpers hoar, with beards that rest on their bosoms.

This is the forest primeval; but where are the hearts that beneath it
Leaped like the roe, when he hears in the woodland the voice of the huntsman?
Where is the thatch-roofed village, the home of the Acadian farmers,—
Men whose lives glided on like rivers that water the woodlands,
Darkened by shadows of earth, but reflecting an image of heaven?
Waste are those pleasant farms, and the farmers forever departed!
Scattered like dust and leaves, when the mighty blasts of October
Seize them, and whirl them aloft, and sprinkle them far o'er the ocean.
Naught but tradition remains of the beautiful village of Grand Pré.

HENRY WADSWORTH LONGFELLOW, in his poem, *Evangeline*, tells us the story of an unfortunate Acadian girl who was taken with other French neutrals from Grand Pré in the year 1755. Separated from her lover Gabriel, Evangeline spent the next years of her life trying to find him. She searched up and down the Atlantic Coast, around the Mississippi, and along the shores of Louisiana. Many years later, after she became a Sister of Mercy, she discovered Gabriel, her lost lover. Though he was dying, her long mission ended successfully—she found the man for whom she had searched for many years.

Most of us at one time or another have seen, read, or studied *Evangeline*. The ordinary text books on literature do not even attempt to give the correct background of this well-known poem based on a tragic period in Nova Scotian history. I've always enjoyed Longfellow's poetry and I think I always will, but there are many who believe it fashionable *not* to read Longfellow. I feel very sorry for what they have missed. The man who wrote "Listen, my children, and you shall hear of the midnight ride of Paul Revere," and "The night shall be filled with music, and the cares that infest the day, shall fold their tents like the Arabs, and as silently steal away," can never be considered out of date.

I realize that there are many who regard the Cambridge poet as merely a formal old gray-beard whose poems they were forced to memorize at school. If they would only read the diary of his life, they would realize that Longfellow was not a grim, unsmiling Victorian at all, but an alive, intensive human person, vitally influenced by all the beauty of life around him. To give the unbelievers just one different picture of the poet, we recall an incident which occurred during his European tour.

One afternoon when he was walking around the Louvre a beautiful statue of Venus caught his eye. On several occasions during that visit he found himself back admiring the statue, and later, at his hotel, he told an acquaintance of his fascination with it. His friend seemed surprised that Longfellow would take such an unsual interest in the Venus statue, beautiful though it was. But Longfellow explained his enthusiasm by saying that it was "an exact portrait of Miss K."

I have always thrilled at the story of Longfellow's *Evangeline*, and on many occasions have followed the action from its start in Grand Pré, Acadia, to the final scene in Philadelphia. But I had never visited Grand Pré itself, and I wondered if the story was really founded on historical fact. It has been the custom lately for many writers to claim that the French, and not the British, were really to blame for what happened at Grand Pré. So I decided to fly northward and discover what I could about the real history behind the poem.

Arriving at the Moncton Airport I was pleased to see my good friend, H. Borden Pye, with whom, during 1947, I visited romantic Oak Island in Mahone Bay. Before we completed the

Evangeline mission, Pye had driven me more than four hundred miles in his car around New Brunswick and Nova Scotia. Fog, snow, rain, and sleet delayed us not, though they were our constant companions almost every moment of the journey. We had chosen the muddy season when all trucks and busses are kept from the roads.

We explored the historical Fort Beausejour not far from Amherst. Here the Acadians had been forced by the French, after their invasion of the area, to take arms against the British. I spent considerable time clambering over the bastions and parapets, and although it was late April, I also tested the thickness of the ice in the water-filled moat. Later we examined the ancient cannonballs in the museum and photographed the old guns frowning over the terreplein. Upon leaving, we almost bogged down in Pye's car when he took a short cut down a dirt road which had turned to a sea of mud, but the car wallowed through successfully. However, I had learned a lesson: never take short cuts over dirt roads in mud season.

With my visit to Fort Beausejour completed, the next journey was through Outer Halifax to Acadia Land itself. The weather was still at its worst, with thunderstorms, fog and rain, but we finally reached our objective late the following afternoon.

The meadows and valleys of Grand Pré presented themselves to us in a soggy, sad state, nearly under water from the two days of rain. Climbing out of the car, we slogged across the grass. A stone memorial cross was close at hand, and we found it was dedicated to John Frederic Herbin, the first Acadian to return from expulsion and live in the land of his ancestors at Wolfville.

Next we visited the Evangeline well, where the real Evangeline, Emmeline Labische, drew water on many occasions. I sat down by the edge of the well and tried to picture the scene which took place 194 years before, when the Acadians were torn from their homes. Then it began to rain harder than ever, and we hurried over to the partial shelter which the church afforded.

At that moment I noticed Evangeline's statue, and rain or no rain, I decided to visit it at once.

The statue which has come to symbolize all Acadia was unveiled by the Viscountess Burnham at Grand Pré on July 29, 1930. Its sculptor was Philippe Hébert. When death took him, Hébert had finished only the clay model, but the work went on to completion. The statue is about twenty feet high, and on the base we read the words *PLEURANT LE PAYS PERDUE.* Evangeline is standing with her body facing east toward the Gaspereau River, where the deportation vessels were waiting in 1755. Her head, however, is turned toward the southwest and the fields which she will never see again. Her face is not that of a beautiful girl, but she is shown rather as a mature, winsome peasant woman who stood with spiritual dignity and heroic pride awaiting her fate. The statue is a striking representation of a valiant soul in solemn sorrow. Evangeline's statue was dedicated just seven years too late to be seen by John Frederic Herbin,* who probably did more than any other man of this century to bring the Grand Pré region into prominence as the land of the Acadians.

After studying the statue, my next interest was the church itself, where the Acadian Museum is now located. We tried every door, but not one was unlocked. Finally, we crossed over through the watery meadow and inquired of the woman station agent at Grand Pré if it was possible to see the museum in the church. After getting some keys from her, which she warned us would probably not work, we started back across the swamp-like field, sinking into the water at times up to our ankles. Before we arrived at the church there came a shout from behind us, and we turned around to see a man running in our direction. "Do you want to enter the church?" he asked. "I have some keys which might help." Our questioner, Mr. Adelbert King,

---

* Herbin's memorial erroneously calls him "Frederick." The correct spelling of his name is "Frederic".

the custodian of the property, reached into his pocket and pulled out an enormous bunch of keys. But when we got to the church, he tried them all, and not one of them worked. I began to be afraid that I would never see the ancient Acadian relics inside the building. But Mr. King ran back to the railway station and soon returned with still another key which opened a padlock and allowed us to enter the church.

"You're the first visitors of the year to get into the museum," King told us, "and I want you to be the first to sign the register for 1949." We proudly signed our names at the top of the new page, and for the next hour we feasted our eyes on the various relics and treasures which recalled the period, two centuries before, when the Acadians lived happily in this promising land.

When we left the church, the rain was still falling. Picking our way through the flooded grass toward the station, we started up the street for the commemorative monument on the east side of the main road. Actually it marks the place where two New Englanders, Colonel Noble and his brother, are buried, but the legend merely tells of the battle in which they fell when attacked by the French and ignores a mention of the Nobles. The one hundred or more New England soldiers who died in the engagement are buried farther down the road, back from where we had come. There is no marker mentioning that burial either.

Our next objective was Wolfville, just three miles away. Here we visited the son of John Frederic Herbin, whose monument stands near the entrance to the memorial grounds. Frederic G. Herbin generously gave us an extremely informative booklet which his father had compiled before his death in 1923. Finally came the time for departure, and we gave a last look at the various places which had figured so prominently in the story of the exiled Acadian settlers. Borden turned the car toward Windsor, and off we drove in the rain.

At Halifax we parted company, and Borden returned to his family in Amherst.

That night at my hotel in Dartmouth when I re-read Long-fellow's *Evangeline*, it had greater significance for me. As soon as I finished the poem, I took out all my material on the Acadians and compared the various accounts in order to eliminate the patently false stories and detect flaws in the usually accepted versions. By two o'clock that morning I was able to place in their proper sequence the events which led to the expulsion of the French neutrals, and an hour later I had reconstructed in my mind the true story of Acadia.

In 1713, with the treaty of Utrecht, England received Acadia from France, and all Acadians were instructed to either take an oath of allegiance to England or move away within a year. At that time there were 1,290 French people living around the Grand Pré region, and most of them were willing to move to Cape Breton Island, which was still part of France. But the British delayed their actual departure and from 1713 until 1730 tried to get the Acadians to take the oath of allegiance rather than move away. Only a few embraced the opportunity. The remainder simply promised to be loyal and agreed not to commit any hostile act against England.

The British Governors changed every few years, and with each change came a discussion of what should be done with the Acadians. In 1729 the newly appointed Governor Phillips announced that all French people must either take the oath of allegiance or leave the country within ninety days. By refusing to allow them to sell any of their effects he thought that he could force them to take the oath.

The Acadians refused both alternatives, however. Phillips relented and allowed them to carry away anything they wished, but he still believed he controlled them, for there was no road leading away from Acadia. The industrious Acadians, however, began to construct a highway from Grand Pré toward Annapolis until Phillips discovered what they were doing and put a stop to it. Finally, in 1730, Governor Phillips and the Acadians agreed that the Acadians should become British subjects, providing they never had to bear arms against their former country, France. From that time on, the Acadians were called the French neutrals.

Once the problem of the oath of allegiance was settled, the people of Grand Pré prospered. But in 1744 France and England were again at war, and the British began to worry that the Acadians would not remain loyal. To be on the safe side, they demanded that the French neutrals turn in all their arms.

In 1747 France began active plans to invade Acadia. The English as a defensive measure, sent Colonel Arthur Noble up from Boston with five hundred volunteers. He quartered his men in twenty-four houses along the highway and left his ships at Gaspereau Landing for the winter. Then Colonel Noble settled down for a long and quiet occupation, never dreaming that the French might attack during the next few months. But Ramesay, the French commander, soon heard of the Bostonian's arrival and made plans for a surprise attack against him.

Just as the French expedition began, Ramesay injured his knee and had to withdraw as leader of the troops. He delegated the command to gallant Captain Coulon De Villiers who made immediate plans for a forced march and night attack on Colonel Noble's army. The French started out in deep snow, and before they could approach Grand Pré another heavy blizzard had set in. On they marched, 346 strong, stopping to rest whenever they could. At the head of the bay, they were met by messengers who told them how Colonel Noble's forces were quartered in the homes of the Acadians. At noon on February 10, 1748, the French began their final march through the snowstorm and by dusk arrived just outside Grand Pré. Waiting an hour for complete darkness, Coulon De Villiers then began his attack.

House after house fell to the determined onslaught of the

French invaders, and before the conflict ended more than one hundred men who had recently sailed from Boston were dead. The New Englanders fought valiantly, but they were completely unprepared. Colonel Noble himself was attacked by a group of French soldiers under Commander La Corne. The colonel jumped from bed and received two musket balls in his body, but he continued firing his pistols. Called upon to surrender, he refused and was immediately killed by a bullet through his forehead. His brother, Ensign Francis Noble, was also killed shortly afterwards. Having lost their leader, the Bostonians surrendered. The surprise attack in the winter snowstorm had been an overwhelming success.

The bodies of the enlisted men from New England were buried at the foot of the bank beside the road leading to Evangeline's well, and Colonel Noble and his brother were interred at the east of the road between two apple trees on the Laird property. The remainder of the New England troops were allowed to march to Annapolis, leaving the French again established at Grand Pré.

With their land changing hands, many of the French neutrals were told to be prepared to bear arms against any future British invasion, and a few hundred Acadians did give in and become temporary soldiers of France.

Back at Fort Beausejour, Commander de Vergor was appropriating money sent him for other purposes than the completion of the fort's defenses so that when Colonel John Winslow landed near Fort Beausejour with 2,000 New England volunteers, de Vergor was not prepared. He implored the Acadians to bear arms against the Bostonians. To a man, the Acadians refused, and de Vergor, after a half-hearted defense, surrendered. Charles Lawrence, cruel and merciless, now became governor. Again in control of Acadia, the British sent one hundred and fifty troops to Grand Pré, where they seized all the arms they could find and quartered themselves in the homes of the Acadians. The inhabitants sent two petitions to Governor Lawrence in protest, petitions which Lawrence regarded as impertinent. A short time later every Acadian priest was removed from Grand Pré and carried away to another part of Canada. Thus the people were left without their spiritual leaders. On July 28, 1755, the fateful decision to deport the Acadians was reached.

Colonel John Winslow, whose diary is extremely important in an analysis of what really happened, had acquitted himself very well in the capture of Fort Beausejour. He now embarked with his forces for Grand Pré, arriving there at Gaspereau Landing on August 15, 1755. After several tours of inspection through the surrounding countryside, Colonel Winslow felt that it was time to carry out his distasteful business. Therefore he drafted a proclamation, part of which I quote:

> To the inhabitants of the district of Grand-Pré, Minas River, Canard, and places adjacent, as well ancients as young men and lads:
>
> Whereas His Excellency the Governor has instructed us of his late resolution respecting . . . the inhabitants . . . We, therefore, order and strictly, by their presents, all of the inhabitants as well of the above-named districts . . . both old and young men, as well as the lads of ten years of age, to attend the church at Grand-Pré, on Friday, the 5th instant, at three in the afternoon, that we may impart to them what we are ordered to communicate to them, declaring that no excuse will be admitted on any pretense whatsoever, on pain of forfeiting goods and chattels, in default of real estate.

> Given at Grand-Pré, 2nd September, 1755.

> JOHN WINSLOW

In obeisance to the proclamation, 418 men and boys crowded into the church at the appointed time and were promptly made prisoners by the New Englanders. From that moment on, the Acadians realized that they were doomed people. Five transports became the prisons for 250 Acadian men and boys. On October 8, 1755, Colonel Winslow completed his list of 2743 Acadians, and the final embarkation aboard the fourteen ships started.

I quote from Winslow's diary:

Began to embark the inhabitants, who went on solentarily and un-willingly, the women in great distress carrying off their children in their arms; others carrying their decrepit parents in their carts, with all their goods, moving in great confusion.

The fleet finally sailed away on October 27.

During the next few years fourteen thousand Acadians were removed elsewhere. The only province to be notified of their coming was Connecticut. In Boston two thousand French neutrals were landed and quartered in tents on Boston Common and in old warehouses down at Point Shirley. New York received two hundred and Connecticut three hundred; the remainder were distributed throughout Pennsylvania, Maryland, North and South Carolina, and Georgia. Wherever the Acadians were put ashore, however, suffering accompanied them. Large numbers fled overland to Louisiana, where their descendants today are legion, numbering upwards of one hundred thousand.

Soon the English began to repopulate the Acadian land with emigrants from New England and elsewhere. Later, because of the American Revolution, wholesale migrations took place and thousands of Tories were transplanted to Nova Scotia and New Brunswick.

After learning how the Acadian evacuation really took place, I began to reconstruct everything which had to do with Long-fellow's *Evangeline*. In Nova Scotia I found many clues. I learned that Mrs. George Haliburton, the aunt of the Judge

Haliburton who wrote *Sam Slick*, told a Reverend Mr. H. L. Connoly the story of an unfortunate Acadian girl who had been separated from her lover by the British during the time of the evacuation in 1755. After searching vainly for many years the girl became a Sister of Charity. Then, one day, she found her lover again.

The Reverend Mr. Connoly came to Massachusetts, and in 1845 dined with Nathaniel Hawthorne and Henry Wadsworth Longfellow. During the meal, Reverend Connoly told Longfellow that he had been trying to get Hawthorne to write a story about this girl and her adventures in attempting to find her lost lover. As the meal progressed, Longfellow grew more and more interested in the Connoly story, and when he could contain himself no longer, he said to Hawthorne, "If you have really made up your mind not to use the story, will you give it to me for a poem?"

"Of course, if you wish it," answered Hawthorne. "Furthermore, I'll not think of using it at all until I see what you have done with it in verse."

Whittier also made an exhaustive study of the Acadian banishment, but postponed his poem until Longfellow had completed *Evangeline*. "Longfellow was just the one to write it," said Whittier later. "If I had attempted it, I would have spoiled the artistic effect of the poem by my indignation at the treatment of the exiles by the Colonial government."

The progress of the poem is best seen by reading Longfellow's journal for the period in question. We find that it took the poet almost two years to complete the poem *Evangeline:*

November 28, 1845.—Set about "Gabrielle," my idyl in hexameters, in earnest. I do not mean to let a day go by without adding something to it. F. and Sumner are both doubtful of the measure. To me it seems the only one for such a poem.

December 7th.—I know not what name to give to—not my new

baby, but my poem. Shall it be "Gabrielle," or "Celestine," or "Evangeline"?

January 8th, 1846.—Striving, but, alas, how vainly! to work upon "Evangeline."

May 20th. Tried to work on "Evangeline." Unsuccessful.

November 12th. I long to be fairly at work on "Evangeline."

December 10th. Laid up with a cold.

December 17th. Finished this morning and copied the first canto of the second part of "Evangeline." . . . I see a panorama of the Mississippi advertised. . . . The river comes to me instead of my going to the river. . . .

February 27, 1847. "Evangeline" is ended. I wrote the last lines this morning.

October 30th. "Evangeline" published.

November 8th. "Evangeline" goes on bravely. I have received greater and warmer commendations than on any previous volume.

Longfellow once told of how he chose the last scene in the poem:

"I got the climax of "Evangeline" from Philadelphia. . . . I was passing down Spruce Street one day . . . when my attention was attracted to a large building with beautiful trees about it. . . . The charming picture of lawn, flowerbeds, and shade which it presented made an impression which has never left me. When I came to write "Evangeline," I located the final scene—the meeting between Evangeline and Gabriel, and the death—at this poor house, and the burial in the old Catholic graveyard, not far away, which I found by chance in another of my walks."

Somewhat apart from the village, and nearer the Basin of Minas,
Benedict Bellefontaine, the wealthiest farmer of Grand-Pré,
Dwelt on his goodly acres; and with him, directing his household,
Gentle Evangeline lived, his child, and the pride of the village.

The real Evangeline, Emmeline Labishe, was an orphan. At sixteen, she was on the eve of her marriage to a deserving, well-to-do man of Saint Gabriel, Louis Arseneaux. Their wedding bans had been published and the nuptial date fixed. Then came the unhappy scattering of the Acadians by the British. In the scuffle which took place when the men were taken aboard ship, Louis was wounded. Finally the vessel weighed anchor. Watching the ship as it sailed away from land, Emmeline cried out in anguish to her step-mother: "Mother, Mother, he is gone."

Later Emmeline herself was taken from her home by the New Englanders, and landed at Maryland, where she was befriended by two men, Charles Smith and Henry Brent. But she could not settle down in Maryland because of her anxiety to meet her lover, Louis, again. She wandered from settlement to settlement, colony to colony, always searching for her lost sweetheart. In Boston, Point Shirley, Maryland, and Virginia she searched in vain. Finally she reached Louisiana, and after a few days spent in hunting for Louis, located a group of Acadians who came from her part of Nova Scotia. Suddenly she saw the object of her long search—Louis, leaning against a huge oak tree.

"It is Louis!" she cried, and rushed for him. But Louis seemed strangely unresponsive, and she called out, "Louis, I am your long lost Emmeline. Have you forgotten me, Louis?"

Louis glanced at her and turned away.

"Why do you hang your head, Louis? I am still your betrothed, and I have kept pure and unsullied my plighted faith to you. Speak to me, Louis."

The man answered, "My poor Emmeline, I am not worthy of you. I have pledged my faith to another. How was I to know where you were?"

But Emmeline did not reply, for her mind was crowded with conflict. Was this the end of all her efforts to find her lover? What did it really mean?

From that moment until her merciful death a short time later, her beautiful countenance was clouded by a sad, bewildered smile, and she never recovered. When she passed away, they buried her at Poste de Attakapas and her grave was kept green for many years by those who knew her. But they, too, have all passed on, and today those who know the real story are few in number.

In recent years it has become fashionable to try to excuse the action of the British in Acadia, and actually many uninformed persons have attempted to prove that the French and not the British were to blame for the evacuation which finally came. Although the British Government was against moving the Acadians and an order was actually on the way to prevent the evacuation, it didn't arrive in time. Therefore the British must share with Governor Lawrence and the New Englander Winslow the responsibility for what occurred.

For two generations it has been popular to find flaws in Longfellow's *Evangeline*, and I admit that there are minor discrepancies. But the general picture which Longfellow portrays is essentially correct. Longfellow had never been to Acadia, Louisiana, or the Mississippi River, and did not have access to Colonel John Winslow's revealing diary, so he was handicapped geographically and historically. Then there are English writers who feel that Longfellow overemphasized the sufferings and tragedy of the entire picture, but the local writers now in Acadia feel that *Evangeline* was a fair statement of facts.

There are just a few inaccuracies in the poem which I should like to record. As the men had already been taken aboard the transports before the women were embarked, there could have been no such scene as Longfellow indicates when he says:

There disorder prevailed, and the tumult and stir of embarking.
Busily plied the freight boats; and in the confusion
Wives were torn from their husbands, and mothers, too late, saw
*   their children*
Left on the land, extending their arms, with wildest entreaties.

Again, there is no plain to the south, as Longfellow states in his poem. Also, since the priests had all been removed earlier that year, there could have been no such scene as described with Father Felician in the chapel. Nor was there a "forest primeval"; a disastrous forest fire had burned out the section in 1710, and the new growth was still immature. Nevertheless, Longfellow's poem, taking everything into consideration, is surprisingly free from errors.

Let us recall the last scene when Evangeline finds her lost lover in the Philadelphia poor-house with the scores of plague victims lying around. Evangeline enters into the corridors filled with patients:

Suddenly, as if arrested by fear or a feeling of wonder,
Still she stood, with her colorless lips apart, while a shudder
Ran through her frame, and forgotten, the flowerets dropped from
*   her fingers,*
And from her eyes and cheeks the light and bloom of the morning
Then there escaped from her lips a cry of such terrible anguish,
That the dying heard it, and started up from their pillows.
On the pallet before her was stretched the form of an old man.
Long and thin, and gray were the locks that shaded his temple;

Vainly he strove to whisper her name, for the accents unuttered
Died on his lips, and their motion revealed what his tongue would
*   have spoken.*
Vainly he strove to rise; and Evangeline, kneeling beside him,
Kissed his dying lips, and laid his head on her bosom.
Sweet was the light of his eyes; but it suddenly sank into darkness,
As when a lamp is blown out by a gust of wind at a casement.

And, as she pressed once more the lifeless head to her bosom,
Meekly she bowed her own, and murmured, "Father, I thank thee!"

Part Two

SAINT JOHN TO CAPE COD

4. The Wreck of the "Asia"

During my stay in Saint John, I was anxious to learn the particulars in the wreck of the full-rigged Saint John ship, the *Asia*. More than any other shipping disaster, this unhappy tragedy of the sea seemed to suggest Longfellow's *Wreck of the Hesperus* because of the death of the captain's eleven-year-old daughter, Lena.

The 192-foot *Asia* was built by Oliver Pittfield at Courtney Bay, New Brunswick, in 1883, for Taylor Brothers of Saint John. On September 6, 1897, the 1473-ton full-rigged ship sailed from Manila with a $100,000 cargo of manila hemp for Boston. The *Asia* made a beautiful picture as she sailed out of Manila Bay, and Captain George N. Dakin was a happy man, for not only was he homeward bound on his last trip at sea, but he had his wife and daughter on board with him. He had never lost a ship and hoped to retire with a perfect record.

On Sunday, February 20, 1898, after a long voyage in which few ships were spoken, the *Asia* neared Nantucket Shoals. Captain Dakin had always feared the shoals around the Massachusetts island, and when a storm of mixed snow and rain hit the *Asia*, Dakin became extremely apprehensive for the safety of his vessel.

The storm which hit the New England coast that day drove shipping back to port all the way along the coast from Rockland to New York. In Boston, scores of vessels were kept in the harbor because of the gale, which at times reached wind velocity of a mile a minute.

Aboard the *Asia*, the course was shifted from north-by-east to north-by-west-one-half-west shortly before noon. At 5:50 the captain ordered sail shortened since the storm was increasing in intensity almost every minute. A quarter of an hour later, the *Asia* crashed against the sandy bottom, and the men aloft came tumbling down from above, all terribly frightened by the shock of striking. But the *Asia* slid over the bar and resumed her dangerous course. Less than an hour and a quarter later, she crashed against the sand again. When night fell, the ship was still standing to the northward. The storm became so bad that orders were passed to shorten sail to the topsails. Hardly had the orders been accomplished, when the ship struck bottom for the third time with a tremendous shock. But the sails were braced up and hauled the *Asia* off the shoals. She sailed clear for a moment, only to crash again against the sandy bottom.

Captain Dakin ordered more sail put on to push the *Asia* across the sand and into deep water. The frightened sailors sprang to the halliards and sheets. The yards were mastheaded and sails hauled out as fast as possible. The added sails accomplished their purpose, and the *Asia* was free again. For several hours she sailed along with plenty of water under her keel. Then, at two o'clock in the morning of the 21st, she fetched up with a grinding, crunching smash on a sandbar from which she could never release herself.

A wild high sea, every wave of which carried a breaking crest, began to pound against the *Asia*, and her beams and timbers soon were cracking and giving way. She then heeled over on her side and every man realized that the ship was doomed.

Although they couldn't know it, the sailors were stranded on the Great Round Shoal, located to the southwest of Monomoy Point, in reality a continuation of the Stone Horse Shoal.

The good ship had fetched up hard and fast. Now increasing to a heavy easterly gale, the wind hit the vessel in terrific fashion, and sheets of rain drove down on the doomed four-masted vessel. Great salty billows swept the *Asia* fore and aft; seething surf and foam washed everything movable overboard.

Captain Dakin, though frantic with fear that his wife and daughter would be lost, was everywhere on the ship, giving advice and rendering help. He did his utmost to maintain discipline and to calm the fears of the others. Suddenly his little blue-eyed daughter came rushing up on deck in her night clothes, followed by her frantic mother.

"Oh, Daddy, what will we do?" cried the terrified child.

"Never you mind, my dear, everything will be all right. Now just you stay with your mother. Don't worry, Lena. It'll all work out," Captain Dakin told his eleven-year-old daughter. Then his wife took the child.

It is hard to visualize the terrors of that dark night on the Great Round Shoal. Captain Dakin was not dismayed, however, in spite of his anguish at the danger to his wife and their little daughter.

It was then that Chief Mate John Cook called the captain aside for a moment. All during the long voyage from Manila he had been a good friend of the lonely little girl, and now that they were in danger, he was ready to protect her from whatever might take place.

"No matter what happens, I'll look out for Lena," he told the father.

When daylight came, the men realized only too well the utter hopelessness of their position. The forward house had washed away during the night; the cabin was flooded; and the spars were all going by the board. Then the mainmast fell, followed at once by the foremast, and the mizzenmast was now the only stick left.

All hands then began to crowd into the lazaret, including the captain, his wife, and daughter. Captain Dakin knew what was ahead. He realized that he was not going to be able to aid his family when the time came, as he would obey the traditions of the sea and be the last to leave the ship. He looked significantly at Mr. Cook, his mate. Cook waved his hand in answer, and that was all the captain needed. He then knew that Cook would save his daughter from the sea if it were humanly possible. Finally all the ship's company had crowded into the lazaret, awaiting whatever the storm had in store.

Without warning a sea higher than the others burst over the side and crushed in the poop deck, almost drowning everyone in the lazaret. The girl and her mother were the first to leave the lazaret, and the chief mate went with them. Captain Dakin shouted that all should leave ahead of him, and he forced the others out of the hatchway.

When it came his turn to go, Captain Dakin was hit by a giant sea which tumbled down into the lazaret and drowned him. His wife afterwards inquired for him, and they told her the truth. She became hysterical, and had to be held by one of the crew. When Lena learned of her father's loss, she accepted the probability of her own death with calm resignation.

The ship began to break up, her bulwarks and part of the port side going first. Everyone then jumped for the mizzen chains. Jacob Staulberg assisted Mrs. Dakin into the rigging, and William Smith took little Lena and passed her across to Chief Mate Cook. As Lena clung tight to Mr. Cook, she began to cry bitterly.

"Oh, please throw me overboard!" Lena exclaimed. "Do throw me overboard so I can go to Jesus. Let me drown, for I know Jesus will take me!"

The mizzenmast stood erect for some time, but at last the sea prevailed and the stick plunged into the surf. It was the beginning of the end. The next part to go was the starboard quarter, and it carried Mr. Cook, still holding Lena in his arms. Mrs. Dakin, James Murray, Charles Stone, Michael Doyle, and Frank Walter also clung to the fragment. The seven persons went scudding away to leeward aboard the starboard quarter section

of the *Asia*. At that very moment the port quarter broke off.
To continue, we quote from William F. Smith, one of the survivors:

Three of us jumped for the port quarter, Jacob Spaulberg, James
Pacus, and myself, and clung to it with death grips. We were
whirled away among the breakers and nearly caught up with the
other raft. We were in sight of them until nearly dark, when they
disappeared.

They appeared to have very hard work to cling to their piece of
wreckage on account of its oval shape. The last I saw of them was
Mate Cook doing his utmost to keep the little one above water. I
think Mrs. Dakin had already been washed off and one or two
others.

All Monday night we drifted through breakers and among tide
rips, suffering intensely with hunger and thirst, for we had not
eaten anything since Sunday. About midnight, as near as we could
judge of the time, we went quite near some kind of a vessel burning two red lights. We judged it was a lightship so thought we
must be somewhere near land. We yelled as loud as we could and
once thought we heard a "Hello there!" but were soon swept out
of sight of the craft.

We were so thoroughly exhausted that when the day dawned
Tuesday morning we were hardly able to cling to our life raft. We
were in much smoother water, however, and began to hope that we
might be near the track of passing vessels. About 9 a. m. we saw a
lightship to the eastward, and soon found that we were drifting in
that direction. Getting nearer to it, we yelled frantically and to
our joy soon heard a hearty response.

A boat was lowered and it was not long before we were safe on
board the Handkerchief Lightship in the kind care of Captain Ellis
and his crew.

The three men, after recovering from their experiences, were
taken ashore to Woods Hole from the Handkerchief Lightship
by the lighthouse tender *Azalea*.

Later in the week the bodies of Chief Mate John Cook and

little Lena Dakin were discovered frozen to death, still tied to fragments of the starboard quarter. The chief officer of the unlucky ship was found, even in death, clinging tightly to the body of the little blue-eyed girl he had sworn to protect from the sea. John Cook had kept his word to the master of the *Asia* —for the girl had not drowned. Instead, they had both frozen to death, lashed to the wreckage of the ill-fated *Asia*.

5. The Great Amherst Mystery

$\mathcal{W}$HILE in Amherst, Nova Scotia, I made it a point to visit Princess Street and walk around a vacant lot where once stood the home of Mr. and Mrs. Daniel Teed. The house had been moved years before, and later torn down, but no one ever had the courage to build again on that spot. I walked around the lot, examining carefully the ruins of the cellar and the general contour of the old walls which still were indicated in the grass. In the building which once stood there one of the most remarkable events in Nova Scotian history took place.

There are many things which cannot be explained in this world, and ghosts are among them. I, for one, do not believe in ghosts, but the story which will be revealed in this chapter is perhaps the most outstanding example of unexplained ghost-like happenings ever recorded. It all began in the town of Amherst, Nova Scotia, back in the year 1878. But before we tell the story, let us discuss ghosts in general.

What is a ghost? Elliott O'Donnell, who lives in Bristol, England, tells us that "hauntings by genuine ghosts are few and far between; but no matter how many or how few they may be, to those who, like myself, regard them as the surest proof of a Future Life, to know that even one exists is an untold blessing." William Oliver Stevens, in his *Unbidden Guests*, says that if we took the ghost seriously enough to study him, in time he might lend a hand in helping to pull the world back to spiritual truth. Hereward Carrington feels that we should consider a ghost not a tall, thin figure, wrapped around in a sheet, walking through the house clanking his chains, but something actually guided by telepathic hallucination.

The Amherst Ghost story is an account of a home completely disrupted by a being which revealed itself through many physical manifestations, allegedly observed by scores of persons.

In the summer of 1878, there were eight people living at the home of Mr. and Mrs. Daniel Teed, on Princess Street. Located near the corner of Church Street, the building was a neat, two-story cottage painted yellow. There were four rooms on the first floor: parlor, dining room, sewing room, and kitchen. A pantry opened into the dining room. The doors of the dining room and parlor opened into a hallway leading to the front door.

Should you enter the front door, you would see the stairway in the hall leading to the floor above, and after climbing the stairs, you would turn to the left on the second floor. Here the entry ran at right angles to the floor below. In the center of the ceiling was a trap door, without a ladder, which led to the loft above. Surrounding the entry were four small bedrooms, each of which had a conventional door and window but no communication between. Two of the bedrooms faced the front of the house and Princess Street; the other two looked toward the stable in back.

Daniel Teed, the master of the house, was a happy normal person with nothing to distinguish him in any way. His wife, Olive, was a good woman, and they had two children, five-year-old Willie and seventeen-month-old George.

Jane and Esther Cox, Olive's two sisters, boarded with them. Jane, or Jennie as she was often called, was twenty-two years old and quite a beauty. Her hair was light brown and fell almost to her knees when not done up. She had a host of admirers of both sexes.

Jennie's sister Esther was short and stout and had cropped dark brown hair. Her eyes were large and gray, with a bluish tinge. She was considered a tomboy. Esther and Jennie shared a room in the front of the house with a window directly over the front door.

Two other boarders lived with the family: John Teed, Daniel's brother, and William Cox, the brother of Mrs. Teed.

Into this pleasant household *something* came. To this day the people of Nova Scotia cannot agree what that *something* was, but it all began after supper one damp, foggy September night.

Nineteen-year-old Esther was already in bed when Jennie came into the room at about quarter of nine. Getting into bed, she noticed that she had left the light on, so she arose and put it out and then returned to the bed in which her sister was already asleep. She bumped her head against the bedpost in the dark, and, as she did so, Esther muttered in her sleep asking if it were not the fourth of September. Jennie agreed that it was. Suddenly Esther gave a scream and jumped out of bed, shouting that there was a mouse in the mattress. Though they searched carefully, they couldn't find the mouse and went to bed again.

The next night, Esther was again certain that there was a mouse in the mattress, and when the girls began to search for it, a surprising thing happened. A pasteboard box which was under the bed suddenly jumped up into the air and fell over on its side. Esther and Jennie agreed not to talk about it, got into bed and fell asleep.

The next night the strange manifestations started in real earnest. Poor Esther began to balloon up in size; her body actually grew larger and larger, and she screamed in pain, fearing that she would burst! Suddenly a loud report shook the room. Three more reports were heard, like peals of thunder, and then Esther shrank back to normal size and entered a state of calm repose.

Four nights later Esther had another attack but jumped into bed with Jennie before it became serious. Then all the bedclothes flew off the bed and settled in a confused heap in a far corner of the room. Mrs. Teed rushed into the room and picked up the bedclothes, placing them on the terrified girls. Again they flew off and landed on the floor. When John Teed entered the room, the pillow under Esther's head slid out, flew through the air, and hit Teed squarely in the face. A short time later two more reports were heard coming from under the bed, and then the room resumed its normal appearance.

Dr. Carritte, the family physician, was called and arrived the following evening. Esther was already in bed. Suddenly almost the entire pillow came out from under her head and then went back to its original position. When it came out again John Teed grabbed it, but it pulled from his hands and went back under Esther's head, seemingly without human help.

Dr. Carritte stood up. "How wonderful that is," he exclaimed, and just then the loud thunderous reports began again. Dr. Carritte looked under the bed but found nothing. He walked away, and the loud reports or explosions followed him. Just then the bedclothes flew up into the air, and before they could be replaced, everyone present heard a metallic sound and writing appeared on the wall of the room. They read in horror the words: "ESTHER COX, YOU ARE MINE TO KILL!"

Day after day the strange events continued to take place. Dr. Carritte later testified that he saw a bucket of water standing on the kitchen table suddenly become agitated and begin to boil. A voice was heard in the house talking to Esther and telling her all sorts of horrible things.

Soon after this, a lighted match fell from the ceiling onto the bed. Then eight or ten other lighted matches fell down through the air. Almost all of them started fires, but members of the family were quick to extinguish them. For several days this fire-setting continued. From cellar to attic, the blazes continued to be lighted and members of the household lived in constant danger of having the house burn down over their heads.

One night Esther shouted that the ghost had appeared to her.

"My God," she cried, "don't you all see him, too? He says I must leave this house tonight, or he will kindle a fire in the loft and burn us all to death. Where shall I go?"

In his desperation Daniel Teed thought of his good friend, John White, and took Esther to White's home. White agreed to let her stay, but the ghost suddenly reappeared four weeks after she had changed homes. A clasp knife which belonged to little Frederick White was whisked out of his grasp and imbedded in Esther's back. Fred pulled it out, whereupon it was taken from him and inserted in the same wound. The others came to her rescue and took the knife away.

In December Esther was taken ill with diphtheria and confined to her bed for a little over two weeks. During her sickness, the ghost did not try to bother her at all. Recovering from the illness, Esther went to Sackville, New Brunswick, for a visit with her other married sister, Mrs. John Snowden, and was free from the ghost in this new location.

Esther then returned to Amherst and occupied a different room. One night she told her sister Jennie that another ghost had just informed her that the old ghost was coming back to set the house on fire. The next day the members of the family gathered to discuss the message in Esther's room, and a lighted match fell from the ceiling as they talked. Within the next few minutes, eight or ten matches fell, but they were all extinguished. That night the loud noises began again.

Now another amazing thing happened. When the noises began, Daniel Teed shouted out to the ghost, asking if it could tell how many were in the room. "Give a knock for each person on the floor," Teed cried.

Immediately there were six distinct knocks for the six persons actually present in the room. From that time on, the members of the family could speak to the ghost in this fashion. The ghost would knock once for a negative answer, three times for an affirmative, and twice if it were not sure of the answer.

Daniel asked the ghost if the house would really be set on fire, and the ghost answered with two knocks. Five minutes later the invisible ghost grabbed a dress from a nail on the wall, rolled it up under the bed and set it on fire. Daniel pulled the flaming garment from under the bed before any serious damage had been done and extinguished the blaze.

All the members of the family were now convinced that the ghost was that of some very evil person who had once lived on the earth and who, for some strange reason, had decided to torture poor Esther. One method of extreme torture was to adopt the strange technique of "moving about in her abdomen, which caused her to swell so fearfully and feel like bursting." The ghost also perpetrated another torture on the girl, but during my visits to Amherst I was merely able to learn that it was of such intimate nature that I should not discuss it.

When the ghost threatened to kindle fires in the White residence, John White asked Esther if she would accompany him to his tavern so that he could keep his eyes on the ghost while he was working. Esther consented, and soon the ghost also began to appear at the tavern. One morning the door of the large cooking stove was opened and shut incessantly by the ghost. Finally Mr. White braced it with an axe handle. Suddenly the ghost lifted the door from its hinges, and sent it flying, along with the axe handle, up into the air to crash heavily on the floor several feet away!

Furious with rage and astonishment, Mr. White rushed out of doors and shouted to Mr. W. H. Rogers, Inspector of Fisheries for Nova Scotia, who happened to be passing by, to come inside and witness this phenomenon. They entered the kitchen, and White rehung the door, bracing it again with the axe handle. At once the door flew off with the axe handle and both landed several feet away!

At another time three large iron spikes were placed on Esther's lap while she was sitting in the dining room of the tavern. The

The three-hundred-foot cliff at Grand Manan Island which James Lawson climbed in 1857 after the
wreck of his ship, the *Lord Ashburton*

The statue of Evangeline

The author standing on a pulp-wood pile at Saint
George, New Brunswick

Keeper Everett W. Quinn and his wife at Saint Croix
Island Light, located half in Canada and half in the
United States

The picturesque bones of the three-masted schooner *Henry W. Middleton* wrecked at Higgins Beach, Maine, in 1898

The author in hiking costume

Pemaquid Point Light, Maine

Anemone Cave on Mount Desert Island, Maine,
with Keeper Gray of West Quoddy Light

Baron Castin, the most famous resident of Pentagoet, Maine

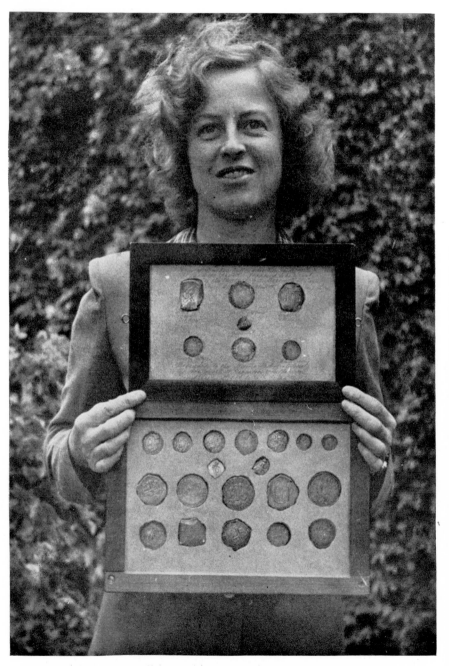

Anna-Myrle Snow, the author's wife,
holding coins from the Castine Treasure

Fort William Henry at Pemaquid, Maine, where Baron Castin
and D'Iberville defeated Pascho Chubb in 1696

The author on top of Trask's Rock, Castine. Here young
Trask played his fife for the Revolutionary forces as they attempted to charge a fifty-foot embankment nearby

(*Right*) The murderer Louis Wagner. This photograph was taken just after his arrest, and he is still wearing the blood-stained coat which he had planned to replace

(*Below*) Smuttynose Island off Portsmouth, New Hampshire. The Hontvet residence, scene of Louis Wagner's crime, is the third house from the left. This drawing was made, of course, several years after the murder took place

The prize-winning photograph by Jimmie Jones of *The Boston Post* which shows the submarine *Squalus* breaking the surface of the ocean July 13, 1939

Bust of Captain Howard Blackburn, the heroic
Gloucester fisherman, by Leonard Craske

(*Right*) The old Nantucket Lightship riding out a gale

(*Below*) The steamer *Portland* which was lost with all hands off Highland Light, Cape Cod, on November 27, 1898

The historic battle between the *Monitor* and the *Merrimac* off Hampton Roads, Virginia, March 9, 1862

Theodosia Burr walks the plank after the schooner on
which she was a passenger was captured by pirates

The portrait of Theodosia Burr Alston, found in a dilapidated hut at Nag's Head. This painting by John Vanderlyn is now accepted as authentic by museum authorities

spikes began to turn red hot, and then they flew through the air to the other end of the tavern, twenty feet away. This happened in the presence of a group of local citizens and has never been explained. Among those present from time to time, who came as unbelievers and went away admitting that some supernatural power was operating were William Hillson, Daniel Morrison, Robert Hutchinson, and the editor of the *Amherst Gazette*, J. Albert Black. All of the men mentioned were well-known citizens of Amherst in 1879.

The Amherst mystery attracted so much attention that Mr. Walter Hubbell, a popular tragedian of his day, became intensely interested in it and decided to debunk the affair as a hoax. Arriving in Amherst on June 11, 1879, the actor visited the home of Esther Cox and met her for the first time. Within a few days Hubbell was definitely convinced that there was something really genuine about the whole affair, and the man who arrived to scoff remained to believe. Not only was he convinced that the ghost was an actuality, but he made plans to take Esther on a tour and exhibit her.

On June 12 Esther Cox, Mr. White, and Walter Hubbell went to the Amherst railway station to take the train for Moncton, New Brunswick, where Esther was scheduled to appear. A large crowd had gathered at the station to see the trio off, and among them was a man who had failed in his attempts to persuade Esther to go on a lecture tour with him. It is believed from what happened later that the man surreptitiously boarded the same train to make trouble for them in Moncton. Arriving in Moncton, the group stopped at the American House, and that same night the ghost began to start a chair rocking fifteen feet away from Esther.

The newspapers of the period covered the entire affair very well, and I now quote from the *Moncton Despatch* of June 18, 1879:

Miss Esther Cox arrived here in care of friends, on Friday afternoon last, and a detailed account of the manifestations and working
of the mystery were given in Ruddick's Hall, on Friday evening
and Saturday. Sunday evening, Miss Cox essayed to attend service
at the Baptist Church, but during the first singing, the ghost which
had been quiet for some days, again manifested itself by knocking,
apparently, on the floor of the pew in front. When told to stop by
Miss Cox, it would cease the noise for a moment, but then break out
worse than ever. Throughout the prayer it continued; and when
the organ began for the second singing, the noise became so distinct
and disturbing that Miss Cox and party were forced to leave the
church. Upon reaching the house on Wesley Street, where they
were stopping, the ghost seemed to enter into Miss Cox, and she
was sick and insensible until morning. Lying upon the bed, she
seemed for a time in great pain, her chest heaving as though in a
rapid succession of hiccoughs, and her body and limbs being very
much swollen. A medical gentleman of this town, who saw her at
the time, stated that the symptoms were those of a functional heart
disease, probably caused by nervous excitement.

The heart was beating at an exceedingly rapid rate, and the lungs
seemed gorged with blood, so that a portion was forced into the
stomach, causing the patient to vomit blood afterwards. A sound
could be distinctly heard in the region of the heart, resembling the
shaking of water in a muffled bottle, supposed to be caused by the
blood in a cavity being shaken by the violent hiccough motion of
the body. As to the cause of the affection, that is a mystery. Toward morning Miss Cox relapsed into a state of somnolence and late
in the day awoke, seeming entirely recovered. She states, however,
that on Monday afternoon, while sitting near the window of a room
on the ground floor, a fan dropped out of the window; she went
outside to recover it, and on returning, a chair, from the opposite side
of the room, was found upside down near the door, as though it
had attempted to follow her out of the room. No one else witnessed
this occurrence.

Again, while writing, the ghost took possession of the pen, and
wrote in a different hand altogether other and entirely different

words from what were intended; in fact, it wrote of itself, the young lady being able to look in another direction, and not to show the least interest in what the pen was writing. A gentleman, who was present at the time, asked the ghost its name, when it wrote in reply, "Maggie Fisher", and stated that she had gone to the red school-house on the hill, in Upper Stewiacke, before Miss Cox did but left when she went. Miss Cox did not know this Maggie Fisher, but it seems that at one time she did attend the school indicated, and that a girl of that name, now dead, had attended previously. Monday night, Miss Cox was again attacked and held under the power of the ghost, much the same as the night previous.

A representative of the *Despatch* called on Esther Cox yesterday afternoon, but, she not being under the power, of course, no manifestations could be seen. The lady appeared quite pleasant and affable, and looked well. She considers her trouble to be a ghost, and is more perplexed with it than any one else. She says she cannot tell, by any premonitory symptoms, when the manifestations are going to commence, is becoming rather frightened concerning it and is very easily annoyed and excited by any noise, except that which she herself may cause. If the ghost is willing, Miss Cox will leave for Chatham, by train today.

The Halifax *Presbyterian Witness* in June, 1879, was outspoken on the matter:

The Amherst Mystery, we are informed on the best authority, is no mystery at all, except to persons who refrain from using their powers of observation and reason. The only mystery is that so many persons who should know better are deceived. The newspapers are greatly to blame for "working up" this pitiable sensation. The story is now going the rounds that the girl, Esther Cox, is to be taken around on exhibition. In the name of humanity, propriety, religion, and decency, we earnestly protest against a proceeding so base and disgusting. If the girl is sick, why should her infirmities be exhibited to the public? If, on the other hand there is nothing to exhibit but very clumsy tricks of legerdemain, the exhibitors will at least appear before the public in a *role* not worthy of character.

The group left Moncton on June 18, headed for Chatham, New Brunswick, about eighty miles to the north. It is believed that the man who failed to obtain Miss Cox on his tour was in the audience the night she appeared on the stage of the Chatham theatre.

As Mr. Hubbell was delivering the concluding remarks of his speech that evening, he was interrupted when an old man in the audience arose, shook his cane, and shouted, "Young man, beware!"

Hubbell continued with his speech in spite of the interruption and had Esther stand up and bow, just as the curtain was rung down. Immediately afterwards there was a great amount of loud talking in the pit of the theatre, and a moment later Mr. White rushed into the wings to tell Mr. Hubbell that a ruffian had attempted to strike him. Hubbell asked White if he had obtained their share of the receipts, and White told him that he had the money.

Ten minutes later the three reached the street and ran into a howling mob. Hubbell grabbed Esther by the arm and started through the crowd. Brickbats and stones were thrown at them, but no one was hit. Finally they reached their hotel, all three completely unnerved by their experience. Mr. White declared that as far as he was concerned the tour was over, for they would surely all be killed before they ended their long journey around Nova Scotia and New Brunswick.

A short time later a friend of the group reached the hotel, where he told Hubbell that another and greater demonstration was planned for the following day. His advice was to leave by the night train for Amherst. Hubbell accepted the advice, and the three went aboard the train at midnight. Thus ended the tour of the Great Amherst Mystery, June 20, 1879.

A few days later, the ghost really caused trouble. At breakfast the lid of the sugar bowl flew off and finally dropped down from the ceiling. Hubbell himself saw it suspended *one foot* from the ceiling before it crashed. Entering the parlor, Hubbell saw a large flower plant sail away from the window followed by a tin pail half full of water which came to rest beside the plant on the middle of the parlor floor. That same day Esther's face was slapped by the ghost.

By now the malignant spirit had been identified as a certain Bob Nickle. There were other ghosts, too, according to Esther: a Maggie Fisher, twenty-one years of age, who had been dead twelve years; her sister Mary; Peter Teed; John Nickle; and Eliza MacNeal. But the ringleader was Bob Nickle, and Hubbell describes him as a scheming scoundrel, sixty years of age, who had been a shoemaker when he was on earth.

Hubbell was remarking one day that the gray and white family cat had never been harmed when suddenly it was lifted from the floor to a height of five feet and then dropped on Esther's back. That night the ghost of Bob Nickle entered the girls' bedroom and tore their night gowns. Two days later the ghost again acted in a terrible fashion. He threw knives around the house and moved the loft trap door. The next day he began sticking pins into Esther's body. Hubbell tells us that he spent most of the day pulling pins from Esther.

On Friday, June 27, a trumpet sounded all day long, and Esther told the others that Bob was blowing it. Mr. Hubbell found the trumpet later, and kept it for the rest of his life.

Later Mr. Hubbell desired a light for his pipe, and spoke out, "Bob, I would like a match if you please." At once a shower of matches fell from the ceiling. Mr. Hubbell declared that he could tell which ghost was in action because of the difference in the knocking. The ghost of Maggie knocked in a soft and delicate fashion, while Bob Nickle knocked with terrible sledge-hammer blows.

Walter Hubbell believed that the true story behind the mystery lay in Esther's terrible experience on August 28, 1878, when she went buggy riding with Bob MacNeal, a young friend. Reaching a secluded part of Amherst, Bob attempted to force her out of the carriage at the point of a revolver. Aiming the gun at her heart, he demanded that either she come with him into the woods or he would kill her. She refused his demands, and he repeated them, again pointing the revolver at her heart, swearing terribly all the while. Cocking the gun, he was about to fire when the sound of approaching carriage wheels made him change his mind.

Leaping up into the buggy where Esther was still seated, Bob seized the reins and drove home at a furious clip. On the drive back into Amherst it rained heavily, and when they reached the Princess Street cottage, Esther's clothing was wet through to her body. She was in a serious, hysterical condition because of her experience. Later, when Hubbell investigated the boy's background, he found that among other strange habits Bob MacNeal had been fond of skinning cats alive and releasing them to run around the neighborhood until they died.

Hubbell felt that the attempt of Bob MacNeal to force Esther out of the carriage and commit an outrage upon her affected her mind and caused a derangement of her entire system. While deranged, he reasoned, her vital magnetism escaped, and thus she became a person subject to the power of the ghosts of the dead. Hubbell also believed that Bob MacNeal was obsessed by the evil spirit of Bob Nickle, the old shoemaker. Upon reaching the grove, the evil spirit of the older man completely dominated the youth. Thus the older man, really acting out the one desire of his devilish nature through the organism of Bob Mac-Neal, forced the boy to act as he did. Shortly after the incident, Bob MacNeal left Amherst for good. An interesting aftermath of the affair was a discovery that both Bob Nickle and Bob MacNeal were shoemakers.

Years later, after the demon had been chased away from

Esther Cox by the "incantations and conjurations of an 'Indian Medicine Man' or 'Witch Doctor' and had promised never to follow or molest her again," Bob MacNeal was visited by the ghost which bothered him for several years afterward.

There is another remarkable thing about the mystery which should be noted. The ghostly manifestations began on September 4, 1878, and always returned with greatest strength every twenty-eight days afterward. The changes of the moon were given as the reason for this twenty-eight day cycle, but other investigators thought that the ghost cycle had more to do with the girl herself.

After leaving her home at the insistence of the landlord, who did not wish his house to burn down, Esther Cox obtained a position working for Mr. Arthur Davison. One day, when Esther was present, Davison's barn burned down, and he had her arrested and imprisoned for starting the fire. The judge and jury did not believe in ghosts and Esther was sentenced to four months in jail. After being in prison for one month, she was released because of public sentiment in her favor.

Many years later, in 1893, the man who had employed Esther Cox, Arthur Davison, wrote a statement regarding the entire incident, from which I quote:

I do not believe in Spiritualism. My own idea is that in some way the magnetic power in this girl became unhinged. . . . Esther Cox worked for me for three months and a better one we never had since we have been married, (20 years). I have often watched her to find out how she came down stairs, she seemed to fly. It proved a bad day for me before she left, as she burned my barn. I may say in passing I read the book published by Hubbell, and while he painted the facts up to make the book sell, the facts were there all the same. She was not good looking, very ignorant, only a common education, could read and write but not spell. She was very much afraid of it. I tried several times to teach her to exert control of her will power, but just as I had gained a point she became afraid and would go no

73

farther nor do anything. My house and where she lived before she came to live with me was only about fifty yards distant and I used to call often to see how she got along. Hundreds did the same.

At first it was only rapping and pounding, but at times it assumed a more serious aspect. One night as I was on my way home, I met the Doctor who attended her. . . . He asked me to go with him and see Esther, as he feared she was going to die. He had then tried everything to arouse her from a semi-unconscious state and as a last resort was going to try a battery. When I saw her she was on a cot bed, and seemed to be dead, but for a violent heaving of her body that is from her breast down to her legs, she would fill up and lift the clothes as you inflate a bladder and then it would suddenly collapse. . . . She had several of these turns but this one I saw; but it is hard to describe it fully but it was the hardest scene I ever witnessed. . . .

Another: And this was the only thing that gave me any fright; I kept a horse and a cow at the time. Esther used to milk the cow. I attended the horse myself. The cow stood at the further end of the barn (say 25 feet from the door) where I kept a box with my curry comb and brushes. This particular evening she had just finished milking and met me at the door. As I stepped inside I saw my curry comb running along the floor about eight or ten feet behind her. You may depend that I stepped out of the way quick too. It struck the door post. I then picked it up, and after that I kept the key in my pocket. The next evening when I came home she wanted the key to go and milk. I handed it to her, she had the milk bucket in her other hand, and just as our hands met, a large 2 quart dipper of water, which had been on the table struck our hands and spilled the water over the both of us, giving me a pretty good wetting, spoiling my cuffs. It appears she had just been using this dipper but it was sitting six or eight feet from us and had to pass through an open door at right angles to get where it did.

My wife saw ashes, tea leaves, scrubbing brushes, soap and mop rags and an old ham bone often flying around and sometimes it put them out in their work, but we got so used to it we put up with all these things as it was hard at the time to get help, especially help like her, until she set my barn on fire, we then had her put in jail, since then I don't know if she has had any of her turns. . . .

> (*Signed*) ARTHUR DAVISON,
> *Clerk of County Court,*
> Amherst, Nova Scotia

After her experiences with the ghost, Esther Cox married, first, a Mr. Adams in Springdale, Nova Scotia, and when he died, a man named Shanahan. She lived in Brockton, Massachusetts, many years before her death in 1912.

In 1908, twenty-nine years after he had first visited Esther Cox and had taken her on the tour, Walter Hubbell returned to Amherst, Nova Scotia. There he found that the house was still standing, and rented a room in it, where he wrote an addition to his book, calling it "Thirty Years After." Before he left Amherst he was presented with a testimonial document signed by sixteen well-known citizens of that town. I quote excerpts from that testimonial:

We, the undersigned inhabitants of the Town of Amherst, County of Cumberland, Province of Nova Scotia . . . having of our own personal knowledge and not by or through hearsay or belief, absolutely known, seen, and heard individually all or some of the demonstrations, manifestations, and communications of an invisible, intelligent and malicious power within the atmosphere that continued its awe-inspiring and mysterious operations in the home of Daniel Teed, 6 Princess Street, Amherst, Nova Scotia, and elsewhere in the actual presence of his sister-in-law Esther Cox (but never manifested itself during her absence from the house) and continued to manifest itself for the period of one year from 1878 to 1879, as narrated by Walter Hubbell the actor . . . which account having been read by us and being known to us as accurate and truthful as to all and each fact . . . we hereto, of our own free will, affix our names to this testamentary paper so that it may . . . go before the world in corroboration and verification of what actually transpired in the presence of the Teeds, Walter Hubbell, and hundreds of the inhabitants of Amherst, including myselves, some thirty years ago.

Signed by us and delivered to Walter Hubbell whom we each know personally, this tenth day of June A. D., 1908.

(SIGNED)

Daniel Teed	*William Ripley*
Olive Teed	*David T. Chapman*
Neander Quigley	*John W. Stewart*
J. A. Simpson	*Lawrence White*
Arthur W. Moffatt	*Rufus Hicks*
J. Albert Black	*Charles Tupper Hillson*
Silas A. McNutt	*Ephraim T. Chapman*
William Beattie	*Barry D. Bent*

In all, I spent several days visiting men of Amherst who could recall the Great Mystery. All agreed that it was not a hoax and that something spiritual and uncanny had occurred there. Frederick L. Blair, about whom I wrote in my chapter on Oak Island in *Mysteries and Adventures*, made a statement for me, which I quote: "I know the Amherst Mystery to be true. There is not the slightest doubt about it. I have heard the rappings in the house and knew that they were coming from there. It was spiritualism—that is the only way it can be explained."

SAINT JOHN TO CASTINE

WITH research work ended in the Maritime Provinces, I made final arrangements for the roundabout hike to Boston and on to New Jersey which was to cover more than one thousand miles. I planned to visit the keeper of West Quoddy Head Light, walk to Mount Desert, tour the Castine peninsula, explore ancient graveyards in Frankfort, and climb around the venerable citadel of Fort Knox. Owl's Head Light; Warren; Pemaquid Point; Christmas Cove; Portland Head and Two Lights, Richmond's

Island; Higgin's Beach; Kittery; Fort Constitution in New Hampshire; and Ipswich and Nahant, Massachusetts, were all on my itinerary and none was on the shortest route from Saint John to Boston.

Early the next morning, with a heavy pack on my back, I checked out of St. John's Admiral Beatty Hotel. Walking down to the waterfront at Portland Street, I visited the site of Fort LaTour, where in 1645 D'Aulnay hanged all the soldiers in Madame LaTour's garrison after capturing the stronghold. La-Tour himself was buried at the fort in 1667, and another visitor told me that LaTour's casket had been dug up there some years before 1930 and reburied.

The next point on my itinerary was Reversing Falls where the Saint John River meets the ocean. Crossing the high bridge over the falls, I climbed far down onto the seaweed and kelp which covers the rocky shore at low tide. The thick creamy foam, or spindrift, rode the spinning surface of the many whirlpools a few feet away. The tide twisted and turned as it fought for supremacy with the outgoing river, individual areas of roaring water varying in height as much as seven and eight feet.

Scores of people have been drowned in the Reversing Falls since the coming of the white man. At the New Brunswick Historical Society in Saint John I had been told by Miss Margaret Evans about two Indians who had attempted to shoot the falls in 1898. One of them was drowned and the other saved with great difficulty. (After his rescue, the story goes, he proceeded to take up a collection from the three thousand persons assembled on the bank.) Several years before the Indian was lost, fourteen picnickers were drowned when their boat overturned at the most treacherous part of the falls.

Giant fishing weirs are located at strategic points along the falls, one of them almost directly under the bridge. The weirs are built very high because of the tide, which has a drop here of about thirty feet. Gaspereau, shad, eels, and salmon are caught in great plenty.

Hiking across to a part of the hilly shore which seemed to have sunk into the ground, I learned that a landslide had taken place there the preceding November. Evidently there was an enormous cavern underneath the hill, for several acres of land had dropped down about fifty feet. An entire barn had been swallowed up, and several residents lost their yards. Many claimed that the Reversing Falls had washed away or undermined that section of Saint John. The real explanation, of course, is a matter for geologists.

Climbing Lancaster Heights, I reached Martello Tower at its summit and obtained a fine view of Partridge Island Light. Ten minutes later I started out of town for the Saint John Airport, located forty miles from Saint John itself at Pennfield. It was late in the afternoon when I walked into Pennfield, but I could still see the Wolves Island offshore and, in the distance, the high cliffs of Grand Manan.

Sunset had come and gone when I reached Utopia Lake, and I began to doubt that I would reach Saint George before the people of that sleepy little town locked their doors for the night. I made it just in time, however, and spent the next seven hours in sleep. Arising at six, I went down to the beautiful falls in the town and then visited the pulp mill with its two mountainous piles of logs.

After passing through Bocabec shortly before noon, I came to a long lonely stretch, and for hours I met few people. I spent that night at a farmhouse and resumed my hike the next morning, reaching my goal at Saint Stephen, across the Saint Croix River from the town of Calais, Maine, by eleven o'clock.

I crossed the bridge into the state of Maine and, after hiking almost due southeast for several hours, I reached Robbinston in time for lunch. But it was the following afternoon before I arrived at my first American destination, West Quoddy Light.

Why it should be known as *West* Quoddy Head Light is something no one can answer—the light is actually on the *easternmost* point of the entire United States! I met Keeper Howard R. Gray, and he showed me around his station. The light is a color-photographer's paradise because of the beautiful contrast of the red and white stripes on the tower against the blue of the surrounding water. The Chinese red finish makes it sparkle and glisten in the sun, and, inside, the red and white paint is equally spotless and bright.

I climbed the tower to get a view of Campobello Island and Grand Manan and later visited the fog signal station and the keeper's dwelling. Here again everything was tidy and spotlessly clean. In these days of much play and little work, Keeper Howard R. Gray stands out as an exception. As I hiked up the road away from the lighthouse, my thoughts were full of praise for this civilian lighthouse keeper who has one of the neatest, prettiest and best-kept lights along the coast.

Another weary hike through a region ravaged by forest fire brought me to Cutler and the Little River. Skirting the western shores of Machias Bay, I entered East Machias and then Machias itself. Here I visited the Burnham Tavern and the tablet at Foster's Rubicon, where a group of determined men resisted British demands in 1775. Off those shores, that same year, fiery Jeremiah O'Brien, aboard the lumber schooner *Unity*, led his fellow Machias townsmen to capture the armed schooner *Margaretta* in what has been called the first naval battle of the Revolution.

I left Machias the next morning, passing Machias Falls. It was several days later when I reached Petit Manan Point and looked across at Petit Manan Island, with its tall, slender 123-foot lighthouse. Off to the south the sloping sides of Cadillac Mountain were visible, but many more weary miles lay ahead before I was to stand where Champlain had stood at the top of Mount Cadillac, 1532 feet above the sea.

Three days later I crossed the bridge leading to Mount Desert Island, and after blundering along two different roads I eventually found the highway which leads to the top of the mountain. Reaching the summit, I found an inspiring view. Far out to sea I could see the powerful beacon on tiny Mount Desert Rock. When off to the west, a glorious sunset spread its inspiring colors, I knew that I should start down at once. By the time darkness caught me, I was almost at the base of the mountain, and I soon reached Bar Harbor and a haven for the night.

The next morning, I walked across to Ship Harbor, or Locust Reach, on Mount Desert where two centuries before my ancestor, Mrs. Isabella Galloway, was shipwrecked with many other Irish immigrants. I went down on the low-tide rocks, wondering at just what spot the ship *Grand Design* had crashed against this lonely shore back in 1740.

Those aboard the *Grand Design* reached shore safely, but many died of starvation and exposure during the first few weeks. A company of young men from the wreck set out on foot to get help, never to be heard from again. Finally, friendly Indians carried word of the shipwreck to Saint George's, now Warren, Maine, and an expedition put out from Saint George's to rescue the surviving members of the ship's company. Mrs. Galloway's husband had died by this time, and when Archibald Gamble asked her hand in marriage she accepted him. Today there are hundreds of descendants of Archibald Gamble and the woman who has become known as "The Widow of Mount Desert."

BARON CASTIN AND THE
CASTINE HOARD

CASTINE, MAINE, my next objective, has always interested me—first because of its fascinating history and, second, because of the remarkable story of Baron Castin and his treasure.

As I trudged along the highway, my thoughts began to form on the subject of treasure in general. Although they are not generally known, there are some hard and fast rules regarding treasure trove in the United States which differ widely from the treasure trove rules of the British Empire.

There are many popular American misconceptions about treasure trove. The name itself can be applied to any gold or silver in plate, bullion, or coin found concealed *in* the earth—or in a house or other private place—but not lying *on* the earth. If the original owner of the discovered treasure is unknown, title to treasure trove belongs to the finder. The owner of the ground in which the treasure is found has no claim whatsoever to any treasure on the property by virtue of his ownership of the land. If a group of persons find treasure, each person shares equally in the proceeds of the venture, but each is under obligation to keep his share of the treasure against the day when the rightful owner may appear.

I remember reading an actual example of the way in which this law works. In New Vineyard, Maine, a man named Leonard Hackett hired three boys to help him clean up his yard. The four of them were digging out gravel and stones near a small building which had been swept by fire when Mr. Hackett noticed the top of an old can. One of the boys, Morton by name, dug around the can and lifted it up, whereupon the bottom fell out and sprinkled the ground with silver coins. The boys discovered two other cans, and the coins were soon transferred to a pail and taken to the Hackett residence for permanent keeping. Later the boys began to wonder if they had not been entitled to a share in the money, which was found to have an original par value of $1,284.67.

The three boys engaged a lawyer, and the ensuing case came up in the Franklin County Supreme Judicial Court in September, 1907. Here it was found that neither the owner of the property, Mr. Hackett, nor anyone else living had the slightest knowledge of how the coins were buried or who had buried them. The judge decreed that the three boys should receive $873.60 to be divided equally among them, and that Mr. Hackett could keep as his share the remainder of the money, just under $300. Unfortunately, it appears that they were not able to realize the par value from the many foreign coins in the treasure trove.

It was around noon when I reached the Castine peninsula. I walked along until I came to the old Dyce's Head Lighthouse. Sitting down in the shade of the fifty-one-foot abandoned tower, I began to review the turbulent history of the region, which has belonged to four different nations and changed governments on nine occasions.

Our first knowledge of the area begins with the year 1604 when Champlain entered the Penobscot River, then called Peimtegouet, and sailed past Castine to reach what is now Bangor. A dozen years later John Smith sailed by Pentagoet and mentioned it as the principal habitation in the vicinity.

Isaac Allerton of the Plymouth Company came to Pentagoet in 1626 and was greeted in English by an Indian who had learned the language from Penobscot fishermen. He set up a trading post there, living and working in peace until the advent of a French captain, Rosillon by name, in June, 1632. Pretending that his ship was in distress, Rosillon put into the harbor at Pentagoet. When he went ashore, he found that most of the officers and men of Allerton's trading station were on a westward trip. He seized the guns and swords of the remaining defenders, forcing them to surrender, and afterwards made them load their own supplies and goods aboard his vessel. He then sailed away, taunting the unhappy men as he left the harbor.

Finally, in 1635, Acadian Governor Razillai sent his lieutenant, Charles d'Aulnay, to capture the Pentagoet trading post of the men of Plymouth and drive the defenders into the woods. D'Aulnay's venture was succcessful and the Acadians became the ruling force in the area. A short time later, Miles Standish and Captain Girling tried to recapture Pentagoet from aboard the *Hope*, but "the stalwart Captain of Plymouth" was unable to overcome the slender garrison of eighteen men, and the *Hope* returned to Plymouth. The Acadian French were not bothered by outsiders again until 1654. However, they spent the next few years fighting among themselves.

Trouble among the Acadians began when Governor Razillai died in 1635 and his two subordinates, D'Aulnay and Charles La Tour, began to struggle with each other for leadership. D'Aulnay had gained control over the Penobscot and Saint Croix regions, and La Tour ruled what is now New Brunswick. The two Frenchmen were strong rivals in both ambition and trade and hated each other cordially. Each was unscrupulous, determined and selfish. Their religious differences—D'Aulnay was a Catholic, La Tour a Protestant—increased their animosity.

D'Aulnay gave firearms to the Indians who fought on his side, and it is said he was the first white man ever to do this. After training the Indians so they could fire the guns, D'Aulnay sailed to Saint John, hoping to capture the strong fort La Tour had built there. After a long siege, D'Aulnay was forced to give up his efforts.

La Tour and his wife then sailed to Boston and appealed to the Puritans, emphasizing the Catholic antecedents of his enemy. La Tour obtained ships and volunteers * and then sailed away to lay siege to Pentagoet, but he failed to capture it just as the Pilgrims had failed some years before. Again, two years later, he attempted in vain to rout D'Aulnay, this time by burning a farm house some distance from Pentagoet and destroying cattle. Finally D'Aulnay learned that La Tour was away from Saint John and attacked his fort with heavy forces. But Madame La Tour put up a strong defense, proving more than a match for

---

* John Winthrop tried to win his friendship by giving him a sedan chair, which had been captured from the Spanish, and was "of no use to us."

Monsieur D'Aulnay. He again gave up the siege and returned home.

Two years later D'Aulnay sent a spy to live in the garrison at Saint John. When La Tour went again on an expedition, the traitor arranged for the overthrow of the fort, and D'Aulnay entered in triumph to carry out personally one of the most vindictive acts in the entire history of North America. After lining up every surviving defender in readiness for execution, D'Aulnay demanded that a hangman's noose be placed around the beautiful neck of Madame La Tour. She was forced to stand by with the rope around her throat, not knowing whether she would be executed or not, while every surviving defender was hanged. Her own life was spared, and she was transported to Port Royal as a captive, but she died there a short time later.

The strangest part of the story was yet to come, however. Monsieur La Tour, his wife gone and his fort captured, became a wandering exile. Years later, when he learned that D'Aulnay had drowned by accident, La Tour returned to Acadia. Here he met Madame D'Aulnay. He extended to her his condolences, and, so graciously did he express his sympathy, that he eventually married D'Aulnay's widow and became the head of D'Aulnay's former domain.

After the beheading of King Charles in 1649, a Major Sedgewick was sent by Oliver Cromwell to capture Pentagoet. He allowed the French settlers to remain in their homes, and when the Treaty of Breda, in 1670, ceded Pentagoet to the French, the English settlers in turn were allowed to remain. By that time, Fort Pentagoet was a four-bastioned defense, with sixteen guns, parade grounds, magazine, guardhouse and officers' quarters.

In surrendering for the English, Captain Richard Walker made a formal presentation of the fortification to Monsieur Hubert D'Andigny, Chevalier de Grandfontaine, who established his headquarters at the fort. By 1671 there were thirty-one persons living at Pentagoet under French rule.

Now enters our story the famous Sieur de Badie, Baron de St. Castin, who dominates the picture for the next generation.

Castin was born in Oleron, France, and became a colonel in Louis XIV's guard. Sent over to Quebec with the Carignan Salieres regiment, he was discharged from the army when the war with England ended. Castin was attracted by the wild, primitive life of the North American forests, and, instead of returning to France, he moved to the headland which now bears his name. There he built himself a weird-looking dwelling, long, low and irregular, constructed partly of stone and partly of wood. A fort equipped with twelve guns was built around the house, and the entire area was palisaded.

If we are to believe all that we read about this man Castin, we shall have to admit that he was an outstanding and fascinating individual. Although held in high esteem by other Frenchmen, he never became friendly with Governor Perrot of Acadia. Perrot, in fact, once had to detain him for seventy days because of a weakness Castin developed "for some females."

In 1686 Castin came into an inheritance of some 5000 livres a year, about $1500. The next year he married Mathilde, daughter of the Indian chieftain, Madockawando. He had three children by his wife and at least one other by another woman. Without question, at one time in his career he was quite licentious and had three or four wives, but after marrying Mathilde he settled down to a life of happy monogamy. Mathilde was a graceful, lovely woman, and Longfellow tells us she had:

> *A form of beauty undefined,*
> *A loveliness without a name.*

This strange, unconventional Baron Castin was so much a part of the Pentagoet area in which he lived that gradually the

peninsula came to be called Castine. The Indians accepted him
and made him a sagamore of the Tarratines. He became the
most important trader in the area, and the Indians brought him
beaver skins by the hundreds to be shipped across the ocean to
France. By 1695 Castin admitted that eight thousand livres a
year was his profit on beaver skins alone. At the height of his
prosperity Castin's total wealth was estimated by some at 250,-
000 crowns "in good dry gold!" This is probably a figure far
above actuality.

Although Castin was busy with his trading, he had time to
harry the English who settled too close to his domain, nor did
the Bostonians allow Castin to prosper without some sort of
opposition. In June, 1688, Sir Edmund Andros, Governor of
New England, sailed to Pentagoet aboard the frigate *Rose*. Castin fled into the woods, for at that time his fort was poorly
manned. Andros took advantage of Castin's absence and stripped
the building of every gun and every piece of ammunition he
could find, taking much of Castin's furniture and merchandise
as well. Returning to Boston, he sent word to Castin that everything would be restored if Castin would ally himself with the
English. Castin not only refused to comply but he aroused the
Indians in reprisals which began the following August. York,
Falmouth, Berwick and Yarmouth were ravaged during this
period.

Probably at times Castin carried on a forbidden trade in furs
with the Bostonians. He often went on raids with the Indians,
however, and he possibly felt that he was making amends for
dealing with the New Englanders by scalping a few of them.
It has been said that Castin was by birth a gentleman and by
choice a savage.

In 1692 John Nelson, a New Englander who was being held
prisoner in Quebec, secretly sent two French deserters to
Boston with a letter saying that the French were planning to
capture the English settlements. Nelson suggested that since

Madockawando was discontented with the French, he might join forces with the New Englanders. The Bostonians decided to use the two Frenchmen, deVignon and Albert, in a plot to capture Castin and bring the Baron back to Boston.

There were three Acadians imprisoned in Boston, and the authorities offered them their freedom if they would join the two deserters in carrying out the plot. They agreed, and arrangements were made for all five Frenchmen to return to French America. But the moment the three former Boston prisoners reached home, they revealed that the two deserters were plotters. Taken back to Quebec, the two men were executed in the sight of Nelson, who soon afterwards was sent to the Bastille in France.

When Castin learned later that the New Englanders had attempted to capture him, he communicated with D'Iberville, and together they made plans to capture Fort William Henry, the allegedly impregnable castle which had been completed that same year at Pemaquid Point.

The first fort built at this location in 1624 was a blockhouse known simply as Pemaquid. Its successor, Fort Charles, was erected in 1677. This stronghold was destroyed in 1689 by the French after Andros had pillaged Castin's home at Pentagoet. The third defense was Fort William Henry, constructed under direction of Sir William Phips at the western tip of Muscongus Bay and completed in 1692. The fort was of stone and quadrangular in shape; its southern wall was twenty-two feet high, and a round tower rose twenty-nine feet in the air at the western end.

As D'Iberville and Castin approached Fort William Henry in French vessels on August 14th, 1696, it seemed impossible that they would be able to capture the stronghold. Baron Castin had brought along two hundred Indians in canoes, and D'Iberville carried a new secret weapon—round, exploding cannon balls, the like of which had never been seen by the defender of the fort, Pascho Chubb of Andover, Massachusetts. The Indians gathered outside the walls of the fort, anxious for a special vengeance against the villanous Chubb, who six months before had violated a truce by killing two Indian truce bearers, Chief Egerement of Machias and Chief Abenaquid of the Penobscots.

At five o'clock that afternoon, Commander D'Iberville sent a summons to Captain Pascho Chubb demanding that he surrender. Chubb's reply was a brave one—that he wouldn't surrender even if "the sea was covered with French vessels and the land with Indians." During the night the French landed cannon and mortars, and when morning came they began shooting the bomb shells into the fort with deadly consequences. Castin seized this opportunity to send a personal message to Chubb suggesting that he capitulate before it was too late. By this time the commander was thoroughly frightened by the exploding cannon balls and wrote back that he would surrender if his troops were allowed to reach Boston in safety. Castin and D'Iberville agreed, and the New Englanders surrendered what was really a very strong fort which could have resisted assault indefinitely.

As the English troops marched out, the red men marched in. After searching the area thoroughly, they found a heavily-shackled Indian imprisoned in a dungeon. He appeared to have been abused. This so aroused their anger that they rushed to attack the English settlers inside the fort, and it was only after a sharp skirmish that the French were able to push the Indians away from their intended victims. But the prisoner and the two trucebearing chieftains were finally avenged, for the Indians from that time until his death kept close track of Chubb. Upon reaching Boston, Chubb was accused of cowardice and put in jail for two months. He afterwards returned to his home in Andover, and there he was killed by the Indians one night, two years after he had surrendered his Pemaquid stronghold.

The French levelled Fort William Henry to the ground, but in 1729 the Pemaquid stronghold was rebuilt and named Fort

Frederick, in honor of the Prince of Wales. It was destroyed again at the beginning of the Revolution by the people of Pemaquid who tore it down because they were not strong enough to man it.

The Peace of Ryswick ended the war between the New Englanders and the French. By this time Madockawando was dead, and when Castin finally returned home, he had tired of the constant warfare. In the year 1701 he left Castine for France, never realizing that he was sailing away from Pemaquid forever. He died in France around 1706.

In 1704, Major Church, the famous Indian fighter, raided Castine, and all settlers there were forced to flee. Church boasted that he had captured every one when Castin's daughter was trapped with her children after she attempted to escape through the narrows. It is believed that she hid the Castine treasure when she fled, but I shall discuss that later.

After Church's raid the French gradually left Pentagoet. For the next fifty-five years, the Bagaduce peninsula was relatively quiet. The English took over the abandoned fort in 1759, with Governor Pownall formally accepting possession of the peninsula in the name of the King of England.

During the American Revolution, the English from Halifax landed at Pentagoet with seven hundred men and took over the ancient citadel, rebuilding it completely as a defense against the Continental forces. The New Englanders, Paul Revere among them, decided to attempt the storming of the steep cliffs of the fortification. Lengthy preparations were made, and Dudley Saltonstall of New Haven was put in command of a fleet which sailed up the Penobscot.

As the whaleboats of the American vessels reached shore, the British troops opened with heavy fire. A young fifer named Trask, huddled in the shelter of a huge boulder on the beach, played his fife while the Americans attempted the steep climb, and the giant rock has been named in the boy's honor. But the

Americans failed to storm the heights, and after losing at least fifty of their men, fell back to the boats. Later they erected a battery north of the peninsula, but instead of pushing forward and overwhelming the comparatively weak British force, Commander Saltonstall foolishly ordered a council of war. The British later admitted that they would have surrendered if challenged, but Saltonstall was afraid to attack. Before the summer ended, reinforcements from Halifax arrived to help the British at Pentagoet, and the American expedition ended in failure and disgrace.

During the War of 1812, Castine again became a British stronghold, and English forces from Castine captured Bangor and plundered Belfast.

The famous Castine treasure, reputedly hidden by Castin's daughter, was discovered in an unusual way, not in Castine itself, but on the banks of the Bagaduce River, in the town of Penobscot, six miles from the site of Castin's fort.

In November, 1849, Captain Stephen Grindle and his son Samuel were engaged on their property in hauling wood down the bank of the Bagaduce to the shore at a place called the Second Narrows, or Johnson's Narrows. They were walking on a beaten path through the bushes when Samuel noticed a coin seventy-five feet above the edge of the water, lying in one of the furrows made by the timbers as they were dragged over the soil. Samuel picked up the coin and identified it as a French crown.

The coin appeared new and bright, although later examination proved that it was two hundred years old. The men fell to work looking for more money, and found twenty pieces before night caught them. A snowstorm began that same evening and they were forced to wait until spring for further digging. The following April they searched again, and found another coin covered with moss on top of a large rock which came up out of the rapidly flowing water of the narrows. By the side of this rock the bulk of the treasure was discovered.

That same month Doctor Joseph L. Stevens visited the scene of the discovery, and although the area had by then been pretty thoroughly investigated, Stevens found several more French half-crowns a few feet from the rock. In all, there were "nearly, if not quite, two thousand pieces"—coins from France, New England, Mexico, Lima, Bogota, Potosi, Holland, Portugal, Spain, and England.

The following year a systematic search was made, but no one ever found a box or tin in which the treasure had originally been placed.

In 1704, at the time Major Church invaded the Pentagoet peninsula, the daughter of Baron Castin was left alone while her husband was in France. When the raiders came, she probably fled with her child and the Castine treasure. Reaching the Narrows, about six miles from Castin's home, she was cut off from an escape, and in the short time before her capture, she hid the hoard beside the rock. She was never able to return and claim the coins. Wheeler, in his fine history of Castine, believed that the coins "might have been left there by the Baron Castin, when he took to the woods, at the time of the visit of Governor Andros, in 1688," but this is impossible, because one of the coins bears the date 1690.

A collection of coins from the Castin hoard are now on exhibition at the Maine Historical Society in Portland.

It was early the next morning when I began my hike around Castine. I went up to the lighthouse again and then walked down the Indian trail which led to the famous Trask's Rock. The trail looked as though no one had been on it for months, with giant trees blocking the path in several places. Progress was slow and laborious, but finally I reached a junction with the trail from over the hill and turned left, where I soon saw on the beach the giant boulder which had sheltered the brave young fifer as he played for the attacking American revolutionists.

My next visit was to the Maine Maritime Academy higher up the hill. Here I met Lieutenant Commander H. E. Small, who introduced me to Captain William W. MacKenzie, in command at the school. Captain MacKenzie told me that the officers and men had recently returned from a Caribbean cruise aboard the *American Sailor*, the 420-foot steamer tied up at the Castine wharf. He invited me to visit the ship, and I went aboard to present my credentials to Lieutenant John Little.

From the *American Sailor*, I went to call at the residence of Clarence A. Wheeler, whose father, Dr. George A. Wheeler, wrote the history of Castine. I talked with Mr. Wheeler and his daughter, and they suggested that I visit the old Unitarian Church where one of Paul Revere's bells once hung. Fifteen minutes later I was admiring the Bulfinch-designed belfrey of the beautiful church built in 1790.

I next visited Fort George and afterwards spent some time reading inscriptions in the cemetery.

Then, hiking down Windmill Hill, I reached the British Canal, walked past Elephant Rock off to the left at the edge of the beach, and began my long journey toward Bucksport.

6. Fort Knox to Portsmouth and the Wagner Murder

$\mathcal{W}$ALKING through Bucksport I was on the lookout for the famous Colonel Buck monument, which allegedly shows the leg of a person the colonel is said to have wronged. I climbed up the banking to the cemetery, jumped the fence—although I learned later that the gate at the rear of the cemetery was open —and photographed Colonel Buck's monument and his grave a short distance away. I'll not mention the Buck legend here except to say that the fabrication of the story is based on an imperfection in the stone of the monument rather than historic fact.

Leaving Bucksport, I crossed the beautiful Waldo-Hancock Bridge, 137 feet above the Penobscot River. As I walked, I saw Fort Knox in the distance on my right, and my interest in old forts induced me to hurry toward this picturesque stronghold. Once there, I met the caretaker, Elijah Morse, who showed me the attractive parade grounds where Civil War troops had trained. I visited the giant Civil War Rodman cannon down on the coverface and wondered if I could squeeze my bulky form into its mouth. I backed in feet first, and sure enough, I soon wriggled my entire body into the mammoth gun. Scrambling out, I visited the granite fort itself. After a tour of this grand old bastion, with all its mementoes of a forgotten day—its secret passageways, fine circular staircases, and long cavernous tunnels—I, for one, was grateful to the State of Maine for keeping the fort in such fine condition.

After a delightful visit with Mr. Morse, I hiked along until I reached Frankfort. There I tried to locate the graves of several of my ancestors, but I found to my amazement that one of the cemeteries had seemingly disappeared. Finally I located a resident who took me to a dense grove of trees, where, deeply covered over by leaves, was the missing graveyard. Neglect has permitted the trees to conquer it, and today, for all practical purposes, the cemetery has vanished forever. It gave me a queer feeling to realize that there, in among the dense woods, were the tombstones of many people, some of whom were my ancestors.

The following afternoon I reached Searsport, where I made my way to the Penobscot Marine Museum, but it was locked tight and I was unable to enter. Continuing my walk, I reached Belfast. At last I was within striking distance of Rockland, Maine, where I must have a hundred relatives. Northport, Lincolnville, and Camden were reached and passed, and when I saw the famous "spite house" of Rockport, I knew that I would sleep in Rockland that night.

A little more than an hour later I had a first glimpse of the Rockland Breakwater Light down the bay, and soon passed the office of the Rockland *Courier-Gazette*. Happily, Editor John M. Richardson was in his office and we had a short chat about my experiences on the hike. I then crossed over to Pleasant Street to receive a cordial welcome at the home of John G. Snow, son of the late Captain John I. Snow who salvaged the *Sankaty* when she burned in New Bedford Harbor.

That night Captain John invited several other old sea captains over to the house, and they kept me entertained with their talk until well after midnight. I was especially interested in the story of the loss of the *Hugh De Payns*, as related to me by Captain Atwood B. Norton. He described the hurricane which hit his schooner down in the West Indies, driving her with winds over one hundred miles an hour. The hurricane was so strong that it blew every stitch of clothes off Captain Norton and his men, and finally the masts went by the board. "Why, I didn't dare to speak for fear the top of my head would blow off," said Captain Norton. "It was a singing wind, much worse than a whistling wind. The storm finally went down and we sat on that wreck with nothing at all to eat or drink for eight long days. We were rescued eventually, but the *Hugh De Payns* went ashore on the Florida coast, a total loss."

After Captain Norton's story, the subject of sea serpents was raised. Ray Angell told of a sea serpent, caught off the Nova Scotia coast by Captain J. W. Peppard, which was seventy feet long, with a dozen legs on each side. That gave me a chance to relate the story of the whaler *Ringold*'s catch of a sea serpent off Rio back in 1877—a hundred foot sea serpent with eyes like a horse and claws like an eagle.

Finally the assembly came to an end after two final stories by Ray Angell—one about the halibut which measured over seven feet from tip of mouth to eyes, and the other of the *Mary Dondero*, a ship with seven decks and no bottom.

I left early the next morning to pay my respects to Keeper Archford Haskins at Owl's Head Light and then walked until I reached Pemaquid. It had been a long journey, and I was pleased to obtain a room for the night and retire.

Early morning found me at Fort William Henry, the fort which Castin and D'Iberville had captured back in 1696. A small marker indicated where those terrible exploding cannonballs had landed. After inspecting the bastion, a replica of the original, I walked southward until I reached Pemaquid Point Light itself, which is untended, though it has lost none of its picturesqueness.

In the two succeeding days, I passed through Damariscotta

and Newcastle and crossed what is called the longest bridge in Maine to the historic town of Wiscasset.

The two schooners rotting at the ancient pier in Wiscasset were my goal, but the thin one-inch planking laid over the decaying wharf didn't particularly encourage me to go aboard. My curiosity was so strong, however, that I began to crawl out on my hands and knees—I knew the old boards would never hold my weight if I stood up. It seemed to take an hour to get out to the schooners on all fours, but finally I crawled up the makeshift gangway and climbed aboard the *Hesper*, the longer of the two ships. I looked across at the *Luther Little*, the other schooner, and recalled her thrilling experience off the South American coast, when her crew mutinied during a fire which had broken out aboard the vessel. The captain first subdued the mutiny and then he put out the fire.

Both the *Hesper* and the *Little* were built at Somerset, Massachusetts in 1917, and both are of 1100 tons displacement. The *Hesper* hogged at her launching when the ways collapsed. Mr. Frank W. Winter later bought the two four-masters at Portland to haul coal and other supplies for his railroad project, but his plan for transportation to serve the farm communities from Wiscasset to Quebec failed to compete with trucks and automobiles. The railroad was closed down, the tracks pulled up, and the project forgotten. The two schooners, which were to transport material to and from the Wiscasset terminal, quietly rotted away at the pier disturbed only by a fire some years ago aboard the *Hesper* which was extinguished after burning the afterdeck.

I took several pictures before I began to crawl back to the pier, expecting every moment that the planking would give way. But when I finally reached firm ground without accident, I wondered at the strange rating which Lloyd's of London still give the *Luther Little* after her many years of inactivity—A 1, the highest classification.

Climbing Wiscasset's hill, I stopped to admire the Nickels-

Sortwell House across the street from where I stood. Constructed in 1807, the beautiful mansion was one of four built by three brothers and a sister. It is a companion to the famous "spite house" of Phippsburg, which was moved in 1925 by my cousin, Captain John I. Snow, to Rockport, Maine, eighty-five miles away.

After another day of hiking I entered Portland the following afternoon. I visited my acquaintances at the various bookstores and then went over to the Maine Historical Society and interviewed Miss Marian Rowe, who gave me permission to photograph the Castine coins in the Society's collection. Next I visited Portland Head Light and Keeper William L. Lockhart, who had seen previous service at Rockland Breakwater, Great Duck Island, and Petit Manan. He described to me the terrible "Oakey Alexander" gale, as it has come to be called, which struck Cape Elizabeth on March 3, 1947.

"One sea hit during that storm at nine o'clock in the morning and its great force carried it over the outer ledge. Before it could hit the area around the buildings, another sea followed and they both hit the fog house together, shattering a sixteen-inch brick wall and knocking the old fog bell down into the gully. I don't think I'll ever witness another such double wave in my life!" Keeper Lockhart then took me out on the cliff and pointed to the rocks where the *Lochinvar* and the *Annie Maguire* had been wrecked years before he came to the station.

Two hours later I reached Cape Elizabeth Lifeboat Station, and met the officer in charge, Boatswain's Mate Everett Marston, who had come to the station in April. A veteran of twenty-four years' service, he had formerly been stationed at the Isles of Shoals and Damariscove. I also met Mrs. Clifton S. Morong at the lighthouse keeper's dwelling there, and she gave me a valuable addition to the *Oakey Alexander* storm story.

"You may remember, Mr. Snow, that the *Alexander* was

wrecked that March 3rd morning. Well, around seven o'clock
that night we saw rocket after rocket climb into the sky far out
to sea. There were fifteen or twenty rockets in all, one right
after the other at first, and then they came in slower intervals.
Finally the last one shot up into the sky fifteen minutes after its
predecessor. We notified the Coast Guard Base, and the *Cowslip*
went out, but when she reached the vicinity there was nothing
in sight—not even wreckage. It must have been the *Novadoc*,
just before she went down, for there was no other vessel in the
vicinity."

The *Novadoc* had also radioed a distress signal early that same
morning. Nothing was ever again seen or heard of either the
ship or the twenty men and two women aboard, and the fate of
the *Novadoc* has become one of the unsolved mysteries of the
sea. The Morongs have added another fragment to our meagre
knowledge of its final disaster.

The next day I noticed a wreck on Higgin's Beach, just to the
south of Cape Elizabeth, and hiked over to find that it was the
bones of the three-masted schooner *Harry W. Middleton* which
came ashore in the fall of 1898 with no lives lost.

Hiking through Old Orchard Beach and Ocean Park, I
reached Biddeford Pool in time to spend the night. Early the
next day I telephoned out to Goat Island Light at Cape Porpoise
and asked Keeper Joseph Bakken if he'd come in and pick me
up at Cape Porpoise. An hour and a half later I landed at tiny
Goat Island where I had dropped so many Christmas presents
each year. There the keeper introduced me to his wife and
their three children. We climbed the tower and then hiked
around the island while Joe Bakken told me about his experiences at Goat Island Light.

"The worst time was the *Oakey Alexander* storm," he began.
"I remember our dog had just had puppies, and when the seas
broke right over the island to smash down the board walk, boat
slip, and rip out the fence, we were so busy that I forgot the

dog. Late that night my wife thought of the puppies. I ran down into the cellar. It was deep in water, but there they all were, the dog and her puppies, floating around in the box we had given her. You can bet I brought them all upstairs."

At noon I returned to the mainland just in time to watch the mackerel fleet unload their catch. One craft, the *Star of the Sea*, interested me particularly when I noticed a woman aboard, dressed in overalls and working with the men. Taking a picture of her, I learned that she was Mrs. Clarence Grant of North Berwick, Maine.

Hiking back along the road, I passed a graveyard high on a hill and went into the enclosure. It seemed crowded with the tombstones of sea captains. A large stone set between two granite pillars attracted my attention.

CAPT. Leander Foss AE 36 was lost on the wreck of the New Barque Isidore together with all on board 15 in number on Cape Neddick Nov. 30 1842.

Late the next day I reached Kittery, Maine, and stopped off at the pleasant graveyard on the hill which slopes toward the water. Located across the street from the First Parish Church, it has scores of inscriptions on the tombs of interest to the visitor.

The gravestone of James W. Remick informs the curious that the stone itself was taken from a trail on Sunshine Hill, the spot where he and his dog Teddy passed so many happy times. Then there is the epitaph written by Robert Browning in memory of a friend he never met, Levi Lincoln Thaxter, husband of the poetess Celia Thaxter:

> *Thou, whom these eyes saw never! Say friends true*
> *Who say my soul, helped onward by my song,*
> *Though all unwittingly, has helped thee too?*
> *I gave of but the little that I knew:*
> *How were the gift requited, while along*

Life's path I pace, couldst thou make weakness strong!
Help me with knowledge—for Life's Old—Death's New!

The sailors who lost their lives in the wreck of the brig *Hattie Eaton*, which was cast away on Gerrish Island in 1876, are buried under a single stone inscribed with a drawing of the brig. Another interesting inscription appears on the gravestone of Mrs. Margaret Hills, who was drowned in 1803 at the age of twenty-eight:

> *I lost my life on the raging seas*
> *A sovereign God does as he please;*
> *The Kittery friends they did appear*
> *And my remains they buried here.*

I called later that afternoon at the home of Miss Rosamund Thaxter, who lives on the old Champernowne estate at Cutts Island, in the shadow of a giant tree. Miss Thaxter is the granddaughter of Celia Thaxter, known for many years as the poetess who lived on a lighthouse. Celia Thaxter is perhaps best remembered for her poem which begins, "Across the narrow beach we flit, one little sandpiper and I." Her father, Thomas Laighton, had been a successful businessman, editor and politician when, disgusted with politics, he chose to become a lighthouse keeper in the Isles of Shoals. The family later bought the estate on Cutts Island where I now sat talking with Miss Rosamund Thaxter.

"I still go out to the Shoals," Miss Thaxter told me, "but it is so different from the days when Uncle Oscar Laighton, Celia's brother, was alive. I adored him. I always sat and held his hand when they sang *Good Bye Sweet Day*. My father was John, Celia's second child. There aren't too many descendants of Celia, for only one of her five grandchildren married, Elizabeth Hubbard, who has three children. One of them is Celia Thaxter Hubbard."

Crossing the Piscataqua River, which runs between Maine

and New Hampshire, I entered the Granite State and made my way to the Portsmouth waterfront, where the boat to the Isles of Shoals leaves. I sat down on the planking and reconstructed the various events which led up to one of the most brutal episodes in Isles of Shoals history.

TRAGEDY AT SMUTTYNOSE

THE Isles of Shoals, located about eight miles out to sea from Portsmouth, New Hampshire, are now chiefly noted for the summer conferences held there by the Unitarians and the Congregationalists. Three-quarters of a century ago, however, they were being discussed for another reason altogether—the murder of two women on a lonely part of the Shoals.

Reaching the little harbor made by Star, Malaga, Smuttynose, and Cedar Islands, I went ashore at Star Island, crossed the breakwater between Star and Cedar Islands, and stood for a moment on the boundary marker on Cedar Island which separates New Hampshire and Maine. Then I hiked along the relatively new breakwater which goes out from Cedar Island and soon reached Smuttynose, the island of mystery and murder. There I saw the ruins of the Hontvet residence, the scene of a terrible tragedy. How peaceful it seemed on this warm, sunny day!

In the year 1870 John and Maren Hontvet left their home in Laurig, Norway, and sailed across the sea to the United States, where they established a home for themselves at Smuttynose, or Haley's Island, one of the eight Isles of Shoals off the New Hampshire coast. They were a happily married couple. Their cottage at Smuttynose faced the cove, and in it they enjoyed the beautiful summers and the long winters together. John was a tall, blue-eyed Scandinavian with bronzed beard and flashing white teeth, and he dearly loved his charming Maren. But Maren had much time on her hands while her husband was off fishing, and she was pleased when her sister Karen arrived to live with them in May, 1871.

Karen came to America to forget an Old World tragedy, for her lover had died in Norway. Mathew Hontvet, John's brother, joined the household the same year, and in October, 1872, Ivan Christiansen, brother of the two girls, came with his wife, Anethe Mathea, to live with the family at Smuttynose. The two newcomers had only been married for nine months. Ivan, quiet and industrious, was tall and light-haired; Anethe was a happy little girl whose bright golden hair reached nearly to her knees. The six members of the household dwelt in peace and security, and afterwards Maren said that this short period when the family was all together was the happiest time of her life.

At that time there were only four inhabited islands at the Shoals. At Star Island, workmen were building a new hotel; there was a lighthouse keeper on White Island; Celia Thaxter, the poet, with her family and servants and the Ingebertsens, a family of fishermen, lived at Appledore; the Hontvets were at Smuttynose. The uninhabited islands were Cedar, Malaga, Londoner, and Duck.

In 1871 a German youth known as Louis Wagner first appeared at Haley's Island. Wagner was a huge man, dark, and very powerful. He was said to have been in difficulty at previous times in his career, and once he himself boasted that "not many had done what he had done and got off in safety." On another occasion, at a fisherman's home, he was arguing with several others who were doing their best to convince him that he was wrong. He finally rushed away, muttering under his breath, "I know I am wrong, but I'll never give in."

In 1872 he moved to Star Island, where he fished alone from a wherry, but he made little money and often called at Haley's Island where the Hontvets befriended him and gave him food. The following June, Hontvet hired him as one of the hands and he moved over to Haley's Island. When Ivan and Anethe landed at Smuttynose, Wagner was still there, and they came to know him and to look upon him as a brother.

In November he left the island and went to the mainland. There he got work on the fishing schooner *Addison Gilbert*, but on January 6 the schooner was wrecked in a gale, and Wagner was "on the beach" again. As the weeks went by and he failed to obtain employment, Wagner grew more and more desperate for money. By March 5 he had been ashore eight weeks and owed fifteen dollars to his landlady, Mrs. Charles Johnson. Wagner was quite outspoken about his desire to raise funds. In the presence of John Hontvet he made the serious statement, "I must have money even if I murder for it." He later repeated essentially the same remark to two other men at different times. The first was Waldemar Ingebertsen, and the second was Charles Johnson, husband of his landlady.

On the fatal day of March 5, 1873, John Hontvet, Mathew Hontvet, and Ivan Christiansen set sail in the *Clara Bella* to draw their trawls to the eastward of the islands. It was their plan to return to Smuttynose for dinner and then go on to the mainland to sell their fish, but when they had drawn their trawls the wind was so favorable for Portsmouth and unfavorable to the Shoals that they decided not to beat back to the island but to sail right for Portsmouth. Their custom of leaving a man on the island to protect the women was broken for the first time. Instead, John Hontvet shouted across to the nearby schooner from Appledore Island and asked Emil Ingebertsen to go over to Smuttynose and tell Maren that he was sailing direct to Portsmouth and would be back later that night.

At four o'clock the men from Smuttynose sailed up to the pier at Portsmouth, where they were greeted by Louis Wagner. They tossed him a line, and he made it fast. As the men came ashore, a quick flush passed over the face of Wagner.

"Are you going out again tonight?" he asked.

"That all depends on the bait," replied John Hontvet. "If it comes by the early train, then we'll get back, but if it comes on the late train, then we won't be back until morning."

The three men were hungry, but they found to their disappointment that they had all left their pocketbooks at home. Louis Wagner was standing nearby, and pricked up his ears when he heard that their money was at home.

"How much do you make fishing, John?" asked Wagner cautiously.

John replied without hesitation, "Oh, I've cleared about six hundred dollars."

Then and there the desperate and penniless Wagner decided to steal out to the island, enter the Hontvet house that night, take the money, and return to Portsmouth before the men came home.

"I may be back later and help you with the baiting," said Louis, but they didn't see him again that night. A short time afterwards he entered a liquor shop and had a glass of beer. Then he walked down to Pickering Wharf in South Portsmouth where he noticed the dory of David Burke tied up at the pier. The thole pins were new, and a pair of oars were lying beneath the thwarts. Wagner had sailed with Burke aboard the schooner *Iris* and had often tied up at the same wharf. Young James Burke, son of David, had just landed from the dory at seven-thirty that evening, intending to be gone an hour.

Wagner, glancing about quickly to see if anyone might be watching, leaped aboard, undid the painter, and was soon far down the river, rowing out to sea with the tide. Everything was in his favor from the moment he planned his scheme until his return. The tide was ebbing, the wind was offshore, and the light of the moon helped him on his way. There was just enough snow on the ground to identify the banks of the river, and the lights of Newcastle and Eliot flickered briefly as he swept down with the current and out to sea. Soon he reached

Portsmouth Harbor Light at Fort Constitution and headed for Whaleback Ledge Light. Now began the longest part of the trip—the seven and a half miles from Whaleback Ledge to Smuttynose Island.

But the sea was relatively calm and the wind was offshore. Minute after minute slid by broken only by the sound of the oars slipping back and forth between the thole pins. To the man in the dory it must have seemed an eternity. The lights of the mainland grew smaller and smaller. Far off to his right gleamed Boon Island Light.* Then the flash of White Island Light came to him over his shoulder in full glow as he neared the Shoals. When the sound of the waves hitting the islands ahead of him came across the water, he pulled with renewed vigor. Alone on the ocean at night, what must his thoughts have been as he rowed on and on during the long hours? Undoubtedly he planned exactly how he would enter the kitchen, take the money from the place he knew it was kept and return to the mainland. Did he feel uneasy at robbing the Hontvets, who had treated him so well? We only know that he rowed on until he reached the snow-covered islands.

On Smuttynose Island that preceding afternoon, the three women had kept dinner hot for the men for several hours. They had scanned the horizon in vain for the sail of their loved ones. At dusk young Emil Ingebertsen faithfully delivered the message to them that the men had taken advantage of the favoring wind and sailed directly to Portsmouth. Karen was disappointed, for she was all dressed and ready to go on the schooner to the city. She planned to match a button she especially liked, and Maren had put the button in her pocketbook as a reminder. After supper the three sat around the fire with the dog, Ringe,

---

* Edmund Pearson, noted writer of true murder stories, makes one of his few mistakes in trying to change Celia Thaxter's correct opinion that Wagner, as he rowed out to the island, had Boon Island Light on his right, rowing with his back facing his destination. Pearson incorrectly believed that the light was on Wagner's left.

curled up beside them. Ten o'clock came and they decided to go to bed. Karen objected to sleeping upstairs alone, so Maren arranged a makeshift bed in the kitchen for her. Anethe and Maren went to bed in the next room, and by ten-thirty they were all asleep.

It was shortly after midnight when Wagner reached Appledore and rowed in between the islands to land at Smuttynose. He pulled his dory up on the southern side, away from the cove, in case the Hontvets should come back earlier than he expected. Striding up to the house, Wagner saw that it was in darkness. At about one o'clock in the morning, he tried the kitchen door and found it unlocked. As he stole into the kitchen, the dog began to bark, and Karen, a few feet away from Wagner, muttered in her sleep, "John, is that you?"

The presence of one of the women in the kitchen was a terrific surprise to Wagner. He had expected to take the money while the women were asleep and leave at once without being noticed. He was only interested in the $600 he expected to find, but still he couldn't let anyone discover him. Seizing a chair, he swung it wildly at Karen, who was now standing on the kitchen floor. His aim was poor, and his blow hit the kitchen clock, which crashed to the floor and stopped.* The crash awakened Maren in the next room.

"What is the matter?" she shouted.

Karen, not recognizing Louis in the darkness, thought he was her brother-in-law, John. With that thought in mind, she answered, "John scared me!"

Maren leaped to her feet and rushed to the connecting door, but she discovered that the intruder had already secured the latch with a stick. Then Karen began to scream again:

"John kills me! John kills me!"

Finally Karen stumbled against the door, and the stick fell

---

* When found later, the hands were pointed at 1:07.

out. Maren Hontvet, rushing in to grab Karen, saw the huge, silent figure of a man outlined against the southern window a few feet away. Now the figure began to advance and struck her twice. Maren pulled her sister into the bedroom with her, slammed the door, and held it shut with her body.

Anethe, who was already wide awake, stood in the room near them.

"Go out the window, Anethe, and then run and hide," cried Maren. Poor Anethe was able to climb out through the window into the snow, but then, paralyzed with fear, she collapsed against the house. Dressed only in her thin nightgown, she must have been a pitiful sight.

"Scream for help, Anethe—run quickly," called Maren, still struggling to keep the door shut against the determined Wagner. But Anethe couldn't make a sound and as in a nightmare, she was unable to move.

Louis Wagner finally stopped pushing at the door and began to listen. Yes, one of the girls was outside in the snow. He went out through the door and around the building, where he found Anethe leaning against the wall of the house. In the reflection of the moonlight against the snow Anethe recognized the visitor.

"Louis, Louis!" she cried, and the man recoiled. He must act fast now, for he had been recognized. Rushing to the front door, he picked up the axe which he had noticed there and ran back to the terrorized Anethe. Starting to run from the building, she sobbed aloud, "Oh, Louis, Louis." They were her last words, for within the sight of Maren, who was standing inside the window a few feet away, Wagner brought down the axe and continued to strike Anethe until she was dead.

When Maren realized that they could not help Anethe, she pleaded with Karen to flee from the house with her, but Karen collapsed and said that she was done for. With a sob, Maren grabbed a skirt and wrapped it around her shoulders, for the night outside was bitter cold. Heading for the cove where she hoped to find Wagner's dory, she heard the screams of her dying sister. The dory was not at the cove, and Maren was trapped on the island. She hid first in one of the old houses, but when Ringe, her dog, appeared, she was afraid his barking might be heard by Wagner.

Looking back at the house, Maren noticed that Wagner had lighted a lamp and that the curtains were down. It was now after two o'clock, and the moon had set. The night was getting colder and colder. But Maren knew that in spite of the cold she and the dog would have to go down to the rocky shore to escape Wagner. She found a hiding place between two rocks, and she took Ringe with her into the opening. Drawing him to her breast so that he would not bark, she lay flat against the ground and waited the dawn.

During the next hour and a half Wagner hunted for Maren all over the island, as his bloody tracks in the snow revealed the next day. The killer of two women, he was unable to find the third and finish his gruesome business. Returning to the house, the madman tore the rooms apart in his effort to find the $600. Actually there *was* about $135 hidden between some sheets at the bottom of a drawer which he examined. But Wagner never found that money. He found only three five dollar bills, some silver coins and a handful of pennies, together with Karen's button which was later discovered in his pocket.

After his search, he went outside and dragged Anethe's body back into the kitchen. Karen's remains were in the bedroom, and it is believed that if he could have found and killed Maren, he probably would have started a funeral pyre of the house itself to destroy the evidence of his crime.

Finally he decided to have some food before returning to Portsmouth. Even though Anethe's body was a few feet away, he sat down at the kitchen table and enjoyed a hearty meal. The teakettle was later found on the stove with his bloody fingerprints all over it. When Wagner had finished his meal, he walked straight to the well outside the house, washed his hands and arms, and left the basin and a bloody towel at the well.

The stars were now fading from the sky, and Wagner realized that he must return or be detected. He went down to his dory and soon was rowing over the ocean toward the mainland.* He finally landed at Newcastle and tried to push the dory out to sea so that no one could connect him with the incident. But the incoming tide brought the dory back, and it was later found near the Devil's Den at Jaffrey's Point.

Louis Wagner, the fiend who killed two women at Smutty-nose for the sum of less than $20, determined to get back to his boarding house without being seen. He presented a horrible sight, his blood-stained clothes covered with ice from the spray of the ocean.

Wagner was forced to climb a rock at the top of a small hill to get his bearings. Seeing the spires of the Portsmouth churches in the distance, he started to walk toward them. It was then about six-thirty in the morning. He hoped to escape notice, but several persons saw him in the next three-quarters of an hour. It was unfortunate for Wagner that the bridge from Newcastle to Portsmouth was damaged and that he had to make a spectacle of himself by inching his way over a plank to reach the Portsmouth side.

Finally Wagner arrived at his boarding house at 25 Water Street. Sneaking up the back stairs, he pulled off his bloody shirt and rolled it into a ball. Later he tucked it under a clean shirt which he had put on and started for the toilet outdoors. Before he reached the back door, he was passed in the hall by Mary Johnson, daughter of the Mrs. Johnson who ran the boarding house. Under oath, she later testified that "there was a bunch sticking out" under Wagner's shirt that was not there before or

---

* Many persons feel that the distance to Smuttynose and back was too far for Wagner to row in one night. Actually, John Hontvet had accomplished it over fifty times, in from three to four hours each way.

after he went out to the toilet. Obviously he dropped the bloody shirt into the privy at that time, for it was later found there.

Shortly afterwards he spoke to Mr. Johnson. He confessed that he was "in trouble and may be taken." He told Johnson that he felt terrible "and must go away." When urged to eat breakfast, he said that it did not appeal to him at all. Finally he left the boarding house, crying out as he shut the door, "Farewell for good!"

Stopping only at the baker's for food, Wagner went to the station and took the train for Boston shortly after nine o'clock. There he attempted to ship out to sea from Charlestown, but, failing once, he did not try again. He walked over into Boston, where he had his beard shaved off and bought a pair of shoes and a suit of clothes. Then he walked wearily to North Street and entered the so-called boarding house of a man named Brown, where a lady friend, Emma Miller, was still on hand. Although Wagner had shaved off his beard, Emma recognized him at once.

"Hello, Louis," she greeted him.

"I am not Louis," Wagner replied. "That is not my name. You are mistaken."

"Well, Louis, if it isn't your name, it is the one you used when you were here before. What mischief are you up to now, Louis?"

After a few minutes the stolid German admitted that he was Louis but that a series of unfortunate incidents had made him afraid to reveal his true identity. He told Emma that he had killed two sailors in a quarrel at sea and that when he landed at New York he had cut off his whiskers to evade the police and reach Boston.

By this time Wagner was exhausted from his superhuman efforts of the past twenty hours. He asked for a mug of spruce beer to revive him. The beer was brought, but the results were quite the opposite from those he anticipated. After drinking the entire mug, Louis Wagner slumped over in his chair and fell asleep on the table.

Now we shall leave Wagner in the Boston boarding house and take up our story at the Hontvet home on Smuttynose Island.

On the rocky beach at Smuttynose, Maren, huddling against her dog, had awaited the dawn with terror. When the sun rose vividly red in the east, she hardly knew what to do. She was half-frozen and paralyzed with fear. Wagner might still be on the island. But, hearing the sound of hammers as the carpenters began their morning's work at Star Island, she called over to them, waving frantically to get their attention. Unaware of the extraordinary events on Smuttynose, the carpenters merely waved back and went on with their work.

Maren then decided that she would have to make her way to the Appledore side of the island in order to get help. Passing her home from a distance, she noticed that the curtains were still pulled down, and wondered if Wagner might not have killed himself as well as the two girls. She crossed the breakwater which ran to Malaga Island, and went to the northern part of the island from which she could see, less than a quarter mile away, two boys playing around the door of the Ingebertsen home on Appledore.

Screaming at the top of her voice and frantically waving her skirt, she finally attracted the children's attention. They in turn went to get Mr. Ingebertsen. He walked down to the shore, pushed his dory into the water, and rowed over to Malaga Island to see what was wrong. Pulling up on the beach, he looked in amazement at Maren's bare feet, her nightdress, and her bruised face. The sympathetic old man was overwhelmed.

"Maren, Maren, who could have done this to you? What is it? Who is it?"

Maren stared at him, dazed, and then her answer came, "Louis, Louis, Louis."

The old man took her aboard his dory and rowed to Appledore with her, and as he rowed he learned the entire horrible
story.

When they landed at Appledore, the old man took Maren to
his house, where she was put to bed and treated for her injuries and
exposure. Then Ingebertsen rushed up to the Thaxter residence
and told Celia Thaxter and his countrymen of the terrible deed.
The men went for their guns and hurriedly rowed across to Smuttynose Island, ready for the murderer if he still remained there.
But all they discovered were the two naked bodies of the
women, Anethe and Karen. Wisely, they decided to touch
nothing, and returned to Appledore to await the arrival of the
Clara Bella from Portsmouth.

The masts of the *Clara Bella* soon appeared above the headland, and the group went down on the shore, awaiting with
anguish the moment they must tell the fishermen what had happened to their loved ones. They signaled for Hontvet to come
ashore at Appledore. Hontvet and Ivan Christiansen noticed
the little group of men on the shore and knew that something
was wrong, but never in their wildest dreams could they imagine the truth. A moment later they landed from the dory and
learned the terrible news.

It was impossible for Ivan to believe what they told him. He
rushed to the Ingebertsen cottage. "Where is Anethe?" he
shouted to Maren.

The girl answered him—"Anethe is—Anethe is at home!"

He ran out and called to John. Together they slid the dory
into the sea and rowed desperately for their home on Smuttynose Island. Others followed them as quickly as possible, but
the two men landed on the beach ahead of the rest and rushed
up to the house.

Ivan stood in the doorway with John at his shoulder for one
frightful second, staring unbelievingly at the bloody and naked
body of his beloved wife. Staggering across the yard, Ivan lost

his senses and fell helplessly to the ground. John soon collapsed also, and the other islanders found them both lying in the snow and brought them back to consciousness.

The neighbors took them to Appledore and helped the schooner make ready for the trip back to the mainland. An hour later John sailed from Smuttynose and landed at Portsmouth after a fast trip across. There he notified the authorities of the double murder. The police of all cities were put on the watch for Wagner, and the city marshal took the next train for Boston, only a few hours after the murderer.

All day long out on the island the slaughtered bodies of the women lay untouched, but at eight o'clock that evening the steamer *Mayflower* arrived with the officers from Portsmouth. John, now back at Smuttynose, stayed with them until their entire investigation was completed. The officers finally left the island, arriving at Portsmouth early in the morning. Meanwhile John returned to Maren. Kneeling by the side of her bed, he broke down and sobbed.

"Maren, Maren, it is too much, far too much! I can't stand it!" But Maren threw her arms around her husband's neck and pulled his bearded head close to her.

"Don't say that, John, for I'll be crazy and I'll die, if you go like that!" John made an effort to contain himself, and promised Maren that he would calm down. But Ivan was beyond reason, and for several days no one could help him. They were afraid he would do away with himself and dared not leave him alone.

Later the bodies of the two girls were carried across to Portsmouth, where they were buried in the local cemetery. Although both John and Ivan were present as the remains were lowered into the earth, Ivan seemed not to notice or care. It was several months before time mercifully brought him back to normal and softened the terrible picture engraved in his mind.

Louis Wagner was captured in the same North Street boarding house where he had fallen asleep after drinking a mug of beer. He was taken back to Portsmouth under armed guard, and his attitude was a little too sanctimonious for the Portsmouth officials. Wagner had decided to take a tardy interest in the Bible and religion.

"Don't you want to know why we are arresting you?" the Portsmouth marshal asked him.

"No, I don't. I have put my faith in the Lord, and there is nothing for me to fear." This hypocritical attitude actually won Wagner many sympathizers. Reaching New Hampshire, the murderer and his captors had to contend with the outraged men of Portsmouth, who tried to stone Wagner as he made his way through the streets.

The day came when the Hontvets confronted Wagner in his prison cell. Wagner glanced up as the sheriff brought in John and Maren, and his face went white. Later, when his courage returned, a bright red spot stood high on each cheek. But he maintained his dogged determination that he was innocent.

"Louis, what have you to say for yourself?" asked Hontvet.

"I'm glad that Jesus loves me," he exclaimed.

" 'Tis the devil who loves you," John cried out at him, and the unhappy couple left the room.

It became the habit of many God-fearing sympathizers to visit Louis Wagner in his cell while he awaited trial, and the murderer, Bible in hand, quoted scripture and convinced many that he was innocent. He told his story remarkably well in simple short sentences. He claimed that on the night of the murder he had baited traps down on the Randall and Caswell Wharf for a few hours, working for the captain of a schooner. As he left the wharf, he passed several men also baiting traps in the shed. He entered a saloon and indulged in two beers, after which he became ill. While walking down Court Street, he slipped and fell on the ice near a little pump in the sidewalk. Unable to get up, he went to sleep by the pump and remained there for several hours. When he woke up at about three o'clock in the morning, he returned to 25 Water Street, where he got into the house by using the back door. He went to sleep, awakened at five and went out again, meeting some men near a bridge. On his way home he heard a train whistle and decided that he wanted to take a trip to Boston. Some time after reaching Boston, he was taken by the police.

Since there are many people who still believe that Wagner was innocent, I shall now prove that his story was utterly false.

Wagner's statement that he had baited traps on a schooner that night and then walked past several men at Randall and Caswell's was disproved by Harrison Berry, who was on the wharf from six-thirty until about one in the morning. "There were three beside myself baiting trawls there," said Harrison Berry, "and I did not see Louis Wagner that night."

Three five dollar bills were taken from the Hontvet house that night of the murder. Wagner spent two of the bills on his new suit and the other was in his pocket when he was arrested.

One silver half dollar had been in Karen's purse, and a silver half dollar was found on Wagner the next day. One silver five cent piece and a silver three cent piece were in her purse and both were found in Wagner's possession the following day. Thirteen coppers were found on the prisoner, and Karen's purse had held a great many coppers for use on the trip to Portsmouth. And let us not forget that Wagner had never paid his landlady the three weeks rent due her and a short time before borrowed thirty-five cents for tobacco. The little white agate button from Karen's purse was later found in Wagner's pocket with the pennies. Can anyone hope to explain these remarkable coincidences in any manner consistent with Wagner's supposed innocence? Of course not!

As to Wagner's claim that he fell on the ice near the Court Street pump and slept there until three in the morning, three different policemen testified that they walked by the pump on several occasions between one and four that morning and saw no one lying there.

His claim that he returned to 25 Water Street and entered by the back door was refuted not only by the landlady, who locked the door promptly at midnight, but by one of the fishermen who tried to use the door later that same morning and found that it was still locked.

Wagner withdrew his claim that he entered the house and slept in his bed when Mrs. Johnson pointed out that his bed was not mussed in the least. He changed his story to say that he had slept on the lounge downstairs. Again he was trapped by his statement, for another man had spent the night on the cot Wagner claimed to have used.

Wagner insisted that the shirt found in the privy outside the house was not his, but Mary Johnson, who mended his clothes for him, identified the shirt as Wagner's by the sewing she had done on it a few days before.

In an effort to pin Wagner down to a definite statement of what ships he saw or men he talked to, the German was placed on the stand and questioned, as follows:

Question: Did you know the name of the person who kept the saloon?
Answer: No, sir.
Question: Did you know the name of the schooner you baited the trawls on that night?
Answer: No, sir.
Question: Or the name of the master?
Answer: No, sir.
Question: Can you tell at what wharf she was lying?
Answer: I don't know the name of the wharf.

Only one man in all Portsmouth knew that the Hontvet schooner had left Smuttynose Island at six that morning and had not returned to the island before sailing for Portsmouth. Only one man knew that there were no men at the island—that neither Hontvet, his brother Mathew, nor Ivan would be at the island all that night. Only one man knew that the money was on the island. He was, of course, Louis Wagner, who met the schooner at the pier, questioned John Hontvet, learned about the money, and acted upon the information. Only Louis Wagner could have murdered the girls.

Wagner's trial began June 8, 1873, at Alfred, Maine, for Smuttynose Island was part of the state of Maine. From beginning to end Wagner maintained his stoic calm, but the evidence produced against him was so overwhelmingly conclusive that at the end of the trial the jury was out only fifty-five minutes before pronouncing him guilty. His execution was delayed several times, and he escaped from jail once, after allegedly winning the affection of the sheriff's daughter. Finally, however, on June 25, 1875, Wagner was hanged along with another murderer. Contrary to popular opinion, this was not the last hanging in the state of Maine.

7. A Unique Rescue

SAILING out to the Isles of Shoals from Portsmouth, I went ashore at White Island and climbed the lighthouse there. While standing at the top of that well-known beacon, I looked out upon the scene of an unfortunate accident which sent a proud, new submarine to the bottom of the ocean some ten years ago.

Hundreds and hundreds of ships have been wrecked along this Atlantic coast, with thousands of lives lost and countless survivors rescued. In 1925, however, a new type of disaster occurred off this coast—the loss of men aboard a submarine. I have always had a great admiration and respect for deep sea divers and sailors who choose to spend their lives on submarines, and, together with the rest of the nation, I experienced a feeling of almost personal loss when I heard that the *S-51* had been struck and sunk by the *City of Rome* off Block Island. Three men jumped to safety before the submarine sank to the bottom, but all the others were lost.

Again, in December, 1927, the submarine *S-4* collided with the destroyer *Paulding*, and every-one of the forty men aboard was suffocated at the bottom of the sea.

Earlier in this book I told the strange story of the wreck of the *Cod Seeker*, in which two men, trapped in the schooner, sank to the bottom of the sea and later were rescued when the vessel floated up to surface again. The story of the *Squalus*, however, is unique. For the first time in history, men were rescued from a submarine which had sunk to the bottom of the sea.*

The loss of the S-51 and the S-4 had proved the need for some method of submarine rescue. Navy Commander Charles B. Momsen was put to work on his new diving lung and began training men to descend more than two hundred feet under water. Commander Allen R. McCann invented a rescue chamber which would go far under the surface of the sea and clamp against the escape hatch of a submarine. The Navy was doing what it could to prevent loss of lives in the future.

On the morning of the twenty-third of May, 1939, the submarine *Squalus* left Portsmouth on a routine trip around the Isles of Shoals with a crew of fifty-nine officers and men aboard. She had already made eighteen successful dives since her completion on May 12, 1939. At seven-forty that morning the *Squalus* submerged. Nothing unusual happened at first, but suddenly the ship listed, swerved sharply, and threw the crew against the bulkheads. The lights soon went off. Water had entered the vessel through the main engine induction valve, flooding the four compartments of the ship abaft the after control room bulkhead. The *Squalus* went down stern first in 240 feet of water.

Lieutenant Oliver F. Naquin, commander of the *Squalus*, felt the soft thud as the vessel hit bottom and realized that the after compartment must have been flooded. He knew that the twenty-six men in the stern of the ship were drowning and that there was no way of rescuing them. He assembled the remaining thirty-two members of the crew and told them, "You all know by now that we're on the bottom. The after compartments are

---

* Because of their work during the disaster, two Boston newspapermen achieved national recognition: Nat Barrows of the *Boston Globe*, who wrote a scholarly book about the sinking, and Jimmie Jones of the *Boston Post*, whose *Squalus* picture was acclaimed as the best photograph of the year. Barrows was killed in the recent airplane crash in India which brought about the death of so many other distinguished newspapermen.

flooded, but we can go forward. We must wait until help reaches us. We'll send our smoke rockets up every hour or so, and they're bound to sight them sooner or later. We've already released the marker buoy so they'll find us without trouble. We'll be able to talk with the surface just as soon as a rescue ship comes along. That's the situation. All right, Gunner, let's have a red rocket sent up."

Gunner's Mate Eugene D. Craven released a red rocket, and every man aboard thought of what must be happening on the surface. The rocket would leap out of the water, eject a red cloud, and possibly a fisherman in the vicinity would notice the red flare.

The captain went on talking. "We're far too crowded here. To spread us out a little, I want Mr. Preble to take some of you men forward and then all of you lie down and take it easy. Don't get up for any reason at all."

Mr. Preble, the naval architect who had designed the *Squalus*, went forward with several of the men and every one aboard the submarine lay down on the deck. The hours passed. The men tried to picture what was happening along the New England coast. In Portsmouth, as soon as the signal was overdue from the *Squalus*, Admiral Cyrus W. Cole would start things humming. The men could imagine Admiral Cole sending word to the submarine *Sculpin* to search for the missing *Squalus*, and they wondered how long it would take before their location was discovered.

At 12:40 that day the *Sculpin* was maneuvering in the vicinity and saw a red smoke bomb released from the *Squalus*. Five hours had elapsed since the sinking, and this was the seventh rocket sent up. The *Sculpin* soon found the marker buoy. Suddenly, the men aboard the *Squalus* heard the scraping of a boat hook on the marker buoy and then the noise of the buoy being hauled across the deck of a ship on the surface. Though their hearts beat fast with hope and expectation, they remained stretched out on the deck according to their orders and waited tensely for the sound of a human voice from the surface.

Finally, at 1:20 they heard the voice of Lieutenant Commander Warren Wilkin of the *Sculpin*: "What is the trouble?"

After Radio Operator John Nichols had explained exactly what had happened, Lieutenant Oliver Naquin stepped over and took the phone: "Hello, Wilkie."

The answer from the *Sculpin* came back at once: "Hello, Oliver."

Suddenly there was a buzzing sound and then complete silence. The mooring buoy had torn loose from the submarine. For a moment or two the *Squalus* had been in communication with the surface—and now—no one could guess how long it would be. The men smiled at each other and pretended there was no need to worry, but the sudden silence had lowered their spirits considerably.

The entire United States Navy had been alerted, however, and in Washington, New London, and Boston, rescue operations were being planned.

Speeding over the highway, which had been cleared by the police all the way up the coast, were three carloads of expert Navy divers headed for Portsmouth. High overhead a twin-engined amphibian brought Lieutenant Commander Momsen, co-inventor of the Momsen diving lung, to the scene of the disaster. For more than twelve years Momsen had been planning for just such an emergency—one requiring deep sea divers to work more than two hundred feet below the surface.

The *Falcon*, the sturdy rescue ship which had done her duty so well in 1925 when the *S-51* sank after her collision and in 1927 when the *S-4* went down, was making her way up the coast. By midnight the 1-4-3 flashes of Minot's Light could be seen as the *Falcon* kept a steady course for the Isles of Shoals Light.

In the submarine at the bottom of the sea, men became dizzy

and sick as the air grew worse and worse. They had been ordered not to change their positions for any reason at all, and as time went on their thoughts grew more desperate. They did not know that two vessels were above them—the *Wandank* and the *Penocook* until, exactly twenty-one minutes after five that afternoon, the piercing sharpness of an oscillator bit through their thoughts. Slowly but surely it spelled out the words in Morse Code:

WILL INFORM YOU ALL ACTIVITIES MAKE FOUR TAPS IF YOU RECEIVE ME.

Now the men on the *Squalus* knew for certain that help was on the way. One of them swung a heavy sledge against the side of the submarine four times. Then came the biting sound of the oscillator as it spelled out the answering message:

CAN HEAR HAMMER VERY WEAK NOW SEND EACH REPLY THREE TIMES.

The hours passed slowly. At 8 o'clock, after no message had been received for two hours, Naquin sent up the following by sledge hammer:

HAVE YOU LOCATED US

There was no reply at all.

Finally, at almost nine o'clock, the oscillator came stinging through the atmosphere again:

WHAT ARE CONDITIONS BELOW

The men swung the heavy sledge again and again, spelling out the message:

SATISFACTORY BUT COLD

The intense cold was slowly sapping away the energy and strength of the men at the bottom. The temperature was only forty-five degrees above zero in the submarine, and it seemed to be getting colder all the time. A little later came the news:

FALCON DUE AT ABOUT THREE IN THE MORNING BELIEVE WE HAVE GRAPNEL ATTACHED WHERE IS YOUR PERSONNEL

The *Squalus'* reply told the graphic news that only thirty-three men were alive:

FIFTEEN IN TORPEDO AND EIGHTEEN IN CONTROL ROOM

And then, as dawn was breaking over the Isles of Shoals Light, several of the men at the bottom of the sea became acutely sick. This was only the beginning of a state which would eventually lead to unconsciousness, but it was enough to worry their commander. He wondered how long it would be before the first man collapsed completely.

The *Falcon* arrived at four-thirty that morning and by eight o'clock was ready to begin operations. At exactly sixteen minutes past ten the men trapped below heard the welcome message that a diver was descending to attach a downhall wire on which to operate for the rescue chamber from the *Falcon* to the *Squalus.*

The man chosen for this important mission was thirty-year-old Martin Sibitsky, at six feet four the Navy's tallest diver. Over the side he went and down, down, through the clear, cold water. At two hundred feet there was a slight delay when the line was snarled. It was quickly freed, and thirty seconds afterwards Sibitsky's feet hit something solid and gray. It was the submarine *Squalus.*

"I'm on the submarine!" he cried into the phone.

Commander Momsen himself was in charge. "That's fine," he replied. "Take your time." Momsen knew that at 240 feet below the surface of the sea a man's intelligence and strength are those of a three-year-old child. The pressure of the water is too great for clear thinking or quick acting.

Ten minutes later Sibitsky reported, "I see a deck plate marked WINDLASS."

Twenty minutes afterwards his next message came through. "I've landed inboard of the port rail and forward of the mast.

I am now six feet from the escape hatch cover. Okay to send the downhaul wire to me now."

When the men below on the submarine heard the sound of Sibitsky's feet on the deck, they were nearly frantic with joy. But through their excitement Naquin's voice came to them, calm and unemotional; he stood close to them in the darkness and spoke in a low tone, "Take it easy men—it may be a long time yet."

Meanwhile Sibitsky secured the downhaul wire to the submarine and returned to the surface.

Two picked divers, John Mihalowski and Walter Harman, entered the rescue chamber, with Inventor McCann ready to direct them from the deck of the *Falcon*. The McCann rescue chamber is shaped like a huge inverted pear, eight feet across and about twelve feet high. Air pressure fed from the ship on the surface keeps the water from rising inside the chamber, which is usually open at the bottom.

McCann signalled for the boom to hoist his invention from the deck of the *Falcon* into the water, and a short time later the rescue chamber was bobbing up and down beside the *Falcon*. The two men inside the chamber were unable to stand because of the valves and gauges which almost filled the top part of the chamber. They adjusted the buoyancy for the descent to the *Squalus*, and then awaited orders to start the motor which would operate the cable running from the surface to the bottom.

"Blow all ballast in the lower compartment," McCann called over the telephone to the two men inside the chamber.

"All ballast is blown," the men replied.

Now the divers reduced the air pressure so that the water came flooding in. Then they started the motor exhaust valve; the downhaul reel began to revolve, and the rescue chamber began its descent. Minutes passed as the diving bell moved slowly downward. Finally the gray hull of the submarine *Squalus* loomed into view, and the rescue chamber settled comfortably around the submarine's outer hatch cover. The divers soon bolted the escape chamber to the cover.

The next few moments are memorable in submarine history. Ankle deep in water at the bottom of the escape hatch, Mihalowski began to swing the wheel of the submarine's deck hatch. The hatch soon loosened, and he threw it open with a quick push. Letting himself down into the lower hatch, Mihalowski made his way carefully until he had found the hand-hold. Then, standing on the lower hatchway, he tapped the cover smartly with a wrench and swung the cover open.

Below in the torpedo room was a circle of joyous faces smiling up at him, and he, too, began to grin.

"Hi, fellows," he said. "Here we are."

They were simple every day words, but they meant life and hope to the men of the *Squalus*.

Seven survivors were chosen to go on the first trip to the surface. Lieutenant Naquin selected them carefully. One officer was needed, and the civilian, Preble, of course, should go with the group. Five enlisted men were chosen to make up the complement, and the seven selected soon climbed the ladder into the rescue chamber, inhaling the fresh air as they went. Once in the chamber, the men sat down on the wide rim above the compartment hatch. Then at thirteen minutes past one they were ready for the ascent.

Harman had already begun feeding fresh air into the torpedo room. "We'll be back," he assured those remaining in the submarine.

After what seemed like several hours, but was actually only nineteen minutes, the diving bell broke through the water of the surface. A great shout went up from the men on the *Falcon*. The order came over the telephone from Commander McCann, "Inside the chamber, open the hatch."

The hatch flew up, and Lieutenant Nichols, the officer chosen for the first ascent, looked out. He was helped to the deck of the *Falcon* and escorted to the sick bay. Then the other six survivors were taken off and followed Lieutenant Nichols to obtain medical treatment.

An epic of the sea had taken place—the first persons in history had been saved from a sunken submarine by a diving chamber.

The next two trips went successfully, but as the rescue chamber made its final ascent with the last eight survivors, the lines stuck at 160 feet. Four divers were sent down to free the lines, but they all failed in their efforts. Hour after hour went by, and darkness came. Finally it was decided to attempt the desperate task of handworking the chamber to the surface. The time was midnight when the order came to blow just enough ballast inside the diving chamber to neutralize the pressure from outside.

Slowly the rescuers blew the ballast from the diving bell, and then four divers began to pull the chamber along the wire cable by hand. Every few feet they had to pause while the pressure was adjusted. If they pulled too fast, the chamber might shoot to the surface out of control, crushing the divers and possibly killing the men inside.

The desperate attempt succeeded. Half an hour later, the escape chamber was on the surface alongside the *Falcon*. All thirty-three of the *Squalus* survivors were safe aboard the *Falcon* after one of the most thrilling rescues of all times.

8. The Newburyport Ghost

EARLY the next day I landed at Portsmouth again and hit across Highway Number 1 toward Newburyport. After walking over the Merrimac River bridge I reached the Newburyport Cemetery, where I paid homage at the grave of Donald McKay, the Nova Scotia ship builder who had left Newburyport in 1845 to begin his construction of the beautiful East Boston clipper ships. He died in Hamilton in 1880, but the records established by his ships will live forever.

I next stopped off to visit the home of the famous eccentric of Newburyport, Timothy Dexter, who allegedly made money by sending a cargo of warming pans to the West Indies where it is said they were purchased by enthusiastic natives and used as molasses ladles. (This is not true, however.) According to legend, when his wife did not show enough grief at a mock funeral he held for himself, he beat her. In 1802 he published his book, *Pickle for the Knowing Ones,* a volume which amazes its readers by concentrating all punctuation marks on a last page devoted entirely to commas, semi-colons, and question marks. That page bears the advice, "salt and pepper to taste."

Now known as the Jackson-Dexter House, the building with its high wood-encased chimneys, swinging gilded eagle on top of the watch tower and columns at the facade gave me a pleasing half hour. I walked around the surprisingly extensive grounds where "Lord" Timothy Dexter had placed many statues of famous men, his own among them.

But the real reason for my visit to Newburyport was to investigate the haunted schoolhouse on Charles Street.

The school was a primary one for boys whose ages ranged from five to fourteen. The pupils came from the humbler Newburyport families. They were the sons of fishermen, tradesmen and mill-workers, and their clothes were tattered and patched.

When first erected, the schoolhouse was an ordinary one-story structure raised upon a three-foot foundation. It had a pitch roof with four windows on each side and an attic above. At the time of the ghost episode, the schoolhouse was in a state of neglect. The faded green blinds and the peeling gray paint of the building gave it an effect of shabbiness, and, all in all, there was something about the school and its surroundings which oppressed the beholder and strengthened his willingness to believe the strange story of the schoolboy ghost.

To enter, one climbed the six steps in front of the school and opened the battered door before stepping into a small hallway. Close and stuffy, the entry gave off an odor eternally connected with schools. Directly opposite the front door was a multi-paned partition window which looked in upon the schoolroom. To the right of the entrance were two sets of stairs, one going up to the attic, the other to the cellar where the coal was stored. Both stairways had doors which were usually fastened with a latch, and there were two large windows at each end of the passageway.

The schoolroom itself was a large one and held seats for sixty pupils, with a teacher's desk at the right of the room. On the walls were several of Coston's maps, torn and soiled. Otherwise the walls were perfectly bare; there was not even a closet in the room. It was perhaps the last place where one would expect to find a ghost.

Many have repeated the story that in the year 1858, the incumbent teacher beat a thirteen-year-old boy until he was black and blue, and after school threw him down into the cellar, where he died during the night. Whether there is any truth to this legend is hard to prove, but the subsequent story that the boy's ghost had been seen in the schoolhouse caused considerable excitement throughout Massachusetts.

In the year 1871 it became generally known that strange disturbances were taking place in the Charles Street School. Peculiar phenomena had occurred from time to time within the building, but no one had paid too much attention because the teachers and the school committee were not anxious to start trouble. The two teachers who ran the school in 1870 and 1871 were forced to give up their positions after their lives had been made miserable by the constant intrusion of a strange power they could neither see nor feel. It was not a being they could scold or whip, and it did not appear at stated intervals. It could not be hunted down and destroyed; it was something intangible and malignant.

Miss Lucy A. Perkins was appointed teacher in the fall of 1871. She was twenty-one, strong and willing to do her duty in the classroom. Shortly after her arrival, the manifestations began in the form of knocks and pounding, the usual devices used by spirits. On one occasion, the sound grew so loud that Miss Perkins could not carry on her spelling lesson; the banging came so rapidly and powerfully that all voices were drowned out. The noises issued from the attic stairs and the entry well. At times they faded until they resembled the tap of fingers, and again they increased in volume until they might have come from the batterings of a mighty sledge hammer.

In an attempt to quiet the fears of her pupils, the teacher suggested that the sounds were probably made by rats and the wind, but eventually she was forced to give up this subterfuge and admit that she really didn't know what was causing the noises.

One afternoon during the month of January, 1873, a series of raps came upon the outer door. Miss Perkins went to admit the visitor, but no one was there. In the schoolroom in front of the pupils' desks was a stove with a cover which was raised by a wire handle. That day the handle was seized by invisible fingers and raised upright; the cover was lifted several inches and then restored to its place.

The teacher's bell was often moved about the room. One day before school began, the pupils outside in the yard suddenly heard the bell ringing, though there was no one in the building. When the teacher came down the street, the pupils told her what had happened. They were more frightened at the bell incident than at any of the knockings or cover-raising episodes.

The schoolroom proper was ventilated by a shutter in the ceiling which could be opened or closed by a cord hanging down into the room. The alleged demon often opened and closed the vent for mischief. Any door in the building might slam without warning, although no one could be seen nearby. One day Miss Perkins heard the door leading to the garret swing open, and as she went out to close it, two more doors swung open. She tried in vain to catch up with the opening doors for ten minutes. The door leading to the cellar had a bolt, and Miss Perkins closed that door and bolted it. Instantly the being slipped back the lock and swung the door open so hard that it crashed into a clothes hook and received a deep dent.

A strange light then began to appear during storms when the sky was heavily overcast. Light seemed to creep in and hover over the frightened faces of the awed pupils. It was an illuminated exhalation, shedding its beam over the schoolroom.

At various times, a strange current of air appeared to circulate above the pupils with unusual speed, creating a noise like that of a great flight of birds. A black ball twelve inches in diameter often appeared in the ventilator, dropping just below the opening and then quickly disappearing. This phenomena was often accompanied by a terrific rushing of wind around the building itself. Gusts of cold air shot into all the crevices, the entire building shook, and the chimney gave off sounds which resembled the playing of a pipe organ. On these occasions the unhappy teacher and her fifty-five frightened pupils would sing at the top of their voices, trying to drown out the noises by song.

One afternoon a boy named Abraham Lydston, thirteen years old, suddenly noticed a child's hand pressed against the partition window, and shouted out, "Teacher! Teacher! The murdered boy's hand!" Soon everyone could see the hand pressed against the window pane. Miss Perkins rushed into the vestibule, but in the two or three seconds she took to reach the hall the apparition had vanished.

Late in October, 1872, the murdered boy's face appeared at the same pane of glass. The teacher ran out again, but there was nothing in sight.

On November 1, 1872, the ghost appeared during a geography class, and stood at right angles to the partition window opposite the teacher's desk. Suddenly one of the boys, whose desk was near the open door, shouted out, "There's a boy out there!" Miss Perkins hurried out and saw the form of a young boy, standing in the vestibule.

"What are you doing out here?" she demanded from the ghostlike figure. The apparition receded from her toward the garret stairs. It was that of a young boy, with blue eyes and yellow hair. He was wearing a brown coat, black trousers and a wide band around his neck of the type used by undertakers to prevent the lower jaw of a dead person from dropping.

The most extraordinary thing about this apparition was that Miss Perkins could look right through it and see the sash and wainscotting on the wall. The ghost was perfectly transparent, but easily visible. Miss Perkins began to tremble, and thought that she was going to faint. As she steadied herself against the wall, the figure slowly ascended the attic stairs after the door leading to it had opened of its own accord.

Regaining her strength, the teacher followed the apparition

up the stairs and finally trapped it in a corner of the building. But when she thrust out her hands to grasp the boy, they met in the middle of his transparent chest, and all she had touched was air. Now the ghost began to disintegrate and soon disappeared.

On the following Friday the apparition appeared again and went through precisely the same maneuvers, but this time it introduced certain innovations. It brought two ghostly friends and spent most of one afternoon hammering away on the attic floor. Once there was a cry: "Damn it, where's my hammer?"

Evidently the ghost found his hammer, for soon he could be heard adjusting the cover of a box and nailing it shut.

The following week the ghost began to laugh softly in a disagreeable manner, most disconcerting to teacher and pupils alike. The teacher asked for volunteers to investigate, and young Lydston agreed to accompany her to the attic, which seemed to be the source of the laughter. But when they reached the attic, the disembodied laugh jumped around them here and there, and they retreated to the schoolroom in great confusion.

By this time there was tremendous excitement in Newburyport over these manifestations. A special meeting of the school committee was held on February 19, 1873. Two of the committeemen stated that nothing was wrong at all, though the chairman, who also served as postmaster, decided that there was much to explain. But there was little action to be taken, and when the newspapers began publishing accounts of the affair, mediums and spiritualists descended on the town to view with their own eyes the schoolroom where the apparition of the murdered boy had appeared.

At another meeting held on February 24th, it was agreed that Miss Perkins should be given a well-deserved vacation. The school was placed in charge of a Mr. Nathan A. Mounton, and visitations allegedly stopped. When Miss Perkins married and moved away, the incident was almost completely forgotten.

Beginning my investigation of the ghost story, I went to the Newburyport Public Library and talked with Miss Grace Bixby. She told me how her mother had repeated the story to her again and again, and suggested that I go to see ninety-year-old George Leeds Whitmore who was living in Newburyport at the time of the sensational events. After two interviews with Mr. Whitmore I had what I needed for my story.

When I first visited Mr. Whitmore's Merrimac Street residence, he admitted that he knew something about the affair which he had never told before. I was impatient to learn what it was, but he answered, "Don't hurry me, son, don't hurry me. It'll all come to me if you just give me time."

I waited quietly.

"Now, I think that I learned the truth about the Charles Street Schoolhouse and Miss Perkins from Tot Currier, who worked in the shop with me years ago. He's dead, and so is everyone else that I knew then, and I guess it won't do anyone any harm to tell the true story at this late day. Why, that happened over three-quarters of a century ago, didn't it?

"The boys who carried out the hoax, for hoax it was, were four in number. They were Tot Currier, whose real name was William, Abe Lydston, Edgar Pearson, and Ed De Lancy—all dead now. They got the idea for the ghost when De Lancy received an object glass which could catch reflections from the sun and throw pictures on any flat surface. It took De Lancy several months to master the thing, but when he did he could shine pictures from within the glass forty or fifty feet away. He really became pretty good at it. The figure he used came out clear and distinct, and when it flashed inside a building, well, it would fool anyone not in on the secret.

"When Ed heard about the noises coming from the school-house he decided to have some fun, so he pulled Tot, Abe, and Edgar into the scheme. Tot didn't attend school, but Abe and Edgar did, and they helped matters from inside the classroom while Tot ran around the attic and the entryway. Miss Perkins, poor woman, is dead and gone now, but they sure had fun with her, and it was partly her fault, because she was pretty superstitious. The day she went up into the attic, she actually fainted. Tot told me all about it one day in the shop, and he explained how he ran out before she came to.—Tot never grew very large, but he really was a little devil. Yes, I suppose the boys were mean to have teased the poor soul that way."

After talking another half hour with the old man, I said goodbye to him and began my lonely hike toward the highway along the banks of the Merrimac River, wondering as I went if the Amherst Ghost story told earlier in this volume might not have a similar explanation.

9. America's First Revolution

$\mathscr{F}$INALLY I reached the Ipswich Town Hall and was preparing to rest my weary limbs when the Seal of Ipswich caught my eye. I slowly read the inscription, THE BIRTHPLACE OF AMERICAN INDEPENDENCE, and at once my mind flashed back to a conversation I had enjoyed with my friend Elliott Morrison Andrews of Boston, whose ancestor, Lieutenant John Andrews of Ipswich, played such an important part in American history.

In the year 1686, the people of New England were enjoying virtual freedom from British control. The charter from King Charles II in 1630 had been their only connection with England. They elected their own legislature and chose their own officials. But King Charles later felt that the New Englanders were getting out of control and sent Edward Randolph to Boston as his special investigator. Randolph reported to the king that the colonists would not obey his commands, whereupon he was instructed to appoint commissioners with real power. But Randolph's efforts were practically ignored. This so angered Charles that he ordered a *Quo Warranto* in the court of King's Bench, whereby the Massachusetts Bay Charter was rendered legally void. As of May 20, 1686, Massachusetts was without a charter.

During this so-called Inter-Charter period, Joseph Dudley became President of the Massachusetts Provisional Government. Duly commissioned by the new monarch, King James II, Dudley governed from May 24, 1686, to the following December 20.

Dudley was succeeded by Sir Edmund Andros, a close friend of James II. He arrived in Boston aboard the *Kingfisher*, Sunday, December 19, 1686 to take over the governorship of the disfranchised colonies. Andros, a staunch loyalist, was a gentleman of high connections and came from an important family. There are many who believe with historian Palfrey that Andros had "a personal grudge against Massachusetts, on account of old affronts" and would be "as oppressive and offensive as the King desired." However, any governor sent to New England just after the people had lost their charter would be hated as the agent of a king they neither knew nor understood.

Sir Edmund Andros set up his government during the first half of 1687 and appointed twenty-five councilors. In March he announced a repressive plan of taxation without representation and ordered every town in his domain to choose a local tax commissioner. The tax to be collected was twenty-pence a head plus a penny a pound on the total valuation of each man's property.

Then he took another step which alienated him from many Bostonians. Belonging to the Church of England, he had no place to worship in that hotbed of Dissenters known as Boston and so demanded that the South Church be made available for him. Protests from church members merely brought a company of red-coats to protect him as he worshipped alone. The Bostonians who were thus forced to wait in the streets for Andros' services to finish were quite naturally resentful. This enforced triumph of the Church of England over the Dissenters was perhaps the first important step Andros took on his road to imprisonment.

In the town of Ipswich, Massachusetts, a meeting of great importance to New Englanders took place on August 23, 1687—a protest against Andros' action in ordering the appointment of a local commissioner to prepare tax lists.

The citizens of Ipswich went on record as ready to rebel

against the representative of the King of England, Sir Edmund Andros, in his demand for the appointment of a tax commissioner. They refused to appoint the commissioner, claiming that "the sd act doth infringe their Liberty as Free Borne English subjects of his Majesties by interfering with ye statutory Laws of the Land."

Needless to say, Governor Andros did not agree with this statement by the Ipswich town meeting and sent his soldiers to arrest its six most active members: John Andrews, chairman of the selectmen and moderator of the meeting; John Appleton, town clerk; William Goodhue; Robert Kinsman; Thomas French and the Reverend John Wise. They were brought back to Boston and imprisoned.

On October 3, 1687, after twenty-one days in jail, the six defendants were brought to trial before a Court of Oyer and Terminer in Boston. The entire colony seethed with excitement and expectation. Judge Joseph Dudley announced what he believed was the brutal truth, that "the people in New England were all slaves . . . and that they must not think the privileges of Englishmen would follow them to the end of the world." The prisoners were convicted and fined from fifteen to fifty pounds each in addition to sharing costs amounting to four hundred pounds. The Reverend Mr. Wise was forbidden to preach and the others were not allowed to bear office. Andros had gained a temporary victory, for every town in Massachusetts now fell in line and appointed tax commissioners. But it became known that Dudley had called the New Englanders slaves, and his statement rankled deep in the hearts of the liberty-loving people of Massachusetts.

The citizens of Boston and the surrounding countryside engaged in secret meetings and discussions which were to lead to important developments within the next few weeks. The exact procedure was never revealed, but when Sir Edmund Andros returned to Boston in March, 1689, after a campaign to the eastward, he noticed a changed attitude in the people's reactions which approached open hostility. Andros' soldiers began deserting by the score, forming small independent bands.

It became noised about that Governor Andros "intended nothing but RUINE TO THEM." The town of Boston was soon in great turmoil. Local leaders met and agreed that unless they acted quickly the discharged soldiers and others would start "a great stir and produce a bloody Revolution," as Cotton Mather's son admitted later. They appointed a delegate, probably Cotton Mather, to prepare a Declaration of Independence, indicating that they expected the worst and, secretly, may have hoped for it.

On April 16, 1689, Sir Edmund Andros mentioned in a letter that a "general buzzing among the people" was quite noticeable. But it was not until April 18, at eight in the morning, that "it was reported . . . that at the north end they were all in arms." Captain John George of the British frigate *Rose* was seized and at nine o'clock drums were beaten throughout the town as if by prearranged signal. The insurrectionists descended upon the leading lieutenants of Governor Andros. They captured Sherlock, Ravenscroft, White, Foxcroft, Randolph, Broadbent and Crafford and hurried them off to prison. When the keeper objected, he, too, was thrust into prison, and Scates, the bricklayer, became the new jailer.

There was a mighty demand for the aging Simon Bradstreet, governor at the time the charter was withdrawn and now nearly ninety years old, to take over the reigns of government. The insurrectionists escorted Bradstreet and several others to the Town House, where they looked down upon the milling crowd gathered in the street. The multitude shouted their approval of Bradstreet and his friends as the only persons qualified to establish the new government. The new executives then gathered at the Town House and nervously read over their declaration.

This first American Declaration of Independence is indeed a

notable document, and is surprisingly similar in spirit to the
Declaration of 1776. I quote from the more interesting and important parts of this lengthy document:

THE DECLARATION OF THE Gentlemen, Merchants, and
Inhabitants of *Boston*, and the Country Adjacent, April 18, 1689.

We have seen more than a decad of Years rolled away, since the
English World had the Discovery of an horrid . . . Plot . . . to Crush
and break a Country . . . entirely.

To get us within the reach of the desolation desired for us . . .
we . . . first have our Charter Vacated . . . before it was possible
for us to appear at Westminister. . . .

We were put under a *President and Council* without any liberty
for an Assembly . . . by a Commission from his *Majesty*. . . . The
Commission was as *Illegal* for the form of it, as the way of obtaining
it was *Malicious* and *unreasonable*. . . . Yet we made no Resistence
thereunto . . . because we took pains to make ourselves believe as
much as ever we could of the Whedle then offer'd unto us. . . .

In little more than half a year we saw this Commission superseded by another, yet more Absolute and Arbitrary, with which Sir
Edmund Andros arrived as our Governour: who . . . planned to
make Laws and raise Taxes as he pleased. . . . We were chiefly
squeez'd by a crew of abject Persons, fetched from *New York* . . .
by these were extraordinary and intollerable Fees extorted from
everyone upon all occasions. . . .

It was now plainly affirmed . . . that the people in *New England*
were all *Slaves*. . . . Accordingly we have been treated with multi-
plied contradictions to *Magna Charta*, the rights of which we laid
claim to.

Persons who did but peacefully object against the raising of Taxes
without an Assembly, have been for it fined, some twenty, some
thirty, and others fifty Pounds. . . . Packt and pickt Juries have
been very common things. . . . Without a *verdict*, yea, without a
Jury sometimes have People been fined most unrighteously, and
some . . . have been kept in long and close Imprisonment without
. . . *Habeas Corpus* allowed unto them. . . .

Writs of Intrusion began everywhere to be served on People. . . .
We do therefore seize upon the Persons of those few *Ill men* which
have been (next to our Sins) the grand Authors of our Miseries. . . .
In the meantime . . . we commit our Enterprise unto Him *who hears
the cry of the Oppressed.*

The contributors to the Declaration of Independence then
composed a letter to Sir Edmund Andros, telling him that the people had taken arms and seized the town. They said that for the
purpose of "quieting and securing . . . the People from . . . emmi-
nent Dangers . . . We judge it necessary you forthwith surrender and deliver up the Government and Fortification. . . .
Otherwise we are assured they will endeavor the taking of the
Fortification by Storm, if any Opposition be made." The letter
was signed by the fifteen leaders in the Town House, including
Simon Bradstreet, John Nelson, William Stoughton and Waite
Winthrop.

Sir Edmund Andros was barricaded at the defenses on Fort
Hill when the letter from the Revolutionists reached him. Andros was soon joined by young Dudley and Colonel Lidget.
The governor asked young Dudley if he would go out to the
homes of the ministers of Boston and request them to appear at
the fort, where possibly they could quiet the people. But Dudley told Andros that he would be captured the moment he left
the fort, and the plan was abandoned.

At the Town House the venerable Simon Bradstreet went out
on the balcony to accept the cheers of the multitudes below.
Colors were run up on Beacon Hill as a signal to the thousands
on the Charlestown side that the moment for action was at hand.
In the harbor, the British frigate *Rose* opened her gunports and
hoisted her battle flags. Captain Winthrop sent a note out to the
lieutenant in command saying that if the *Rose* fired a single shot
into the town her master Captain John George, who had been
captured by the revolutionists, would be executed.

This bold note accomplished its purpose. Though the lieu-

tenant in command of the *Rose* pretended that he would soon
fire, he never did, and finally accepted defeat and sent in his sails
as a token of surrender.

But the excitement was not yet ended. Watching his chances,
Governor Andros signalled for a boat to approach from the
frigate and went down on the Battery Wharf with ten of his
associates. The unruly mob had outguessed the group, however,
and captured the boat as it landed at the wharf. In the boat were
hand grenades, small arms and "a quantity of match"! Governor
Andros and his party hurried back to the fort when they saw
that their scheme had miscarried.

A battalion of soldiers led by John Nelson of Long Island,
Boston Harbor, then appeared at the fort and ordered Governor
Andros to surrender. For a moment it looked as though the guns
of the fort would be fired into the unruly crowd of soldiers and
civilians, but after due consideration Sir Edmund Andros decided that his best move was to surrender. It had been a blood-
less revolution.

After his acknowledgment of defeat, he was taken up to the
Town House, where Mr. Bradstreet waited to receive him.
William Stoughton was the first to speak, and told Andros in no
uncertain terms that he had only himself to blame for "the disaster" which had befallen him. Andros was confined for the
night in Mr. John Usher's house and the next day taken to Fort
Hill and imprisoned. Later he was incarcerated at Castle Island,
where he made two unsuccessful attempts to escape. He was
foiled in his first escape when an alert guard noticed military
boots showing under the woman's clothing Andros was wearing
as disguise, but the second time he got as far as Rhode Island
before being apprehended.

Happily for the people of New England, affairs in England
were also reaching a state of crisis. A new king brought over
from the continent took the throne away from James II to rule
as William of Orange. Increase Mather, who had fled from

Boston to England, had obtained audience with the king and was interceding as best he could on behalf of the New Englanders. On July 4, 1689, exactly eighty-seven years before the Declaration of Independence was drawn up in Philadelphia, King William told Increase Mather that he would approve the results of the American Revolution of 1689, without, however, renewing the old charter.

The following month the king sent a Royal Letter ratifying the government of New England, but actually the colonists did not receive all the liberties for which they asked.

Stuart opposition to William of Orange was still strong in England and did not collapse until the Battle of the Boyne on July 1, 1690. But with the defeat of the Stuart supporters, there was no more danger to the New Englanders from across the sea. They would not be punished for their revolution in New England, for in England the same thing had happened, and they would be allowed many of the things for which they had rebelled.

It was not until the 1760's that England and New England were once again in conflict, and then the difficulties could not be resolved without a great war. Whether or not the accession to the English throne by William of Orange prevented this country from realizing her independence in 1689 rather than 1775 is a question which offers interesting debate.

10. An Epic of the Sea—
Howard Blackburn

PERHAPS the most dangerous calling among seamen is that of the halibut fisherman, who works at his task throughout the entire year. The possibilities of collision and shipwreck are an ever-present hazard; the fisherman's dory, heavily loaded with gear and halibut, may capsize. But the normal dangers of halibut fishing are increased tenfold when winter sets in. In addition to the jeopardies of the furious wintry gales, there is always the chance that a sudden storm will cut the men off from their ship.

Many terrible storms have hit the fishing banks, but one of the worst on record, a storm which is still discussed by the children of the fishermen who were out in it, was the *Blow of '62*.

On February 24, 1862, a gale swept in from the northwest so suddenly that it caught the Gloucester fishing fleet on George's Bank. Seventy ships were trapped at anchor. In the fearful confusion that followed, thirteen vessels were lost with their entire crews, and two other schooners went down without loss of life. No ship escaped without serious damage.

In Gloucester, as the fleet came in, the entire town went down to the waterfront to watch and to learn the tragic news that fifteen proud vessels would never return. A hundred and twenty men died in the *Blow of '62*, seventy women were widowed and a hundred and forty children lost their fathers.

In all eight thousand men of Gloucester have been lost at sea, and hundreds have suffered terribly before rescue.

The halibut fishermen of Cape Ann have had their share of tragedy since the first Gloucester halibut schooner, the *Nautilus*, left port, March 5, 1830. Even on that trip there was a near-disaster. The men were fishing from their dories and the *Nautilus* was drifting along when storm clouds began to gather. All but one dory hurried back to the *Nautilus*. Benjamin Marble, a fisherman who had been in a great hurry to get his dory overboard first, was the only one still out. The rest of the crew began to worry, for darkness was falling and there was no sign of Marble. Suddenly one of the men noticed a pair of oars on the dock. Marble had forgotten them in his haste! The *Nautilus* immediately began to cruise around for the missing fisherman. Just as night fell and the storm was about to break, they discovered him. A moment later, the storm struck with tremendous fury, and all agreed that Marble never could have survived in his dory.

The first halibut fishing trip in Gloucester narrowly escaped a tragic ending.

On another occasion, soon after the custom of fishing in pairs began, a dory capsized in a gale. One of the men decided that he'd be better off in the water than lying on top of the dory beside his comrade in the freezing wind. Holding his breath, he went under water, grabbed the painter, took a half hitch in it and was then able to stand in the loop of the hitch with only his head above the surface. Seven hours later he was picked up. His mate had long before succumbed to the cold and slipped overboard.

Without question the greatest epic among Gloucester fishermen is the story of Howard Blackburn, a tale which will be repeated as long as the men of Cape Ann go to sea.

On the morning of January 25, 1883, the Gloucester fishing schooner *Grace L. Fears* lay at anchor on Burgeo Bank, thirty miles out to sea from the southwest coast of Newfoundland. The men were just leaving the schooner in their dories. As

Howard Blackburn and Thomas Welch, two staunch crew members of the halibut fishing fleet, pulled away from the schooner, a thin, light snow drifted down, which soon increased to a heavier fall. Finally the dory mates could not see their schooner in the gathering storm. Their sight was soon limited to less than fifty feet. But they kept at their fishing and eventually filled the dory with halibut.

The snowstorm, which had begun in the southeast, soon swung to northwest, and the two men became confused as to the direction of their schooner. After hauling their trawl they began to row toward the place where they believed the schooner was anchored. There was no sign of her nor could they hear any signal from bell or fog horn.

Now the storm grew worse. As the wind rose stronger and stronger, the two fishermen decided to anchor and wait for a possible clearing. Three hours later the snow stopped, and although it was dark, they could make out the riding lights of the *Grace L. Fears* off to windward. Pulling up their anchor, they set to with a will—it had become a matter of life or death. Harder and harder they pulled on their oars, but they couldn't seem to gain against the terrific wind at all. Finally they put all their strength into a grim half hour of even more strenuous rowing. They didn't gain a foot! The powerful wind kept them from their goal. Exhausted beyond all endurance, they let go the anchor and settled down to wait the dawn.

Soon the anchor began to drag and the dory started to drift. She fetched up, and a wave broke over the craft. Only by bailing frantically were they able to keep her from capsizing. The temperature dropped lower and lower, for one of the coldest periods of the year was hitting the Newfoundland area. Ice began to form on the dory, increasing her weight and causing her to settle dangerously low into the water. The men heaved overboard the trawls and all but one fish (saved for an emergency) to prevent her from sinking.

That night, while the temperature remained below zero, the men alternately bailed water and chopped ice. When dawn came, they looked hopefully for the *Grace L. Fears*, but she had vanished completely. Blackburn and Welch knew that their only chance of survival was to reach Newfoundland, now an unknown number of miles to the northeast.

After they had rowed for several hours, the wind increased and soon the waves became so high that the two men had to give up their efforts and put out a sea-anchor, which Blackburn constructed from a broken buoy keg and a gurdy.* In order to free his hands for making the sea-anchor, Blackburn pulled off his mittens and threw them into the water at the bottom of the dory so that they wouldn't freeze. At the same time Welch grabbed a bailer and began to scoop out the water and floating ice. By mistake the mittens were also thrown overboard.

Soon Welch noticed that Blackburn's hands were turning white and realized that his dory mate's fingers would soon be frozen and that there was nothing which could be done to prevent it.

For the rest of that day the men bailed and broke ice. Finally, removing the rubber boot from his right foot, Blackburn took off the sock and tried to put it on his hand. But the hand was so swollen that he could only pull on the sock as far as the heel. Finally the sock became so stiff that he tried to hit it against the gunwale to knock off the ice, and, in so doing, tossed it overboard.

Just before darkness fell, a sea broke over the dory and almost filled it. All that day Welch had been hopeful that they would be picked up, but when the wave hit he seemed to lose heart. Blackburn bailed out again and told Welch to move around or he would freeze.

---

* Also called a hurdy-gurdy. It is a crank or windlass used to pull trawls.

"What's the use?" asked Welch. "We can't live until morning, and we might as well go first as last."

A short time later Welch became delirious. He asked for water, and when he couldn't get that, pleaded with Blackburn for a piece of ice. As he ate the ice, he began to mumble to himself, calling Blackburn twice by name. By eleven o'clock that night he was suffering terrible agonies, moaning in piteous fashion. A few minutes later when Blackburn got up to bail, he saw that Welch was dead.

Blackburn placed the body of his dory mate in the stern and then removed one of Welch's mittens, but he found that he was unable to pull it over his own swollen hand.

When the morning of the third day came, Blackburn alternately bailed and rested. That night the sea began to quiet down a little and by dawn it was calm enough to haul in the sea-anchor. Somehow, Blackburn had to reach Newfoundland. His hands were almost completely frozen and had lost all flexibility. But still he must row. He bent his stiff and freezing fingers around the oar handles, and kept them there until they had frozen solidly to the shape of the oar. Blackburn then began rowing for the Newfoundland shore. As he fell to his task, the frozen flesh of his hands and fingers began to grind off like powder.

Early in the day he saw, far in the distance, the snow-covered hills of Newfoundland. Blackburn rowed steadily but the snowy shores were still ahead of him when evening fell. Again he put out his sea-anchor and awaited the sunrise. Hungry, thirsty, and in pain, he locked his arms around the thwart and moved his aching body back and forth all night long so that he would not freeze to death in the sub-zero temperature.

At sunrise the next morning, Sunday, the water was peaceful and the weather seemed much warmer. Blackburn hauled in his sea-anchor and fell to rowing again. At two o'clock that afternoon he reached and passed the River Rocks. Seven long miles ahead lay the mainland of Southern Newfoundland. But as he neared the shore, all he could see were high, towering cliffs. There was no place where he could land.

Following the coastline, he eventually reached Little River, a small stream some twenty-one miles from Burgeo, an important harbor on Newfoundland's southern coast. The high banks of the river didn't offer much hope, but he rowed doggedly until finally he saw a house on the north side of the river. The building looked deserted and he moved on in search of a settlement of some sort. But he made such poor headway against the strong current that after rowing three-quarters of a mile he let the dory drift back to the deserted house. There was a landing stage near the building, and he tied up the dory, giving her too much slack, as he later discovered.

He walked up to the house and found it wide open, with no doors in the frames and the snow in the building two feet deep. In what was once a bedroom Blackburn found a bedstead with wide boards across it and, hanging from one of the beams, an old fish net and a reel. He shook the snow from the boards, turned them over, and then used the net for a blanket and the reel for a pillow. He shivered all night long on the improvised bed, knowing that if he slept he would freeze to death.

Blackburn got up at various times during the night to scoop snow from a table top. He used his arms so that the dead flesh on his hands would not contaminate the snow. Then he bent over and ate the snow as if he were bobbing for apples. But the more snow he ate, the thirstier he grew for a drink of real fresh water.

Monday morning he found that his dory had split open on a rock and that the plug had been forced out, filling the dory with water. Tom Welch's body was still in the boat but practically everything else had washed out. Blackburn decided to put his friend's body in a safe place until he could get help. Lifting the corpse from the dory, he allowed it to sink twelve feet to the bottom of the cove in a little sheltered area between the rock, the wharf, and the shore. Blackburn then pulled his dory up on a rock and made emergency repairs. After exhausting himself trying to find a well, he gave up and determined he would row up the river again, even though it was getting dark. Luckily there was a full moon that night, and by its light he rowed his leaking dory several miles against the strong current, hoping to find a fresh-water brook, for by this time he was desperately thirsty.

All that night he rowed. The moon disappeared but he continued up the river until dawn. Finally he came to a little settlement. Resting on his oars, he noticed groups of people leaving their houses to go out on the river ice. Slowly and painfully he rowed toward them. When the dory hit the ice they caught it, and two of the settlers jumped aboard to bail her.

Blackburn's first thought was of his dead dory mate, twelve feet under the water at the wharf.

"Get my dory mate, men!" muttered Blackburn. "I'll go with you. I left my pal Tom Welch down the river."

One of the men spoke up. "You come in the house with us and we'll get your mate." Blackburn crawled out of the dory and three of the settlers began to row his dory down the river for Welch's body.*

A little group began to question Howard Blackburn about his experience, and as he began telling them what had happened, a man, pushing his way through the crowd, saw that Blackburn was desperately in need of attention. The good samaritan, whose name was Frank Lishman, took Blackburn away from the curious crowd and into his own home.

There Blackburn eagerly drank the first fresh water he had had since he left the schooner almost five days before. When

---

* The body of Thomas Welch was recovered and later buried at the Burgeo church yard on April 12, 1883.

he asked for more, they refused it to him knowing that too much water would kill him in his condition. As they cut the rubber boots and the clothing from his body, they prepared a tub of brine for his hands and feet. His limbs were then submerged in the tub, and as the frost began to leave his body, Blackburn suffered torture almost beyond endurance. He wished that he were dead, lying alongside of poor Tom Welch in twelve feet of water.

"How long must this continue?" he cried out in anguish.

"I'm sorry," said Frank Lishman, "but your hands and feet are so terribly frozen that you'll have to stay there a full hour."

The minutes dragged along, but finally that part of the ordeal ended, and Blackburn's limbs were covered with a poultice of cod-liver oil and flour. Put to bed, the Gloucester fisherman was fed hot spruce tea and bread. The agonizing pain in his arms and legs prevented him from sleeping, but in the morning he was allowed a tub of warm water in which to bathe. He was carried to a bench in front of the fireplace, and the Lishmans began to loosen the wrappings from his hands. The little finger of his right hand which had been broken when Blackburn smashed it in the dory now dropped off when they undid the bandage.

Mrs. Lishman cut away the dead flesh and skin, and new bandages were applied. "It'll be nine days before your hands start to heal," she told Blackburn. "You're the worst case of frost-burn we've ever seen. You know, you really should be dead!"

Blackburn, as the time went by, could hear odd scraps of conversation from the front room. Every morning a well-wisher dropped in to visit Mr. Lishman.

"Captain Lishman, how is the dory man today?"

"I don't think he'll live to sunset," Lishman answered.

Day after day Blackburn heard the same answer to inquiries about his condition, until finally one morning Lishman gave a different answer: "You know, I think he'll live after all."

Before the ordeal ended, however, Howard Blackburn lost all his fingers and toes and half of each thumb. A third of his right foot, from which he had taken the sock in the dory, also had to be amputated. Over seven weeks elapsed before the final amputation was made.

Word of Blackburn finally reached the American Consul at Saint John's and on April 23 Blackburn thanked his saviors and went to Burgeo, where he stayed a full month. He then returned to Gloucester by way of St. Pierre, Halifax, and Boston. Word of his experience had arrived before him, however, and his accomplishment was destined to be talked about for years to come.

The sum of five hundred dollars was donated to Blackburn, and with this money the former fisherman started a tobacco store. Later he opened a tavern on Main Street where fishermen could come in from the sea to drink and talk. It was difficult at first, picking up change with no fingers, but he soon became expert at it. With the assistance of Captain J. W. Collins, he wrote a booklet of his experiences, and Captain Collins' brother, Paul E. Collins, made three drawings of the incident.

Added to the income from his tavern, the sketches and booklet brought him enough revenue to get by and actually save money. When he had enough money laid aside, he tried to pay back the five hundred dollars given to him after his ordeal. But his benefactor refused to accept the money, and Blackburn turned it over to a fund for Gloucester widows and orphans.

After a while, Blackburn began to long for the sea. When the Alaskan gold rush began, he sailed to San Francisco and planned to go on to Alaska, but he injured his knee and had to return to Gloucester. He then bought a thirty-foot sloop which he named the *Great Western* and decided to sail her alone from Gloucester, Massachusetts, to Gloucester, England. After a trip crowded with adventure and danger, Blackburn arrived in England to be showered with roses and feted by the Lord Mayor of

Gloucester. He sold the *Great Western* there and returned to America by steamer to make plans for his next voyage.

This time Blackburn built a smaller sloop, the *Republic,* and crossed the ocean alone again, landing in Portugal thirty-eight days out from Gloucester. In his twenty-five foot sloop he visited Portugal, France and England. Some years later he sailed on the *Republic* from Gloucester, Massachusetts, to New York, up the Hudson, through the Erie Canal, through the Great Lakes, down the Mississippi, and was finally wrecked off the coast of Florida. He himself was uninjured, but the *Republic* was damaged beyond repair.

Next he left Gloucester in a fifteen-foot fisherman's dory and sailed it out beyond Cape Sable. Here the craft capsized, but Blackburn righted it, bailed it out and continued his trip. When he reached a point off Cape Breton Island, a bad squall struck him and he capsized twice more. After the third capsizing he decided it wasn't going to be a successful voyage and sailed back to Gloucester.

In 1931 I visited Howard Blackburn at his home on Main Street, Gloucester, and was amazed at the dexterity this finger-less fisherman showed when he picked up a die from the kitchen floor. He told me something that is not generally known—that on his second trip across the Atlantic in 1901, he encountered a real sea serpent. The creature was fifteen feet long and had a small fish or turtle in its mouth.

"I did my best to try to lasso the serpent, but I failed," admitted Blackburn. "If I had brought it back to Gloucester I'd have made them sit up, all right." We both began to laugh at the thought of a man without hands lassoing a sea serpent in the middle of the Atlantic, and I almost forgot the reason for my call.

"I'd like to know just how many hours you spent in the dory when you were lost from the schooner," I said.

"I've figured it out long ago. Exactly 104 hours," Blackburn answered promptly.

The very next year Howard Blackburn became ill and soon was confined to his bed, never to leave it. During his last illness he had visitors almost every afternoon. Chief Justice Oliver Wendell Holmes, John Hays Hammond, A. Platt Andrew, Nathan MacLoud, and Leonard Craske were among those who called.

Blackburn died May 4, 1932, at the age of seventy-four, leaving an estate of $17,000. Though his hands and feet were crippled early in life, he lived to overcome adversity and to win the respect and admiration of everyone in his community.

This account, which I received from Howard Blackburn himself, is *the* Gloucester story of all times. His feat stands unchallenged by the experience of any other Gloucester fisherman. It should be remembered through the years as a great example of man's triumph over the cruel sea. When Gloucester men themselves say with deep respect in their voices that Blackburn was a "hard, tough fisherman," we can be sure that he was a great man. The people of Gloucester are united in their belief that no other American fisherman has ever lived to tell of such an experience.

11. *Swallow Cave*

$\mathcal{A}$s I HIKED along the Massachusetts coast-line, it became more and more familiar. The Reef of Norman's Woe, Rafe's Chasm, Beverly and old Hospital Point Light, Marblehead and Marblehead Neck, each had its moment of interest as I trudged by on the way to my particular objective—Nahant.

There is much about this tiny seagirt village which has always attracted me, for at Nahant there seems to exist a dramatic atmosphere not present at any other North Shore town. Even the names of the various locations are fascinating—Castle Rock, Irene's Grotto, John's Peril, Pulpit Rock, Dorothy's Cove, Spouting Horn, and best of all, Swallow Cave.

As I walked through Lynn, I remembered the first time I had ever visited Nahant. In the fall of 1932 my wife and I left Winthrop by canoe on a bright clear day, bound for Nahant. By the time we had arrived there, a brisk northeast wind had set in, and we had difficulty in landing at Swallow Cave. We reached the shore without tipping over, however, and after thoroughly exploring the cave, we started back to Winthrop. By now the waves were four and five feet high, and I didn't have much hope of our landing right side up. But finally, after an hour's frantic steering and paddling, we approached Grover's Cliff in Winthrop, paddled in to the beach just ahead of a giant breaker, and pulled the canoe up in the lee of Fort Heath. Much to our surprise, we didn't have to swim at all.—Late that night the ocean washed out the narrow gauge railroad tracks less than a quarter mile from the place where we had landed.

In my other books there are many Nahant stories, including the legend of that massive boulder, Egg Rock. On a certain fall day around 1815, Faustino, the Italian sweetheart of a Greater Boston girl, sailed out to Egg Rock from Nahant. His object was to pick for her some of the forget-me-not flowers which grew on the crest of the boulder. But Faustino perished in the sea while trying to reach Nahant, and Alice, his betrothed, later died from the shock of her lover's drowning. It is said that Alice's spirit returns every year to the rocks of Nahant, where her voice is still heard calling for her lost lover—"Faustino! Faustino!"

Another Nahant story took place in 1819 when the New England sea serpent gave his best performance of the century just off its shores, and several of Boston's leading citizens, without the help of alcoholic stimulation, recorded their impressions of this unusual event.

Swallow Cave, however, had so far eluded all my efforts to obtain its history. I was determined to visit the Nahant Library again in an effort to glean more information about the cave which historian Fred A. Wilson mentioned in his *Annals of Nahant*. I spent a full day in the library, and with the gracious assistance of the librarian, located the original material which included the story I wanted.

The account begins with the physical features of Swallow Cave, describing the entrance as about five feet high and the depth of the cave as twenty-four yards. "The ceiling is carved by nature into tall but irregular Gothic arches and rises through the whole passage from eighteen to twenty feet. The sides are ruggedly perpendicular, and the floor uneven by its elevations and cavities. Perpetual humidity reigns in this dreary cavern from the continuous droppings of water through the crevices of the ceiling. There is a slight bend in this singular cave, and through a fissure of rocks, from which one enjoys a fine view of the sea, you step along the rugged beach and grope your way up the side of the hill opposite to that you just descended. It is called the Swallow Cave from the great number of that species which hatch their young and inhabit there the greatest part of the year, and are even said to exist in it during the winter in a completely torpid state."

In the year 1675, during King Phillip's War, forty Narragansett warriors paddled across Massachusetts Bay from Pocasset on Cape Cod, hid their canoes in the woods near the entrance to the Saugus River and raided the town of Lynn that night. The men of Lynn struck back and overcame the Indians, forcing them to retreat into the darkness toward Long Beach and Nahant. The Indians did not know where they were being driven and fled far in advance of the pursuing white men. When they reached the vicinity of Swallow Cave, one of them discovered the opening in the rocks, and all forty Indians soon were hiding inside.

The men of Lynn lost the trail and finally returned to their homes, determined to come back later and destroy the last of the Indians. While they gathered their forces for a counter-attack, the Indians were allowed to live at Nahant unmolested.

Two weeks later a captain was appointed to drill twenty-five men for battle with the Indians, and these prospective warriors were equipped with "broadswords and muskets," each man carrying "a Bible in his hand and a Westminister catechism in his left pocket." Before embarking on the perilous trip to Nahant, however, the captain decided to visit Wonderful, the witch, who lived near the Salem shore.

Wonderful made her living by fortune-telling and was a harmless, sharp-tongued woman. She had a brilliant mind and had often discovered lost property and accurately predicted coming events.

When the Lynn captain and his men knocked at the door of

Wonderful's hut, it was indeed a dismal night. "Come in!" shouted the witch, and she walked toward the captain, holding a candle. Its feeble yellow blaze formed the only illumination in the hut. Wonderful fastened her piercing stare on the captain, and he noticed that her withered and aging skin was in striking contrast to the youthfulness of her flashing gray eyes.

"Welcome, my brave soldiers," she cried. "Success to your enterprise. You see, I know where your game is!" At that moment her candle blew out, and they were in darkness. Wonderful's voice came to them in the blackness of the hut. "Before tomorrow's sun has set you'll be sure of the wild, yelling devils."

Just then a door banged in the shed outside.

"Comrades, are we betrayed?" shouted the captain. "Take care what you say, Wonderful."

"Why, my brisk man," answered Wonderful, "I haven't lived seventy years for a blustery soldier of thirty to question me. I know that you are after the Indians, and I know that you will find them, forty in number, on the Nahant shore, waiting to dip their tomahawks into the blood of your families. I've been counting the clouds and watching the cattle all week.

> *Mingle, mingle, mingle, mingle,*
> *Away, apart, together, single,*
> *The Indians on the shore you'll see,*
> *Your death or life—remember me."*

After the captain and his companions had left the hut, they discussed Wonderful's predictions and decided to leave at once for Nahant. Three hours later they were cautiously making their way toward the rocks. Suddenly, in the vicinity of what is now the Forty Steps, their captain warned them to lie down. The soldiers remained motionless for several minutes. Then the outline of an Indian brave appeared silhouetted against the sky.

"Hark," shouted the Indian to his companion. "I saw the form of an English soldier."

"Impossible," came the answer. "The English dare not come here. Our sharp hatchets are ready to avenge our wrongs, which are deep and hot and need much blood to cool our fevered brains."

The recumbent soldiers watched the two Indians walk slowly away from them and disappear toward what is now called Swallow Cave. Twenty minutes later one of the Lynn men spoke up.

"Listen—I think I hear the roar of the war drums."

"Oh, no, that is the surf at Spouting Horn," came the captain's answer, "but to ease your mind I'll take my blunderbuss and go over to the spot where the two Indians disappeared. If you hear me fire, come and help, but stay here until you hear my gun."

Ten minutes later he was cautiously peering down over the cliff at Swallow Cave. He saw a fire burning and several Indians sleeping soundly on the rocky floor. Two giant red men were awake, however, checking the sharpness of their hatchets and tomahawks. One was boasting to the other of how they would kill every last person when they attacked the English settlement at Lynn the next day.

When the captain heard of the Indians' plans, his anger overcame his judgment, and he decided to fire at once at the giant who had spoken. Just as his grip on the musket began to tighten, he heard behind him the voice of Wonderful, the witch.

"Shed no blood, my friend, or you will live to regret it," said Wonderful. "I promise on one condition to deliver the enemy without loss of a single drop of human blood. I wish you to allow me to visit the Indian encampment alone." The captain agreed, and a short time later Wonderful returned with the Indian who had boasted in the cave.

"White man," said the Indian, "our mother here says that you spared my life by not shooting me. An Indian knows both bravery and gratitude. But you must know we grieve that you have taken our homes here away from us. Is this not so?"

The captain was quick with his answer. "This is no time for parley," he cried, "Will you surrender?"

"On one condition—that we be allowed to bring our canoes back from their hiding place on the Saugus River and then may leave for our lands at Pocasset. If you refuse this simple request it would be better that we swim in our own blood."

"All right, then swim!" cried the captain and aimed his pistol at the Indian chieftain. But the pistol missed fire, flashing on the flint.

"For shame," cried the witch. "Remember your promise."

The Lynn captain gained control of himself, and admitted that Wonderful was right. "I consent to let them return," he began, "but the Indians must pledge their solemn oath that they will never fight us again."

The Indians, after a discussion of some length, gave their oath. The crisis was over.

The men of Lynn returned to their homes, and the Indians went up the Saugus River to the point where they had secreted their canoes, pulled them down to the bank and paddled back to Nahant. Early the next morning the inhabitants of Lynn climbed to High Rock to watch the procession of Indian canoes starting across the water toward Graves Ledge and the Brewster Islands on their long journey back to Cape Cod.

Wonderful the witch later admitted that she had been secretly placed under Indian protection because of her ability to foretell the future. Shortly after the Nahant compromise she predicted her own death, and surely enough, the soldiers found her lifeless body two weeks later in the hut. The citizens of Lynn decided to bury her high on the hill overlooking Swallow Cave, the scene of her peace-making.

A hundred years ago the superstitious ones claimed to have seen Wonderful's ghost among the rocks around the cave, and the older people could hardly pass the place without recalling the singular escape of the Narragansett Indians from an engagement which was never fought—the Battle of Swallow Cave.

12. The Woman in the Purple Cloak

IN THE town of Winthrop, Massachusetts, there is a small peninsula of land which runs from Great Head to Shirley Gut, known as Point Shirley. This part of Winthrop has had a more interesting history than all the rest of the town put together, for long before Winthrop was separated from Chelsea, Point Shirley was a thriving community known as Pullen Point.

Back in 1753 a group of prominent Bostonians journeyed down to Pullen Point to make preliminary plans for establishing a fishing industry there. The proprietors invested a substantial sum of money, built fishing warehouses and flakes and purchased six new schooners for their venture. They sent men, horses, and supplies out to far-distant Sable Island, and by mid-summer of 1753 they were ready to do business. Governor William Shirley was invited down to Pullen Point for the opening exercises, and on his arrival, he was informed that in his honor, the proprietors wished to change the name of Pullen Point to Point Shirley. The pleased executive gave his consent, and the peninsula has been known as Point Shirley ever since. But the fishing industry met with early trouble when one of its vessels ran aground and several others were captured by the French. This heavy loss was too much for the proprietors, and they abandoned their enterprise in despair.

A few years later the deserted fishing buildings were used by exiled and homeless Acadians, and there are those who say that Emmeline Labische, the original Evangeline, once came to the Point in search of her lost lover.

During the War of 1812, on December 17, 1814, the mighty battleship *Constitution* sailed out to sea through Shirley Gut to escape the watchful British fleet. The farmers of what is now Winthrop gazed with awe and admiration as "Old Ironsides" successfully negotiated the narrow passage to reach the ocean. Captain Stewart of the *Constitution* continued on his course with several British ships in vain pursuit.

The *Constitution* is still afloat at the Boston Navy Yard, but Shirley Gut, that narrow waterway between Point Shirley and Deer Island, gradually became shallower, and by 1932 mariners ceased to use it altogether. Today there is a wide road running across from Winthrop to Deer Island, and Shirley Gut is no more.

Salt works were put up at Point Shirley shortly after the War of 1812, but they were abandoned with the discovery of inland salt which was cheaper to produce. Paul Revere's sons and grandsons established copper works at the Point in 1841, but these, too, were abandoned in 1869. Summer cottages were built soon afterwards, and now the Point Shirley area is heavily populated, winter and summer.

In the month of October, 1868, omnibus carriages were still running to Point Shirley from Maverick Square. From the last coach, one day at about five in the afternoon, there alighted at Point Shirley an unknown woman dressed in a peculiar purple cloak.

A young boy, Wallace Wyman, watched the stranger climbing down from the stage. As he leaned against the rail fence on his father's farm, he wondered why the woman had arrived at Point Shirley so late in the day. The stage coach on which she had come was now starting back for Boston and there would be no other until the next day.

Now the strange woman in purple advanced slowly up the hill to the place where Wallace Wyman was standing.

"Young man, is this Point Shirley?" she asked.

"Yes, my lady, it is."

The woman studied the boy carefully before she continued.

"Then I have come to the right location. You look like an honest lad, so I'll tell you why I am here. Last night I had a dream, a very vivid one in fact, and I dreamed that I was standing at an old fort on a hill. Then there was a strange voice which kept repeating over and over to me. . . . 'You are at the old fort at Pullen Point. . . . There is treasure all around you, especially to the north, east, south, and under your very feet.'

"Young man, that dream was so real that when I woke I couldn't believe I had been dreaming. I couldn't sleep any more that night, so I dressed and went down to the library where I opened several books on Boston. Finally I found one which mentioned Pullen Point, and it said that the location was now known as Point Shirley. I was determined to go there. The idea obsessed me.

"Even then, as I live in Dorchester, it was quite a journey. Finally, by two o'clock, I crossed the penny ferry at the foot of Hanover Street in Boston and arrived in East Boston at Maverick Square, where I took the next stage to Point Shirley. Now I want to know if there is an old fort here and if so, where I will find it."

"Yes, there's a fort. It's on the top of the hill, and the old stones are still there."

"The stones are there. Why, I saw them in my dream, piled one above the other. Take me there at once, my lad."

Ten minutes later the Lady with the Purple Cloak and young Wallace Wyman arrived at the old stone fort which had been at the top of Point Shirley Hill since the days of the American Revolution.

"Yes," began the mysterious Lady in Purple, "this is the exact location of my dream. It all comes back to me now. There is treasure in the ground on which we stand, my lad, make no mistake about that. And there is more treasure over on the island behind the one in front of us. Then there is more treasure up there to the north, behind that high promontory. I know that I won't ever find any treasure, but I am passing the information on to you, my lad. Some day, if you are industrious, you'll find a fortune on this hill."

Just then she was interrupted by a high-pitched voice shouting, "Wallace, Wallace! Come to supper."

"That's my Ma," cried Wallace, "and I'll have to go now."

He ran down the hill and disappeared into the house. After supper he came out again, although by this time it had grown quite dark, and he walked up to the old fort. The Lady with the Purple Cloak had vanished. He searched all over Point Shirley, but never again did he see the woman who had arrived on the last stage coach that evening. There was no way she could have left Point Shirley except on foot, and surely the woman could not walk six long miles to Maverick Square at that time of night.

He often wondered in the following days what could have happened to her, but he never learned. He did, however, go up to the top of the hill and dig here and there for the treasure which she had said was buried nearby. But he soon gave up and after a few years nearly forgot the entire incident.

Wallace Wyman grew to manhood and became a fisherman. One morning in 1887, when he was in his thirties, he arose early to go out and haul his traps. After pulling on his heavy rubber boots he walked down to the back shore, pushed his rowboat into the water and soon reached his anchorage. While slipping his moorings, he noticed three strangers leaving a schooner anchored in the offing. They rowed ashore with a firm stroke and passed within fifty yards of him on their way to the beach, where they landed a quarter mile north of the old salt works.

As he hoisted sail on his own craft, he noticed that the men had shovels and picks with them. They soon pulled their skiff up above the reach of the incoming tide, and then struck off at a rapid clip toward the old Point Shirley fort.

He thought no more of it and sailed out of the harbor to haul his traps. Late that afternoon when he finished his work, the wind had died down and stranded him near Great Brewster Island. He realized that he was in for a long scull home, and it was after dark when he neared Point Shirley. He noticed, however, that the strange schooner was still at anchor in the offing and that the dingy was alongside.

"Here's a chance to find out who those men are," Wyman thought to himself, and he sculled up slowly to the side of the schooner. Glancing through a porthole, he saw the three men, with guns drawn, sitting around an ancient rust-covered sea chest, which was literally filled to the brim with gold and silver coins.

"They'll shoot me first and ask questions later," Wyman thought in horror. Just before he pushed off from the schooner, he heard one of the men mutter to the others, "The treasure of Long Ben Avery, after a hundred and fifty years!"

Wyman sculled silently off into the night. After going home and eating his supper, he took a lantern and climbed to the old fort. In the exact spot where he and the Lady in Purple had stood years before, there was a yawning pit. He climbed down to investigate further, and at the bottom of the pit saw the outline of a chest, about fourteen inches long and eight inches wide, with the rust from the hinges still clinging to the dirt. At this sight, Wyman bitterly realized that untold riches had been within his grasp all his life.

Later when the old wheelhouse of the ship *Columbia* was stripped for metal, Wyman acquired the house, sailed it across to Point Shirley, set it up near the beach as his home and settled down to live comfortably in it by himself. The years passed uneventfully. By the 1930's Wyman was a man of seventy, though vigorous and active. He still lived in the pilot house of the old

Columbia, but Point Shirley had become a thriving community in the meantime, and the old building was by then hemmed in with modern dwellings. It was here that I found him in 1936 when I was collecting material for my history of Winthrop.

Some of the most interesting evenings of my entire life were those I spent at the old Point Shirley pilot house. One night Wyman told me the story you have just read. And he told me, too, that treasure has actually been found in each of the places mentioned by the Lady in the Purple Cloak!

13. *The Steamer Portland*

*M*ORE than half a century has elapsed since the beautiful white-and-gold trimmed steamer *Portland* sailed from Boston on her regular run to Portland, Maine, November 26, 1898. The paddle-wheel steamer, built at Bath, Maine, in 1890, was 291 feet long and of forty-two foot beam. Since this trip took place the Saturday after Thanksgiving, there were more passengers than usual who wished to make the return journey to Portland that night. Many were returning to Maine from Philadelphia, New York, and points south after spending the holiday with their families.

That November morning the weather was pleasantly fair, with a light breeze. As the day wore on, however, the clouds above Boston grew heavier, the first signs of a growing condition of grave danger. A tremendous cyclone from the Gulf of Mexico was about to join forces with a storm of only slightly lesser proportions roaring across from the Great Lakes.

Meanwhile, the loading of the steamer's freight continued at India Wharf in Boston. Passengers who had made reservations for the trip began to come aboard. Some of them later cancelled their accommodations, but the majority, more than one hundred persons, sailed with the ship. With passengers and crew, there were 176 people aboard the *Portland* by sailing time.

The general manager of the Portland Steam Packet Company, John F. Liscomb, received warning of the approaching storm from New York and tried to communicate by phone from Portland with the steamer's captain, Hollis H. Blanchard. Failing in this, he left word that the *Portland's* companion ship, the newer *Bay State*, should not leave Portland until nine o'clock, when the size of the storm could be better gauged. When he returned at 5:30, Blanchard talked over the phone to the *Bay State's* captain, Alexander Dennison, called because of his comparative youthfulness "the Kid Pilot."

Captain Dennison repeated to Blanchard the manager's suggestion to hold the *Portland* until nine o'clock that night. Captain Blanchard replied that the *Portland* would sail on schedule at seven. He added that, judging by the direction of the storm, it would not reach the city of Portland until after the steamer had safely docked. Dennison, said Blanchard, would be proceeding southward, and would run into the storm before he reached Boston. But Captain Blanchard, who had been ordered to sail that night, thought it wise for the *Portland* to sail on time so as to reach her destination before the storm.

The fact that the two captains talked over the phone that day has given rise to the popular legend that Captain Blanchard sailed contrary to the advice of the general manager. The motive ascribed to him was that he was anxious to prove his professional superiority to Captain Dennison by steaming into Portland Harbor while the *Bay State* was still at the wharf. There seem to be no foundation in fact for this rumor, though it dies hard.

There has always been a heated controversy as to whether or not Captain Hollis H. Blanchard was ordered to sail that night. A few years ago I interviewed Miss Grace Blanchard, granddaughter of the captain. She told me that her father, Charles Blanchard, visited his father shortly before the *Portland* left the pier and had a conversation with him. The two men talked with each other briefly in the pilot house.

"My father asked my grandfather if it was necessary for him to sail," Miss Blanchard said. "The wind had started to come up and they knew that there was a heavy snowstorm in New York.

Grandfather Blanchard said to his son, '*I have my orders to sail, and I am going!*' Those were the last words ever spoken by my grandfather to a member of his family."

Captains of passenger vessels invariably feel the responsibility for the many lives which depend upon their skill and judgment. Those who really knew Captain Blanchard were convinced that he was no exception. His decision was based upon long experience, and at least twelve other sea captains have admitted that under similar conditions they would have reasoned and acted as he did.

At 6:07, fifty-three minutes before sailing time, the final notice arrived with the information that it was still snowing in New York, but that the wind had backed around to northwest. This news gave Captain Blanchard further confidence that he could reach Portland ahead of the storm as he had done many times before. At precisely seven o'clock that November evening the final departing whistle from the *Portland* split the chill night air of Boston's Atlantic Avenue, and Captain Hollis Blanchard sailed into the unknown.

It is falsely believed that the *Portland* was not seen after leaving Boston on her way up the coast. However, Captain William Thomas of Bailey's Island, Maine, master of the fisherman *Maud S.*, saw the lights of the *Portland* when he was nearly four miles southwest of Thacher's Island. Since his wife was supposedly on the steamer, Thomas was naturally watching for the *Portland* with more than ordinary interest. From his vantage point, less than two miles away from the side-wheeler, it seemed to Thomas that the steamer was closer to shore than usual. He said to his crew, "There goes the *Portland*. She will probably run close to Thacher's." It was then two and a half hours after Blanchard had sailed from Boston. Nothing at that time led Thomas to believe that the captain of the *Portland* was foolhardy in continuing her journey. (Incidentally, Thomas' wife was not on the *Portland*, having made fortunate use of the privilege of changing her mind.)

Captain A. A. Tarr of Thacher's Island light off Gloucester agreed with Thomas about conditions at the time the *Portland* passed by. He said that the weather seemed so nearly normal when the ship was scheduled to pass the island that he did not even bother to look for the sparkle of her lights. We have the additional evidence of another man stationed at Thacher's Island. Captain Lynes B. Hathaway of Brockton, master workman of the Lighthouse Department, at nine-thirty or shortly thereafter saw the *Portland's* lights as the steamer passed within five hundred feet of the shore between Thacher's and the Londoner Ledge. The *Portland*, then on schedule, continued up the coast.

Around eleven o'clock, less than ninety minutes after Captain Hathaway saw the steamer, Captain Reuben Cameron of the schooner *Grayling* sighted the *Portland* twelve miles south by east of Thacher's Island. Thus, without question, the vessel had changed her course. The *Portland* came so near to the *Grayling* that Captain Cameron burned a Coston flare to warn the steamer away. The paddle-wheeler at this time seemed to be rolling and pitching badly, although her superstructure appeared intact.

Also in the vicinity was the schooner *Florence E. Stream.* At approximately eleven-fifteen p.m. her master, Captain Frank Stream, passed a paddle-wheel steamer which must have been the *Portland*, as there was no other vessel of her type in the area. Half an hour later Captain D. J. Pellier of the schooner *Edgar Randall*, then fourteen miles southeast by east of Eastern Point, Gloucester, noticed a large vessel bearing down upon him out of the night. Pellier swung the *Randall* away and escaped a collision but had no time to see that the ship was a paddle-wheel steamer. At the time, he believed that the steamer's superstructure had been damaged, but the accuracy of his vision from the lurching deck of a small schooner is a matter of conjecture.

Meanwhile the storm had increased in intensity. In Portland at noon there had been a north wind blowing at nineteen miles per hour, which increased at two p.m. to twenty-six, changing to northeast at three o'clock, then increasing to thirty-six miles an hour that evening. After swinging around to north at six p.m., the wind shifted to northeast an hour later. There were spells of wind which blew during this period at almost a mile a minute. In Boston the official records indicate that many gusts as high as seventy-two miles an hour were registered. Occasionally the velocity reached almost unbelievable intensity. The barometer at Boston dropped from 29:70 at seven to 29:44 at twelve.

Shipping all along the coast scurried for shelter. Vessel after vessel, failing to reach a safe harbor, was tossed ashore along Nantasket Beach and the North Shore of Massachusetts, and every coastal town and city in the path of the storm was fearfully battered. Giant breakers swept through many main thoroughfares, and the tide, as measured at Cohasset, rose even higher than it had during the record gale of 1851 which toppled Minot's lighthouse.

Just how far on her scheduled journey did the *Portland* go? There were those, including the late yachting enthusiast and newsman, William U. Swan, who believed that the *Portland* reached a point north of Boon Island off Portsmouth on her voyage up the coast. This belief is hard to reconcile with the known facts. If the side-wheeler passed the Londoner Ledge off Thacher's Island around nine-thirty, she could not have attained a position near Boon Island, many miles to the north, changed her course and still be twelve miles southeast of Thacher's Island ninety minutes later at eleven p.m. Logically it would seem that the *Portland* got further than five miles north of Thacher's Island on her scheduled route.

Captain Frank Scripture of Rockport, Massachusetts, later

said that when the *Portland* sailed from Boston there was no reason why a prudent master should not leave that port. But Captain Scripture had never experienced a storm as sudden as the one which descended on Cape Ann that night. Probably when the blast caught Captain Blanchard somewhere north of Thacher's Island, he headed the *Portland* toward the open sea to ride out the gale as he had done before.

Judging by what we know of the fate of the *Monticello* in another storm off Nova Scotia, it is possible and even probable that the *Portland* began shipping seas and soon developed a list to starboard. In that case, though her port paddle-wheel came out of water, the starboard wheel kept turning, and, heading toward the open sea, Captain Blanchard could offset the drive of the gale pushing him toward the southwest. The net result of the various conflicting forces placed the *Portland* off Cape Cod early the next day.

At five-forty-five that Sunday morning, Keeper A. C. Fisher of the Race Point Life Saving Station heard four blasts from a steamer's whistle. He went out, glanced at the clock, and rang the gong for the surfboat in case rescue work was ahead. Although he telephoned Peaked Hill Station to be on the look-out and sent a man down to the beach, neither ships nor wreckage could be seen at that time. "Conditions were the worst I have ever known," Keeper Fisher said later.

While neither Fisher nor his men saw any sign of the *Portland* early that morning, when the eye of the hurricane passed across Cape Cod between nine and ten-thirty, several other persons saw the *Portland* wallowing in the huge offshore seas some five to eight miles from Cape Cod during a brief clearing in skies. The clear weather lasted until ten-thirty, and then the storm returned with all its former fury. By two o'clock it was worse than ever.

At the end of the afternoon, the bitter wind continued to fill the air with snow and sand, making it nearly unbearable for

Surfman John Johnson of the Peaked Hill Bars Station as he plodded along the beach. He knew that another life saver was pushing toward him from the Race Point Guard Station several miles away and that ahead was the Half Way House which marked the division of their patrol. Arriving at the Half Way House, Johnson met his fellow watchman, Surfman Bickers, exchanged a story or two, spoke of the gale, and started back along the windswept beach.

The darkness increased. At seven-twenty Johnson thought he saw something thrown up by the incoming tide. Keeping his eye on the object, he fought his way down to the shore, picked up his find and hastily retreated to the bank above the surf. In the dim light of his lantern he examined the object. It was a life belt, and on it he read the words *Steamer Portland of Portland*. He had no reason to suppose anything more than that the boat had lost a life preserver.

Here is his statement:

"I was bound west toward the station, when I found the first thing that landed from the steamer. It was a life belt and it was one-half mile east of the station. At seven-forty-five o'clock that evening I found the next seen wreckage, a creamery can, forty-quart, I guess. It was right below our station, and nine or ten more of them, all empty and stoppered tightly came on there closely together.

"Jim Kelly succeeded me on the eastern beat, leaving the station at eight-twenty p.m. and at nine-thirty he found doors and other light woodwork from the *Portland* on the shore. When I found the life belt the wind was north northeast."

Actually, the *Portland* was at that time in the last stages of foundering. Thomas Harrison Eames tells us that "the pounding of the sea under her guards opened her up and allowed tons of water to rush into the hull, flooding engine room and boiler room, drowning the men and depriving the ship of her power."

It was not until eleven o'clock, around high tide, that the

wreckage began to come ashore in large quantities. Edwin B. Tyler of the Race Point crew found doors, electric light bulbs, wash stand tops and other wreckage, and when the midnight watch returned the beach was buried with debris from the *Portland*. Mattresses, chairs, upholstery, windows, doors and paneling all came ashore just before midnight.

The next morning the Cape Cod shore was littered with wreckage piled eight and ten feet high. In with the *Portland's* remains were fragments from the ninety-six-foot granite schooner *Addie E. Snow*, which had also gone down with all hands. A short distance away the upper part of the cabin from the steamer *Pentagoet* was discovered embedded in the sand. The wreck of the *Snow* was later discovered a short distance from the *Portland* on the bottom of the sea. Thirty-six bodies were eventually recovered and identified from the *Portland*, but not one body was ever found from either the *Snow* or the *Pentagoet*.

Several watches found on the victims had stopped at about nine-fifteen, and since the *Portland* was definitely seen afloat later than that on Sunday morning we can safely assume that she made her final plunge at around quarter past nine that Sunday night, November 27, 1898.

Because the wreckage of the *Addie E. Snow* and the *Portland* came up on the beach together, it is entirely possible that a collision may have occurred between the two vessels. An engine room gong with a lignum vitae clapper later floated to the surface and was brought into Boston. In order for this to be freed from the engine room in the bowels of the ship, the *Portland* must have split apart before she sank, as the *Monticello* did when she went down off Nova Scotia. The question is: Did the *Portland* break in two because of a collision or did she split in two of her own accord?

Relics from the *Portland* are many. I have heard that there is scarcely a cottage along the Outer Beach at Cape Cod that does not have its *Portland* souvenir. There are said to be four wheels of the *Portland* in existence. The captain's speaking trumpet was sold to a westerner in 1899, and an oil dealer converted a life raft into a container from which to sell kerosene on the streets of Boston. Cy Young of Hyannis amassed a great amount of *Portland* material, storing empty coffins, cabin posts, bunks, doors and life belts in the cellar of his antique shop in Province-town, where he sold them for forty-five years after the disaster. Hundreds of paper knives and miniature oars were carved from stateroom blinds and doors, and stateroom door numbers com-manded a high premium. Today, although half a century has elapsed since the disaster, these relics are seldom sold but are handed down as precious heirlooms from generation to gen-eration.

Through the years, relatives and friends of those lost aboard the side-wheeler have been drawn together by a common bond. It was their custom to meet at India Wharf in Boston, from which the *Portland* sailed, and hold memorial services for their loved ones. The group became known as the *Portland* Associ-ates. On each November 26, at precisely seven o'clock in the evening, one of the members read the names of those who were lost. With the reading of the final name, another member dropped flowers into the harbor from the pier. Then those as-sembled would discuss their individual versions of the weather that fateful night or repeat to each other their own anxieties and emotions when they first realized that the *Portland* was missing.

At the first report that the steamer had not been heard from, mild alarm had given way to doubt, then deep anxiety, and, finally, the cold, gripping fear which accompanied the awesome certainty that their loved ones and the *Portland* had been lost at sea. The *Portland* story became one which was told and retold with undying interest through the years.

The last president of the *Portland* Associates was John A.

Thornquist of Medford, Massachusetts. As the half century anniversary approached, it was decided to hold the final meeting on November 26, 1948. A solemn group of eighty persons gathered that evening on India Wharf, and, exactly fifty years after the *Portland* had sailed from that same wharf, began their final exercises. The 176 names were read, the prayers were given, and flowers were scattered into the sea. The next day President Thornquist led a smaller group to Highland Light, Cape Cod, where in the presence of many Cape Codders he unveiled a tablet to the *Portland* victims. The memorial plaque was placed against the sturdy sides of Highland Light, overlooking the waters where the side-wheeler plunged to her doom on that same day fifty years before.

Hundreds of persons who were in Boston when the *Portland* sailed claimed that they planned to be aboard her but for one reason or another were delayed and missed the boat. Some say that they were in a barroom taking a last drink, others that they were on a street car which was held up. My only comment is that the barrooms and street cars of Boston must have been packed with humanity that day, judging by the great numbers who have chosen to identify themselves with the *Portland* in this manner. Actually, of course, there were only a few authentic cases of persons who did not sail as they had planned. The story of Mrs. Anna Young of Boston is one of the true accounts:

"I was resting in my stateroom. The whistle of the *Portland* was sounding for all visitors to go ashore. Suddenly there was a knock at the door, and a message from my mother was delivered. Mother believed a storm was coming, and she had a premonition that I shouldn't sail. Carrying my child, I ran for the gangplank just as they started to lift it, and they waited for me. When I got ashore I heard the final whistle of the *Portland* as she left the wharf."

Another true story of a lucky hunch was told by Mr. George

Gott of Brooklin, Maine. Mr. Gott was standing on the wharf before going aboard the steamer when he noticed the strange behavior of the ship's cat. She was systematically removing her litter of kittens from the ship to the corner of a great barnlike shed on the wharf. Again and again she boarded the vessel and brought another kitten ashore. Then and there Mr. Gott decided that if the *Portland* wasn't good enough for the ship's cat that night, it wasn't good enough for him, and the side-wheeler sailed without him.

For the past fifteen years I have been collecting information about the steamer *Portland*. I have in my possession letters from several of those whose information was vital in piecing together what we know about the side-wheeler. Many other letters, over four hundred, in fact, mentioned the possibility of getting a diver to go down to the *Portland* and examine her.

In 1944, I visited Captain Charles G. Carver in Rockland, Maine, who told me of his contact with the *Portland*. He had been scallop-dragging about five miles north of Highland Light and brought to the surface quite a lot of material which was identified as coming from the *Portland*. A short distance away he also located a small granite schooner, probably the *Addie E. Snow*. His interest centered in the *Portland*, however.

"I have no doubt but that we had our drags on what is now left of the steamer *Portland*," Captain Carver told me. He mentioned pulling up six champagne bottles, several doorknobs, dishes, plates, silverware and frame fixtures. One doorknob had the insignia of the old Portland Steam Packet Company engraved on the handle. Since the *Portland* was the only vessel of that line lost off Cape Cod, I knew that he must have been over the wreck of the ill-fated side-wheeler.

Captain Carver examined his records to give me the exact location of the *Portland*, and I made plans to send a diver down to the hull of the vessel. (Not one of those who had suggested

that I arrange for diving operations volunteered to help finan-
cially in the project.) I contracted with Diver Al George of
Malden, Massachusetts, to descend to the hull of the old steamer.
He spent the last week of June and the first day of July, 1945,
working at the location, after which he prepared and signed a
statement covering the vital part of his diving activities. His
account follows:

In the month of June, 1945, I was commissioned by Lt. Edward
R. Snow to descend to the bottom of the ocean off Cape Cod at a
location previously found by Captain Charles G. Carver of Rockland, Maine. Highland Light bears 175 degrees true at a distance of
4½ miles; the Pilgrim Monument, 6¼ miles away has a bearing of
210 degrees; Race Point Coast Guard Station, bearing 255 degrees,
is seven miles distant.

Arriving on the location during the last week of June, I carried
out the plans for finding the *Portland*. I ran on a course 115 degrees
true from the Peaked Hill Bar Buoy. I made a sweep after reaching
a point 1¾ miles from the buoy, using a span of 600 feet of cable.
We swept the entire location within a radius of three-quarters of a
mile. On the second time across I made fast to what I knew was
some large submerged object. After buoying it, we swept the entire
vicinity to make sure the object was the steamer *Portland* and not
some other wreck. Of this I am certain: This wreck is the only
wreck in this vicinity which corresponds to the bearings given by
Captain Carver. Therefore it must be the steamer *Portland*.

Realizing this fact, I then got rigged for diving. I slid down the
sweep wire and within three minutes of the time I had left the
Regavlas I had landed on the *Portland* which was over on its beam
ends and heavily sanded in. It may surprise the average person to
realize that the visibility here is less than 18 inches.

It was a weird sight. Crawling along the sloping hull of the vessel,
I nosed my helmet forward until I ran into a mast heavily covered
with marine growth (mussels, seaweed, etc.). Reaching my hands
out, I found I could not span the mast. I followed the mast up until
it went off out of my reach at a space between two gigantic boulders

on the bottom. The mast appeared to be broken off 15 feet up.

It would seem as though the *Portland* had hit bottom on her beam ends and then through the years had worked its way into the sand until it is buried almost completely. Only the bare hull of the ship seems in position.

All superstructure evidently has been spread around the ocean bed long ago. The boulders are much higher than my head. I could not tell whether it was the foremast or the mainmast. Going down on my hands and knees, I could make out the ripples of sand on the bottom of the sea and could see little shells from time to time.

The tide was running about one knot and it was slack water. My brother telephoned down from upstairs that he had 300 feet of line run out to enable me to stand on bottom in 144 feet of water.

It was a strange experience standing there alone with the ill-fated *Portland* and probably what remained of the passengers and crew still imprisoned in her sand-covered hull.

I wish I could give one the awesome picture. While visibility was a foot and a half, vague shadows could be made out up to five and eight feet away. Giant devil weed and long streamers of other varieties of seaweed shrouded me in a big black cloud of marine life.

As there probably will be many who might think that the *Portland* sank gently to the bottom to remain practically intact for the 47 years since the disaster, I must impress on their minds the true picture of the present conditions. The entire hull of the vessel which protrudes above the sand is a blackened shapeless mass of watersoaked wood, seaweed, mussels, scallops, and scores of different types of marine growth.

I spent less than a half hour on the bottom, then I gave the signal to be hoisted up to twenty feet from the surface where I hung for ten minutes, then I was hoisted to ten feet from the surface where I remained suspended for fifteen minutes. I then was brought over the side and my dive had been completed.

I realize that the purser's bell, the keys, the doorknobs, and the many other articles which have been brought to the surface from this shipwreck indicate many more articles could be retrieved. I have been told that a small fortune in uncut gems in the purser's safe would well-repay the lucky finder. In my opinion, however, although I would be happy to undertake the search, the chances are greatly against anything more of practical value ever being found. If anyone would consider financing such an enterprise, the cost would be prohibitive.

Al George

Each year I receive more letters from *Portland* enthusiasts. Many of the writers suggest that I conduct further research work on the hull of the steamer (at my own expense) and thereby find the purser's safe. It has been said that the safe contains many uncut diamonds, but I am extremely skeptical, and even if the diamonds were there, the chances that they would be found are infinitesimal. Tens of thousands of dollars would be necessary to obtain conclusive results, and unless those who urge further diving on the *Portland* pay for the work themselves, it will never be done.

Perhaps it is just as well to let the old steamer rest for the remainder of her existence at the bottom of the sea, undisturbed by visits from the world above the surface. There is much that we should like to know for certain about the side-wheeler, but the chances are greatly against the appearance of new information at this late date. In any event, the last voyage of the *Portland* will remain forever New England's greatest saga of the sea.

Part Three

CAPE COD TO SANDY HOOK

14. The Nantucket South Shoals Lightship Station

FROM the Hyannis Airport on Cape Cod I flew out to Nantucket, the Far-Away Island, and then across forty-two miles of ocean to the South Shoals Lightship, one of the most isolated floating beacons on the entire Atlantic Coast. This small, tossing vessel, bright red with large white letters spelling out the word NANTUCKET on her hull, is anchored in thirty fathoms of water. She is probably the most important lightship in America, for every liner, freighter or warship approaching New York looks for and listens to the Nantucket Lightship. Many unusual adventures have befallen the brave men stationed on this rolling, pitching guardian of the deep—adventures which for some ended in death and for others in suffering and hardship. But to the everlasting credit of the service, the heroes of the Nantucket off-shore station have never faltered in the face of danger, whether from storms or steamships.

I have never visited the Nantucket Lightship without a feeling of admiration for the men who are virtually imprisoned there. How would *you* like to be stranded on a vessel way out in the ocean, sailing nowhere, seeing nothing but the same expanse of water day after day?—It isn't a natural existence, of course, but it is a necessary and vital one. Few of the officers or crew enjoy it. I shall never forget the remark made by one of the captains of the Nantucket Lightship, when he had to go back to his floating station. "If it weren't for the disgrace," said the old captain, "I would rather be going to State's Prison." And he meant it. What a strong sense of duty have these men of the New England lightships!

In 1847 Lieutenant Charles H. Davis discovered the shoals which still bear his name, and plans for a lightboat * were made soon afterwards. Although Captain Samuel Bunker of Nantucket was appointed to be the first lightboat keeper in 1853, it was not until June 15, 1854, that he reached the station with his vessel. Captain Bunker and his crew of five successfully weathered the summer and early fall at the station near the South Shoals, but when the blasts of a wintry gale hit the vessel, she broke adrift. Captain Bunker had the lightboat on a course for a safe harbor, but, smashed and battered by storms and high seas, the ship finally went up on the beach at Montauk Point, Long Island. She had traveled over a hundred and twenty miles in her wild ride from the station off Nantucket, with only a leg-of-mutton sail to guide her.

This first Nantucket Lightboat should never have been placed on the station. She was merely a rebuilt whaleboat of a type too small to make a profitable whaling trip.

Congress now appropriated a substantial sum to build a lightboat which could last throughout the winter at the dangerous South Shoals. This new lightboat, built at the Kittery Navy Yard, became known as the *Number 1*. In January, 1856, she began the lonely vigil which was to last for over a third of a century. She fought the storms and seas at her isolated watch station winter and summer until 1892, breaking loose many times but always returning.

The lightboat was constructed with an inner and an outer hull of white oak, and salt was poured between the two hulls to "keep her sweet." The holes made for this purpose were closed by plugs fastened to the bulwarks by short strands of tarred

---

* The term lightboat instead of lightship was used for several years.

rope, which formed a black line from stem to stern and served as a quick means of identification. The two lantern masts on the old *Number 1* were each seventy-one feet high, and there was a stick behind them which could be rigged for sail.

Through the courtesy of Mr. Gustavus B. Holt of Hingham, Massachusetts, I have been able to examine several of the original log books of the Nantucket Lightships. The concise wording of the records is typical of the true sailor. Here are some excerpts:

Jan. 5—1876 Midnight trimmed lights. Sunrise put out lights. At 7:30 commenced heaving in chain, found the chain foul, got in 25 fathom, found we could gain no more held on to clear it. and 9 a.m. parted the chain lost 65 fathoms. 2 p.m. made sail heading W. by N. light air. 5 p.m. the wind breezed up.

Jan. 6—7 a.m. sounded in 27 feet, set the square sail and kept off NW by N. 10 a.m. made Norman's land. Bearing N by W distance 10 miles. the wind heading us off could not weather it. noon wore ship to the westward.

Jan. 7th—Wore ship to the Eastward, Gay Head bearing N E by E distance 33 miles. 7 a.m. the Gale moderated took the reef out of the Foresail and set the Squaresail. Noon made Gay Head bearing NNW. distance 20 miles.

Jan. 8—Midnight light wind from NW making a SW course. 1 P. M. Gay Head bearing ESE kept off . . . 5 P. M. came to anchor in Tarpaulin Cove in 10 fathoms water.

Jan. 10—At anchor in Tarpaulin Cove—At 3 p. m. the Verbena came alongside with chain & mushroom. At 5 p.m. got our chain aboard.

Jan. 11—At 9 a.m. schooner drifted across our bow and carried away the squares and yard. At 11 a.m. got underway in tow of steamer Verbena. At 3 p.m. came to anchor in Hyannis Harbor.

Jan. 12—At 3 a.m. the Verbena came along side and put aboard the mushroom weighing 5495 lbs. chain 1⅞ inch.

Jan. 13—At 6 a.m. got underway in tow of steamer Verbena. At 8 a.m. passed Handkerchief Lt Vessel. 10.25 a.m. passed Sankaty, wind strong. At 2 p.m. came to anchor on our station. Sunset set the lights. 11 p.m. trimmed the lights.

On May 15 1876 Spoke schooner Charles Shearer from a sealing voyage to Cape Horn bound to Stonington.

June 17 1878. At 8 p.m. a boat from schr Rescue of New Bedford from Fyall for N.B. with 90 passengers and short of provisions. let them have two barrels bread some suggar & potatoes 48 days from Fyall.

The great gale of October 13, 1878, was the worst in the career of the *Number 1*. Sweeping in from the northeast, the storm quickly parted the ship's cables and the lightship began a long and dangerous journey to the south. Before the gale had ended, she had traveled eight hundred miles to a point just off the islands of Bermuda. When she finally reached home port, the *Number 1* had to undergo repairs which kept her away from her station a total of three months.

At midnight January 3, 1879, a heavy gale blew in from the west-northwest, and by morning the sea was fearful. At six o'clock a gigantic wave broke over the port bow and smashed the forward bearer on the lifeboat, staving in the bow. It was bitterly cold, and the lightship was icing up rapidly. By nightfall the entire vessel was caked with several inches of ice, and it was impossible to raise the lantern to its proper position on the mast. After pulling it up a few feet from the house, the men secured it there for the night.

The next day it was sufficiently calm to allow the crew to chop ice from the ship, but the ice re-formed all through the day and the following night. On the fifth of January another strong wind sent tons of spray aboard the lightship, and again the men were busy chopping until sunset. The following day the weather began to moderate, and the entire crew earned a well-deserved rest from the double dangers of gale and ice.

On Christmas Day, 1880, a great storm began which was to have serious consequences for lightship *Number 1*. Before nightfall Captain Thomas James stated that the vessel was "laboring hard and jerking on the chain," with the sea "very rough."

The log book tells the story of the following days:

Dec 26 Blowing a hurricane.
Dec 27 Midnight heavy gale the ship pitching hard. 2.15 A. M. parted the chain. 4 a. m. commenced heaving in the chain. The ship rolling and pitching bad. Making our drift WSW. Noon got in the chain. Parted 62 fathoms from the mushroom. Made sail & wore ship to the westward. Heading W. making SSW course.

The lightship then lay to under trysail. Four days later, in thick snow, the men passed a steamer. The weather finally quieted enough by noon, January 1st, to enable them to make another observation.

On the third day of the new year they began to sail back to their former station, but on the return trip another snowstorm caught them and pushed them away again. After a terrific buffeting by the elements, Captain James found himself off Gay Head, Martha's Vineyard Island. The next land he sighted was Point Judith, and then he raised Vineyard Sound Lightship bearing east by south. At seven a. m. on the sixth of January, 1881, the captain sighted Beavertail Light bearing northwest eight miles away. The lightship then ran into a thick fog and anchored in five fathoms of water over the Middle Ground.

At ten o'clock "the steamer *Monahasset* spoke us and took a dispatch," writes the weary captain, and at "two P.M. U. S. Steamer *Dexter* spoke us. By midnight the weather was pleasant." At two o'clock in the afternoon of the following day Captain Gibbs arrived with the tug *Hunter* and towed the lightship into Woods Hole.

That period from December 27 to January 9 had been one of the hardest in Nantucket lightship history. For almost two weeks, the awkward lightship, never intended for active duty, had wallowed in the trough of dangerous seas as it was buffeted by the storm. A week later, with new chain and anchor, the Nantucket Lightship *Number 1* was back on station.

Of course the men stationed on the lightship were more frequently rescuers than rescued. On February 16, 1881, the lookout aboard the *Number 1* signed a raft flying a signal of distress three miles away. A crew let over the lifeboat and rowed in its direction. Reaching the raft which was slowly drifting out to sea, they found three seamen aboard. One gesticulated feebly as they came alongside, but the others did not move. All three were taken aboard the lifeboat, but it was soon found that one of the sailors was dead. Brought back to the lightship, the dead man was given a sea burial, and the two survivors were eventually nursed back to health and sent ashore at the first opportunity. They were Second Mate Emil Olson of Norway and Seaman John Sheridan of Dublin, Ireland, survivors from the bark *Hazard* which had hit on the Old Man Shoal and gone down soon afterwards.

Gustav Kobbé, a well-known magazine writer of the 1890's, must have had a deep interest in the light-houses and lightships, for he visited Matinicus Rock Light in Maine and Minot's Light in Massachusetts. He also sailed out to *Number 1* at her station in the year 1890. When it was learned that he was going out to Nantucket Shoals station, several of his friends commented on his proposed visit. One told him that the loneliest thing he had ever seen was a polar bear floating on an icecake far at sea, but that the second loneliest object was the South Shoal Lightship. Kobbé was also given to understand that even the most experienced sailors were sometimes seasick aboard the lightship.

The tug *Ocean Queen* took Kobbé out to the old *Number 1*, but before they arrived a thick fog set in which delayed them several hours. Those who have been lost in a fog at sea know that it is uncanny the way the tolling of a fog bell can abruptly advance and recede while the vessel you are on has barely changed her position And that is what happened to those aboard the *Ocean Queen*. Three times they lost the fog bell, and three times they found it. Suddenly, after more than four hours had passed, the fog vanished and the lightship lay directly in front of them.

Kobbé spent some time aboard the lightship. He noticed the day-marks, red hoop-iron gratings forty-four feet in the air, and was particularly interested in the two great octagonal copper-framed lanterns built around the masts themselves. These were each five feet in diameter and weighed more than a ton. At night they were hoisted to a point twenty-five feet above the rolling deck. When morning came, the smoking lanterns were lowered into little sheds built to receive them. Once inside the houses, they were further secured by hinged covers which closed snugly about the lantern and mast together, thus preventing a sea from sweeping into the house.

Kobbé was interested in the manner in which meals were served aboard the *Number 1*. When the weather freshened, little pegs were fitted into holes in the table to keep the dishes from sliding off. In spite of all precautions, however, every so often the ship would give a terrific lurch and the entire meal would land on the floor several feet away. Those who have experienced an ocean crossing may think that on a rough passage dinner is a difficult matter, but a lightship meal in a bad storm is a far worse experience. One day on the Nantucket Lightship, a pork roast jumped from the stove to an occupied bunk, and while its recipient appreciated the quick service, he objected to the manner in which it was delivered.

To pass the time aboard the lightship, the crew of the *Number 1* made baskets which sold well on Nantucket Island and elsewhere during the summer months. Toiling laboriously through the long winter months, the men made scores of these small, attractive baskets, usually in nests of three to eight.

Because of the change of draught in ocean liners and the desire of the Lighthouse Department to avoid the dangers of the

Davis South Shoal altogether, the lightship station was moved about the year 1891 to a place approximately ten miles further off shore from Nantucket. The rougher seas ten miles out proved too much for the old *Number 1*. After breaking away from her moorings twice in the year 1892, the old lightship was later assigned to a quieter part of the ocean near Savannah, Georgia. In 1930 she was condemned and sold.

The new Nantucket Lightship, the *Number 9*, was also unequal to the task and a few months later was withdrawn. After a varied career which included service at the Hedge Fence Shoal, the *Number 9* was sold in 1925. She is now a floating gasoline station in Boston Harbor. The *Number 39* next tried her hand at the difficult station, but she, also, failed to live up to expectations and was transferred.

In the autumn of 1893 a new vessel, the *54*, took the *39*'s place, but she, too, proved a poor deep sea craft when she almost sank in the first severe gale which hit the station. The *39*, therefore, was put back on station to await the construction of an entirely different type of lightship, one specially built for conditions thirty miles at sea in an exposed position.

This new vessel was the *66*. Until she was finished, however, the *39* was anchored in her place. Finally, in 1896, the *66* was completed and rushed out to the station. By this time the government decided to move the Lightship Station once more. The new position was over twice as far from Nantucket Island as the original lightship had been. Far outside of Asia Rip itself, forty-two miles from Nantucket, the *66* was given a unique task.

The *66* was the first ship in the world to receive a wireless message. In 1901 the *New York Herald* sponsored a plan to demonstrate the value of wireless at sea. The *Herald* established a wireless station at Siasconset, Nantucket, and a wireless outfit on the South Shoals Lightship *Number 66*. The first message ever to be received from an incoming liner was sent out from the *Lucania* on August 16, 1901, when the steamer was fifty-two miles away. The message was then relayed from the Nantucket Lightship to the Siasconset Station ashore, and in a few minutes the telegraph cable had relayed the information to New York City.

For several years the wireless station aboard the *66* was a wonder to contemplate. Today, of course, radio messages are commonplace.

In 1905 the relief lightship, *Number 58*, was struck by a heavy gale which buffeted her about in the boisterous seas until she sprang a bad leak. A message was sent ashore asking for help at once, but it was four-thirty the following day before the lighthouse tender *Azalea* reached the scene. Such heavy seas were running that several hours more went by before a hawser could be secured between the vessels. Finally, the *Azalea* started for New Bedford with the leaking lightship. Around noon, however, the condition of the *58* became so serious that it became necessary to abandon her.

It was a dangerous task to transfer the thirteen members of the *58*'s crew to the relatively safe deck of the *Azalea*, but within a short time all were aboard. Ten minutes later, somewhere south of Nantucket, the old *58* went down in twenty-five fathoms of water. The *Azalea* reached New Bedford Harbor that afternoon with a strange story of adventure at sea.

In the *Azalea's* records, we read:

Sunday Dec 10, 1905, the Azalea left Merrill's Wharf, New Bedford to reach Relief Light Vessel #58 which was leaking and in a sinking condition on Nantucket Shoals Light Vessel Station—got crew together—Bent storm sails, main stay sail and leg mutton main sail—left at 7:05 P. M. for Relief Light Vessel 58 Nantucket Shoals...

MONDAY DEC 11 1905

At sea—passage to Nantucket Shoals Sighted Relief Light Vessel 58 at 4 a. m.—arrived up to her at 4:45 a. m. burning costen lts.—spoke her—found she was in no immediate danger of sinking, but leaking badly and leak gaining . . . layed off & on by her until 10 a. m. when sea moderated enough to get hawser to her. by attaching piece of wood on heaving line and drafting it across her bow—Took her in tow and started for port. Light vessel listing to starboard—At 12.15 p. m. R. Cutter Gresham spoke us, and offered to assist us, but we were pulling all hawser would stand. . . . At 3 p. m. when about 18 miles by log N W of station Light ship signaled Must abandon ship—Asked him if he could use his boat and he signaled Yes—Tried to haul in hawser, but could not. . . . so cut it. . . . Steamed to leaward and Engineer Davis & 5 men came on board from Lt Ship. Mate & 3 men went back to Lt Ship and took off Capt Jorgensen and others. making 13 all told. . . . Could not hoist up boat—hoisting bolts being too small for hooks of blocks let her go adrift. . . . At 3:43 started for port—At 3:53 the Lt. Ship was seen to founder on her starboard beam in about 25 fms water and about 14 or 15 miles NW of station

George E. Eaton
1st Mate

In the year 1907 Lightship *Number 85* was completed and placed on the Nantucket station. Seven years later, on December 5, 1914, she broke adrift during the great storm which also pushed the six-masted *Alice M. Lawrence* to her doom at Tuckernuck Shoal. The *85*, blown fifteen miles from her station, later returned to her post. The lightship was commanded at that time by First Mate Walter Warnock, in the absence of Captain David B. Studley who was on leave.

Less than two years later the German submarine *U-53* sank four vessels in the immediate vicinity of the Nantucket Lightship. On the sixth of October, 1916, three steamers, the *Strathdene*, the *West Point*, and the *Christiana Knudson*, were torpedoed, and a schooner, the *Victor and Ethan*, was also sent to the bottom. The crews from the sunken vessels rowed to the lightship, and 115 shipwrecked survivors crowded aboard the lightship. They were given the best of treatment, and later were taken ashore.

In 1923 the new *Number 106* replaced the *85* at America's most perilous sea station. In spite of her relatively few years of service, she was succeeded by the *117* in 1931.

The *117* was longer and larger in every way than any earlier lightships. Outfitted from stem to stern with every modern device, the new Nantucket Lightship was equipped to make the life of her crew easier, safer and more comfortable. Electric refrigerator, radios, hot and cold water, bathtubs of the latest design, an oil burning kitchen range, an electric windlass and boat hoist, all combined to make the *117* the best lightship ever built for the station.

In May, 1931, Captain David B. Studley, veteran lightship master, brought the new vessel out to her Atlantic post.

She stood her test in the first great storm, but in the gale of January 25, 1933, the *117* broke from her moorings when a wind estimated at between seventy and eighty miles per hour struck the Nantucket area. Just after she parted her chain, word was flashed to all shipping at sea:

BE CAREFUL NANTUCKET LIGHTSHIP OFF
HER STATION

The following day the *117* was thirty miles away, but by January 30 she had returned to her station. Later, when she put into port for repairs, it was found that her cable had broken seventy-five fathoms or 450 feet from the anchor. The cable had previously been tested to stand a strain of 150,000 pounds on her 1⅛ inch thick links. In fact, similar chain had already held up to pull of 369,250 pounds.

But the most spectacular event in the short but dramatic career of the *117* was still to take place. Returning to her station after repairs had been completed, she survived a minor collision when the liner *Washington* ran into her during a dense fog, January 6, 1934. Radio aerials, a mast grating, and a boat davit on the *117* were carried away. With inexcusable carelessness, the captain of the *Washington* did not consider the damage great enough to mention when he radioed that he had passed the lightship that afternoon. But the lighthouse department thought it necessary to issue a warning for all vessels to be more careful in approaching the *117*. Less than five months later, however, the *117* was the victim of another similar accident.

At 11:06 a. m., Tuesday, May 15, 1934, the gigantic 47,000-ton White Star Liner *Olympic*, bound for New York, was proceeding toward her destination in a dense fog at sixteen knots. Suddenly the lightship appeared directly in her path. The captain instantly ordered the engines reversed and in a few seconds the speed was reduced to four knots. But it was too late. Within sixty seconds after sighting the lightship the knife-like prow of the *Olympic* cut completely through the tiny lightship, sinking her almost at once.

Scarcely more than a minute before, the lightship's radio operator, John F. Perry of Provincetown, was sitting at his desk when he heard a cry of terror from someone out on deck, "The *Olympic* is on us!" Throwing open the door, Perry saw the great prow of the White Star liner bearing down on them through the fog. Running forward just as the crash came, he escaped the bow of the *Olympic* by inches as she slowly but surely sawed through the beam of the lightship. After one final glance at the huge white letters OLYMPIC towering high above him, he found himself under water.

His own words follow:

"I was dragged down by the suction. Just when I thought my ears would burst from pressure, the old *117* released me and I shot up to the surface. I saw an empty sea, covered with fog, and a big patch of oil spreading over the surface. I thought that I was alone and never would be found. I tried to kick off my shoes to swim better, but I could not make it. I paddled around for a while, and then a short distance away, on the rise of a big wave, I saw the white ring of a life preserver. I swam toward it and secured it. It was one of those which floated free from the wreck of the Nantucket. I regained my energy as I floated on this life perserver."

The fog lifted a short time later to reveal the vast bulk of the liner some distance away. As he floated in the water Perry recalled that he had made certain the radio beacon had been operating from six o'clock in the morning up until the moment of the accident at 11:06. He wondered why the *Olympic* had blundered into a collision with a fixed, anchored lightship.

Soon the lifeboats from the British liner came along and picked him up. Also rescued from the sea were Captain George W. Braithwaite, First Mate Clinton E. Mosher, and L. V. Roberts, an oiler.

Captain Braithwaite had been reading in his bunk when the crash came. Unable to swim, he foundered helplessly in the water when the *117* went under, but was rescued by the lifeboat crew of the *Olympic*, which reached the scene less than fifteen minutes after the crash. Badly injured around the head, sixty-nine-year-old Captain Braithwaite was hospitalized and died later as a result of his experience.

Those who were lost from the lightship were Chief Engineer William Perry of Reading; Justin Richmond, oiler; Isaac Pina, cook; Alfred Monteiro, second cook; John Fortes, seaman; Matthew Rodrigues, seaman; and Ernest George, seaman, all of New Bedford.

The disaster was blamed on the ocean liners' dangerous custom of riding the lightship beam to its source of power and turning off at the last minute to veer to New York. The *Olympic* miscalculated, stayed on the beam too long. An ironic note was that on May 2, fourteen days before the disaster, all steamships and steamship companies had been notified of the possible dangers of riding the beam. In the cautionary circular these strangely prophetic words were included:

Apparently the great advantages of radio beacons . . . have given a false sense of security to navigators. . . . It is of the highest importance in using radio bearings for approach that at a sufficient distance before reaching a lightship the course be set clear.

The White Star line arranged for the building of a new lightship to take the place of the *117*. It was called the *112* and the first master was Captain Guy V. Emro, now on the Pollock Rip Lightship off Chatham, Massachusetts.

In the wheel house of the *112* is a memorial tablet to a civilian, believed to be the only known case in lightship history where this has been allowed.

On July 19, 1936, Captain William H. Wincapaw flew out near the Nantucket Shoals Lightship to allow a group of newspaper photographers to take pictures of the *Queen Mary* as she approached New York on one of her record-breaking trips. Something went wrong as they flew over the gigantic liner, and the men on the lightship watched with horror as the plane crashed in the sea. One of my best friends, Edwin Thompson Ramsdell of the *Boston Post*, died as a result of the crash, but all the others were saved. Those of us who mourned Eddie Ramsdell, one of America's earliest and best flying photographers, placed a memorial plaque on Nantucket Lightship *112*, anchored near the scene of the fatality. Mr. Henry Gillen, prominent Boston poet, composed a fitting eulogy which was placed on the tablet:

> *Knightly in warring and the peaceful ways*
> *Soaring he mirrored life with splendid art*
> *Leaving the memory for our lonely days*
> *Of courage flaming in a kindly heart*

Roy G. Whittemore, now with the personnel department of the Coast Guard in Boston, is an old lightship man who tells interesting stories of his career in the service. His comments about the *112* follow:

"With the advent of Pearl Harbor they soon withdrew the Nantucket Lightship *112* and sent her to Portland, Maine, where she served during the war as the examination vessel for Portland Harbor. She went back to her station around January, 1946. The *112* is the best lightship of all, for the White Star Line saw to it that she had comfortable quarters and many features which the usual lightship did not have.

"I can honestly say that in spite of the collision with the *Washington* and the disaster of the *Olympic*, I would still choose the South Shoals Station every time. I went out there in 1936 and spent two years at sea. There's nothing to worry about, really. In heavy weather the cable snaps and we drift a few miles away, but we always get back. When it's foggy we lie in our bunks and listen to the whistles. But the *112* is a fine weather ship—one of the few built especially for her station. The old ships were not designed for this far-from-land service.

"When we'd go out on deck to greet the ocean liners from Europe, they'd give us a special salute. At night the *Normandie* would illuminate her stack for us so we could see the French colors. Then she'd blow her three-whistle salute. The sword fishermen would come over when we'd signal that we'd noticed a swordfish, and later we'd get a generous slice of the fish itself.

"The longest time I was ever out there was eighty-nine days. Another thing I liked, when you'd go ashore it'd be for a full month's vacation. You really needed a vacation after looking at the same men all the time. I suppose you've heard about the captain and the engineer who ate and sat at the same table day after day. They got mighty sick of each other's faces and general characteristics after a few years. Well, they finally rigged up a canvas curtain so they didn't have to watch each other eat. As soon as the meal was over, the curtain would go up.

"The very distance at sea makes the Nantucket station safest.

If you broke free from the Vineyard or Pollock Rip, why you'd be ashore in no time, but forty-two miles out to sea there's plenty of room to move around."

The beam of the Nantucket Lightship flashes three times every nine seconds, and is equipped with a warning radio beacon which operates when a vessel is too close to the station. Whenever there is a danger of a ship's hitting the lightship, the warning beacon emits a distinctive warble note for one full minute directly after the regular radio beacon transmission.

Boatswain Arthur D. Gosson is now the commanding officer of the *112* at its deep, rolling station off the Nantucket Shoals. There he keeps his lonely vigil far from his family and friends, summer and winter, good weather and bad.

Rarely do we hear praises sung for the lightship men of America, but in spite of this, a deep sense of responsibility guides them through the long watches of the day and night. A salute to these gallant sailors is contained in the following poem by C. Tucker, which Ex-Commissioner George W. Putnam has allowed me to use:

> *When a sailor gets to thinking*
> *He is one of the best*
> *Let him ship out on a lightship*
> *And take the* acid test
> *And if he still feels like bragging*
> *I don't think that all his tales*
> *Will be of deep sailing*
> *But of the ship that never sails.*

15. Murder on Gay Head

Gay Head on Martha's Vineyard, home of the Gay Head Indians and scene of countless shipwrecks, received its name because of the many colors in its cliffs. The headland assumed coastwide importance when Gay Head Light was built there in 1799.

At that time, Ebenezer Skiff was appointed Keeper of Gay Head Light with a salary of $3.85 a week. Six years later, Skiff believed that since his living costs were increasing he should be rewarded with a raise in pay. After long consideration, he composed a letter to Albert Gallatin, Secretary of the Treasury, in which he told of the terrible wind storms on Gay Head, the lighthouse glass, continually coated with dust from the cliff, and the spring which was located more than a mile away. He explained that his task of keeping the glass clean was extremely difficult since he was forced to carry water from the distant spring.

Because of this unusual letter, Skiff received an increase of ninety-six cents a week. Then, without the government's knowledge, he added to his income by becoming a school master and teaching the Indians who lived in the surrounding country-side. Skiff was the only white man on Gay Head.

In 1815, the lighthouse keeper decided to ask for additional pay and wrote to the government in practically the same words he had used in 1805. He went on to add that he was forced to get wood from the mainland, as the Gay Head Indians were down on the beach below his lighthouse before he could arrive there and always managed to take every bit of driftwood which came ashore. His second letter secured him another ninety-six cents increase in pay.

Such problems were Ebenezer Skiff's chief concern when, in 1821, a mysterious stranger, Richard Johnson of New York, landed at Gay Head. Johnson was befriended by the old Indian Jonathan Cuff, whose son, David Cuff, had just married a young Indian girl named Mary. When Mary's baby was born in August, 1822, Johnson was still living with the Cuff family.

Mary Cuff was an extremely industrious housewife, and whenever a storm hit Gay Head, she was always the first to get down to the beach to salvage whatever material might be washed ashore. Her husband David often helped to carry logs up the high cliffs, and if there was an unusually heavy log, Richard Johnson, still at the home of the Cuffs, would help out.

A tremendous gale swept the coast in late February. During the storm the brig *Pilgrim* was wrecked. She had been heavily loaded with precious mahogany logs. Everyone at Gay Head tried to salvage as many of the logs as possible, but Mary Cuff was ahead of them all, getting up one and even two hours before sunrise, leaving her husband to mind the baby. Mary Cuff and Richard Johnson had a terrible argument over the ownership of one of these logs. Johnson threatened Mary with death if she didn't leave his log alone, but she defended her rights and won out. On the surface Johnson seemed to have forgotten the incident. But later events proved that he had not and that actually he had another nameless score to settle with Mary.

A week passed. On the morning of March 2, 1823, Mary arose from her bed in the Cuff home an hour and a half before sunrise and walked swiftly across the fields toward the lighthouse. Reaching the edge of the cliff, she paused for a moment. Then she jumped down onto the path and followed it at a steep angle to the beach far below. There she trudged up and down the shore searching for wood, avoiding the giant boulders and the clay pits with the skill only one of her race could show. Shortly afterwards Richard Johnson quietly dressed and followed her.

Meanwhile the lighthouse keeper, Ebenezer Skiff, arose an hour before sunrise, as was his custom, ate a hearty breakfast and prepared to extinguish the lamps in the lighthouse tower. At exactly five minutes before six, or a quarter hour before sunrise, Keeper Skiff climbed up to the top of his lighthouse and put out the lamp.

At that moment there came up to him from the bottom of the cliff the scream of a woman in mortal terror. Then he heard a harsh answering shout, seemingly of a man in great excitement. Just the two cries—nothing more. Keeper Ebenezer Skiff went about his work of extinguishing the lights and thought no more of the cries he had heard.

The morning wore on. At the Cuff home, Mary's husband continued to watch their baby but for some reason was not particularly concerned about his wife's prolonged absence. The afternoon passed.

That night the weather grew very bitter, and the next day was so unseasonably cold and snowy that no one went out. The following day Jane Wansley, an Indian girl who lived a mile from the light, went down over the cliff. She walked along the shore, and there, near the most beautifully colored part of the cliff, Jane discovered the body of her friend, Mary Cuff. There were tracks in the snow and sand around Mary's body which had been partly filled in by the snowstorm.

Jane ran up the cliff as fast as she could and into the home of Ebenezer Skiff.

"Eben," she cried, "Mary Cuff's dead down at the foot of the cliff." The lighthouse keeper quickly put on his coat and hat and ran down over the cliff to the beach. He soon found the body of Mary Cuff. She had obviously been killed by a series of severe head blows.

Mary's husband was notified of the tragedy. Though he maintained a stoic indifference, the rest of the little Indian village was stirred as never before, for a murder at Gay Head was a rare occurrence. That evening the elders of the settlement met at the lighthouse. The local authorities felt that there was enough evidence against Richard Johnson to arrest him, but it was impossible to conduct a murder trial at Gay Head or any other town on Martha's Vineyard. Word was sent to the mainland and a trial arranged for.

The trial of Richard Johnson was scheduled to come up at the Barnstable Courthouse in July, and when the time came a schooner was chartered and everyone connected with the affair was taken aboard. For the first time in twenty-four years Keeper Ebenezer Skiff turned the running of his lighthouse over to a Gay Head Indian and went with the other twenty-eight people—witnesses, sheriffs, and the prisoner—to the mainland.

The trial began with the old-fashioned ritual and ceremony of which the Commonwealth of Massachusetts is so proud. The procedure resembled that of the ancient British Admiralty hearings when condemned pirates paraded to the court and back before the astonished but admiring eyes of the local inhabitants.

And then on July 8, 1823, the charge was read in the Barnstable Courthouse, a charge which read:

RICHARD JOHNSON, late resident of a place called Gay Head, without the bounds of any town but within the county of Dukes County, aforesaid, not having the fear of God before his eyes, but being moved and seduced by the instigation of the Devil, on the second of March, in the year of our Lord one thousand eight hundred and twenty three, with force and arms, in and upon one Mary Cuff, feloniously, wilfully, and of his malice aforethought, did make an assault, with a certain dangerous weapon, made of oak wood, and called a club, of the value of one cent, with his right hand, then and there had and held, the aforesaid Mary Cuff, in and upon her left eye and temple of her the said Mary Cuff, then and there did kill and murder against the peace of the Commonwealth aforesaid and contrary to the form of the statute in such a case made and provided. . . .

The trial was not a long one, and the facts brought out were essentially those which have been related here. Mary Cuff's husband, David, admitted that he had told no one about his wife's disappearance for almost two days. Another family of Indians stated that they had found what they believed was the murder weapon, covered with blood, and had taken it inside their house and burned it. Two Indian girls gave the most definite evidence against Richard Johnson, claiming that they had seen him running to and from the scene of the death.

The jury was duly charged. There seem to have been four main points which were brought out for the defense, reasons for the decision which eventually came: Why didn't Mary Cuff's husband tell someone that his wife was missing from home? Why did Keeper Ebenezer Skiff do nothing about the cries which he heard at dawn? Why did the Indian family burn the murder weapon, if murder weapon it was? What was the standing in the community of the girls who claimed they saw Richard Johnson at the cliff the morning of the murder?—In regard to the last question, the two girls who testified against Richard Johnson, Abaigail Nevis and Jane Wansley, were declared by one of the most influential men at Martha's Vineyard to be unreliable. To quote his exact words, "Both girls are bad for truth and not to be believed on oath."

The Cape Cod jury pondered over these questions and finally declared that, as far as the evidence showed, Richard Johnson could not be called guilty. Two days later Richard Johnson was allowed to go free. He sailed away to New York and never returned to Martha's Vineyard.

Now comes the strangest part of the whole affair.

In May, 1949, in the course of research on another subject I was looking through the New York *Commercial Examiner* for the period covering the storm of 1829. Much to my surprise and shock I came across a headline which read THE TRIAL OF RICHARD JOHNSON FOR THE MURDER OF URSULA NEWMAN.

Of course, I went on to read the details. On November 23, 1828, Johnson shot the Newman woman in a rage. For this crime, he was tried, sentenced and later hanged. During his trial it came out that Johnson suffered from a strange mental sickness in which he considered himself the parent of children actually not his own. When the mother of the child in question protested, he would fly into a rage, and there is no way of telling how many times his rage had resulted in murder. This belief of parentage was certainly the reason for his killing Mary Cuff with a club and shooting Ursula Newman five years later in New York.

I wonder if anyone living in that little Indian settlement at Gay Head ever heard that Richard Johnson finally was punished but that it took another murder in another state for his punishment to take effect. You see, truth *is* stranger than fiction, as Ebenezer Skiff must have decided if he ever found out—which, of course, we shall never know.

16. Block Island and the Palatines

From Providence, Rhode Island, where I met my wife and an old friend, Tom Johnson, I arranged to fly out to the scene of the Palatine story on Block Island. Soon we were soaring southward, piloted by Norman Bishop, and in a short time we saw the pear-shaped island spread out below us. We descended toward what would be the stem of the pear, and passed over the North Light, far out on Sandy Point, and then circled the island so that I could make a few moving pictures.

Approaching the high cliffs at the southern side, we flew fairly low so that we could see the Southeast Light, built like a fortress at the edge of the cliffs. My curiosity was aroused by a white V-shaped object near the tower, and later I discovered that it was inadvertently arranged by the keeper's wife who had hung up her washing to dry in the sunshine. From the air, the clothes seemed to form a perfect symbolic V for Victory.

Finally we came in over what Norman Bishop called the airport. It was in reality a glorified pasture, with high telephone poles just beyond one end of the field. The small landing area was entirely enclosed by a stone wall, as all pastures seemed to be on the island. But in spite of the unorthodox features of the airport, we made a perfect landing at Block Island.

I knew that the history of the island where I had landed was long, interesting, and varied, but the most spectacular event of all was the strange "Palatine" wreck and what the inhabitants called the "Palatine Light." We visited the marker erected in 1938 where the Palatine graves are located and then toured the island and interviewed everyone who might know something of the affair. Mrs. Mary Rose Clark took us into her home and showed us the two pitchers which she said were salvaged from the wreck of the *Palatine* as it drifted out to sea. She also admitted having heard the cries of the Harbor Boys, about whom I'll tell later, but she said she didn't believe the story.

"I've seen what is called the 'Palatine Light' on at least two occasions, though I don't believe, as others do, that it is the burning ship."

Mrs. Mitchell, companion to Mrs. Clark, spoke up once or twice but refused to be quoted. Later we learned why—she did not consider herself a real Block Islander, having come over from the mainland as late as 1900.

When we left the Clark residence we took a taxi back to the airport. The driver was talkative and interesting, and I asked him if he was born on the island. "No, I'm not an islander," he answered, "but they're beginning to accept me. I took all their hot air, but now I've made the grade."

We arrived back at the airport in the pasture, (incidentally, it will probably be enlarged to a fine flying field before you read this) and within a short time we were out over Point Judith on our way back to Providence.

Back on the mainland, it was many weeks before I had worked out the problem of what really happened to the Palatine passengers and their ship, and in the course of my research I learned many other stories of the early days at Block Island.

Block Island has had many names. First the Indians called it Manisses, which means "Little God." In 1524 the French explorer Verrazzano told his ruler, King Francis, that the island was "full of hills, covered with trees, and well-peopled." He named the location Claudia in honor of the king's mother. When explorer Adrian Block sailed in the vicinity, the Dutch called it Adrian's Eyland, but it soon became known as Block

Island. In 1672, the appellation New Shoreham was made a prefix, so that the real title is still "New Shoreham, otherwise Block Island."

In 1660 Dr. John Alcock of Roxbury, together with six other Massachusetts men, bought the island for four hundred pounds. The next year a barque left Braintree and another vessel cleared from Taunton, both carrying settlers for the new colony at Block Island. These early colonists found many natural resources on the island, including lumber for the houses, peat deposits for fuel, and sea moss and sea weed for food and fertilizer. Of course, clams, fish and lobsters could be obtained in abundance.

By 1750 the peat deposits were being relied on exclusively for heating purposes. The trees had all been cut down. Block Island is still suffering from lack of trees—even today there are only a few on the entire island.

The earliest Island tragedy occurred in 1636, when in July of that year Mr. John Oldham was brutally murdered after allowing several native Indians aboard his boat. His friend, John Gallop of Boston, was cruising in the vicinity at the time and noticed something strange about Oldham's vessel. He sailed over and found fourteen Indians on deck, with no sign of Oldham. Gallop and his crew opened fire, killed eleven Indians, captured another and tossed him overboard, but later spared the lives of two Indians who had hidden below. Under a large fishing net they found the body of John Oldham, "stark naked, his head cleft to the brains, and his hands and legs cut as if they had been cutting them off, and yet warm." Oldham had been killed by the Block Island Narragansett Indians because he traded with the Pequots, the hated enemies of the Narragansetts.

When he heard of the murder, Governor Henry Vane in Boston ordered Captain John Endecott and Captain John Underhill to take a hundred troops and subjugate the Indians. Arriving at Block Island, Captain Underhill went ashore in a small boat with twelve armed men. As they landed, they were confronted with sixty Indians, "very tall, of active bodies, and having their arrows notched."

In the encounter which followed Underhill narrowly escaped death when an arrow glanced off his helmet. The white men were driven back and caught between the beach and the surf. Finally they managed to reach their vessel and open fire on the Indians, whose arrows would not shoot that far. Meanwhile, Colonel Endecott's forces landed farther up the beach, overcame the Indians and pushed them into the swamps. The white men burned the Indian homes and destroyed their corn.

Returning to Boston, Captain Underhill remembered that when he left home for the punitive expedition, his wife had insisted against his will that he wear the helmet which later saved his life. His comment was pithy: "If God in his providence had not moved the heart of my wife I had been slain. Let no man despise advice and counsel of his wife, though she be a woman."

Up to around 1878 there were Indians living at Block Island. In 1830 the red man Aaron Church turned pirate and helped the notorious buccaneer Charles Gibbs capture the brig *Vineyard*, murder the captain, and loot the ship of the $54,000 aboard. Later, off Southampton Light, they set fire to the *Vineyard*, left it in two small boats, and watched the brig burn and sink. Aaron Church was drowned when the dinghy in which he was rowing hit a bar and overturned. By 1878 Aaron's uncle, Isaac Church, was the only Indian left on Block Island.

Block Island, because of its isolation, has always been subjected to raids in time of war. The conflict between France and England toward the end of the seventeenth century gave French raiders an excuse for going ashore at Block Island.

In July, 1689, three vessels of unknown nationality anchored off the east side of the island and sent a boat ashore. A man who

called himself William Trimming of England announced that he
was in need of a pilot, saying that he was under the command of
George Astan, a well-known English privateer. He asked for
wood, water, and a pilot for Newport Harbor. Several Block
Island pilots immediately sailed out, but once they were on
the deck of Trimming's vessel, they were clapped under
hatches and forced to reveal what they knew of the island's
defenses. Trimming turned out to be a French sea captain.

The French now lowered three boats, with fifty men in each
craft, and rowed for the island. The inhabitants were soon over-
powered and all Block Island soldiers taken prisoner. The invaders ravaged the island, insulted the women and tortured
many of the men.

One Block Islander managed to reach the mainland to try to
get help. That night a ribbon of bonfires burned all the way
from Pawtucket Point near Westerly to Sakonnet Point. The
fires alarmed the French invaders, and they left the island the
very next day. Two men-of-war were soon sent out from Newport for Fisher's Island, where they captured and killed the
deceitful Captain Trimming and made prisoners of his crew.

A short time later the French and English fleets clashed in
sight of Block Island, and many of the shells and bullets hit the
banking near its shore. The engagement was indecisive, however, and the French sailed away. But they came back again
and again to raid the island and steal pigs, cattle and poultry.

On one occasion, a pirate, Paulsgrave Williams, associate of
the notorious buccaneer Captain Samuel Bellamy, forced three
Block Islanders to join his crew. The kidnapping took place on
April 18, 1717, just eight days before Bellamy lost his life in the
Cape Cod surf when his ship, the *Whidah*, was wrecked. We
quote from the records of the period:

> Block Island ales New Shoram
> Aprell ye 18th 1717.

We the subscribers testifie and say that as we went on board of a large sloop, Paulsgrave Williams Commander . . . three of our men . . . were forcibly taken from us . . . by violence. . . . The men were George Mitchell, William Toesh, and Doctur James Sweete; and furthere Deponents say not.

Thomas Daniels
John Rathbun
Thomas Pain

During the revolution there were many raids on Block Island by bands of Tory refugees. Late one afternoon when the surf and wind were very high, ten of them were seen approaching the island in a light open boat. As they came close to shore, they headed for the Old Harbor Point Landing. By this time the sun had nearly set, but crowds of islanders gathered to watch the Tories attempt the landing. When the boat was within a few hundred yards of the wharf and safety, the waves grew higher and higher. Strain as they might, the ten raiders could make no headway against the terrific wind. Then a great voice cried from the boat, "Pull, boys, pull for your lives."

Just after this, the boat was swallowed up in darkness. Cries for help were heard a short time later, and when morning came the boat had gone down. Since that time the ghosts of the Harbor Boys, the Tories who were drowned near the Old Harbor Landing, are said to appear at Block Island periodically. Many people claim to have heard their cries.

About the year 1795 a small vessel anchored in Cow Cove shortly before dusk. Three of the crew went ashore and entered the carriage road which ran from Sandy Point to the Harbor. When they had taken certain measurements and sights, they began digging in the middle of the road. The next morning they were gone, but the man who had been watching them, Mr. Isaiah Ball, found the imprint of a large earthen pot. In the surrounding earth Ball discovered a single silver coin, probably a Spanish two real piece, similar to the United States twenty-five cent piece, inscribed with the designation M 94. No one has ever learned anything more about this mysterious episode.

The first lighthouse on Block Island was at Sandy Point in 1829. In 1837 a new tower was built, and a third was erected around 1857. Since appointments were political, there was an interplay of lighthouse keepers depending on what party held the presidency. The fourth lighthouse, built of stone, was erected in 1867 a safe distance back from the vagaries of the sandy beach. It is still standing today.

Block Island's southern light, a two-story brick dwelling with an attic and octagonal tower, was built in the summer of 1874 by L. H. Tynan of Staten Island. This is the structure which seemed so formidable when we approached it from the air. The tower itself is fifty feet high and stands on a cliff 152 feet above the water. At times the glow of its light can be distinguished thirty-five miles away, although the official list indicates that twenty-one miles is the farthest that the curvature of the earth allows the light to be seen.

Another story of interest concerns three blind brothers who were famous characters at Block Island a hundred years ago. They were known as Blind Varnum, Blind Henry and Blind Nelson. The brothers were deaf-mutes in addition to being blind, and because of their unfortunate afflictions they attracted considerable attention.

Blind Varnum was an expert at catching short lobsters—lobsters which were below the legal standard. Knowing that he would be punished if he actually *caught* the lobsters, he devised a scheme whereby the lobster became the offender and he himself the victim. He swaddled his feet with heavy rags, and over the wrappings he placed several pairs of oversize stockings. Then he waded out into the water around the rocks, working his feet down into the sand and into the crevices under the rocks.

When he felt the pinch of the lobster on his toes, he grabbed the creature by the back and soon had him safe in his sack. He had not broken the law because the lobster had actually caught him, and he had acted in self-defense.

One day, however, the surf was greater than he realized, and Blind Varnum waded out too far. Just what happened is not too clear, but his lifeless body came ashore several days later. Blind Varnum had been caught by his last lobster.

THE PALATINE AFFAIR

THE most important episode in the maritime history of Block Island was the Palatine affair. Unfortunately, almost everyone who has written about this event has made some rather serious and unfortunate errors, and it is only to be expected that many of these errors have come to be accepted as fact. After a careful study of the original records and all the other material available, I shall now attempt to tell as clearly as possible what really happened to the Palatines at Block Island.

In August, 1738, the 220-ton ship *Princess Augusta* of Ramsgate, England, sailed from Rotterdam for America with 350 refugees from Palatine, a section of Germany on the Rhine River. The emigrants were leaving their own country because of religious troubles and had brought all their worldly goods with them. Many who were fairly well-to-do were accompanied by their servants. In addition to the refugees, there was a crew of fourteen on board the *Augusta*.—The origin of the passengers is undoubtedly responsible for the misnomer *Palatine*. As far as I know, there never was such a ship in this part of the world.

The *Augusta's* water supply had been put aboard at Rotterdam, but unfortunately for both Captain Long and a majority of the passengers, the casks provided for the water, "had before contained White and Red Wines." Fresh water was poured into mouldy barrels and thereby contaminated. Of the 364 persons on board ship, three hundred were poisoned by the water. Two hundred and fifty of these died and were thrown overboard, among them Captain Long and several of the crew.

A new master, Andrew Brooks, was placed in charge, and the stricken ship continued on its way to America. Exactly what Captain Brooks' plans were we shall never know, but his conduct indicates that he had some ambitious scheme by which he would greatly profit at the expense of the surviving Palatine emigrants.

On December 19 Captain Brooks sighted land, but to this day we cannot be sure where he made his landfall. He claimed that it was Cape James in Latitude 38 degrees, which would place the *Augusta* near Cape Henlopen in Delaware. Judging from subsequent events the ship was actually off Cape Cod.

Around midnight of the 19th, Captain Brooks weighed anchor and stood to the southward until two o'clock, then wore ship to the northeast against a northwest wind. The wind increased to a gale, and the storm battered the *Princess Augusta* to such an extent that the crew cut away the mizzen mast. A leak developed near the "Square of the Stern" and the ship became almost impossible to sail. The weather grew colder and colder, and many of the ship's company began to freeze. Christmas aboard the vessel was hardly noticed because of the terrible suffering.

By December 26, the survivors had been subjected to a fearful series of "Cold violent Winds, Snowstorms & the Like." At eight o'clock that morning the *Augusta* made a landfall off the east end of Long Island, and Captain Brooks decided to "endeavor for Rhode Island." The following morning he sighted Point Judith bearing northeast five miles away. Hoisting their "ancient" or flag to the main topmast shrouds to indicate they were in distress, the vessel then "laid to under topsails."

But no ship came to their rescue. Some time later Captain

Andrew Brooks brought the surviving passengers together on the deck and they all agreed to make another attempt to reach Philadelphia, with New York and Rhode Island their next two choices.

Here is part of the sworn statement of Captain Brooks to the warden of Block Island:

Then we steered away to go between Block Island & Long Island and it was so exceeding thick of snow and wind about NNE we could not see much above three times the length of said ship and about 2 of the clock the said Capt. Andrew Brooks saw something loom as a cloud & instantly ordered the helm hard a port. But before it could be done the ship struck the shore and stuck fast. And in about 2 hours after justled off, but had not got above 3 times her length before she struck again & struck very hard and beat a plank off her bottom 8 or 9 feet long.

According to Brooks, the *Princess Augusta* was wrecked at Block Island on December 27, 1738, at 2 o'clock in the afternoon.

After the vessel struck, there was great confusion aboard the ship. Many tried to get ashore, but Captain Brooks ordered them back. Watching his chances, Captain Brooks launched his small boat into the dangerous seas and reached shore safely. There he met Simon Ray, Chief Warden of the Island, who accompanied him back to the *Augusta*. The tide had gone out, leaving the vessel's bow high on the shore. Ray expressed the opinion that the ship would float off at high tide, but Captain Brooks said that a piece of her bottom was "drove on shore, and that she had a great deal of Water in the Hold." Hearing this, Ray told him to let go his sheet anchor, lest she float off with the "Palatines' Goods."

By this time there were almost one hundred passengers clamoring to get ashore. They were anxious to remove their possessions, but they were told by the captain that nothing could be taken from the ship. The wretched Palatines finally climbed down over the side of the ship to the sand and made their way in little groups to the deep snow above the rise of the tide. There the cold, raw wind beat on them mercilessly, freezing their hands and feet. Two helpless old women died before morning.

The men of Block Island now distinguished themselves by their humane, unselfish acts. There were two cottages a mile to the south of the wreck, and every survivor was carried to them through the snow until the rooms were filled with victims. The stronger Block Islanders carried the survivors on their backs; other immigrants reached the cottages on horses. Even blankets were used to transport the victims: four Block Islanders, each holding a corner, walked through the snow with a Palatine sufferer in the woolen blanket.

With two cottages soon filled to overflowing, the other passengers had to be transported through the deep snowdrifts an additional three, four, and even five miles for shelter and food. Although the immigrants were starving, Captain Brooks had some fifteen thousand weight of bread aboard the *Augusta* which no one could touch because the master claimed he could not break into the cargo. Nevertheless, he had already carried goods belonging to himself and the surviving sailors ashore. Perhaps he rifled the chests and trunks of the Palatine passengers and stored the spoils in his own trunks ashore. This, at least, seems a likely explanation for his strange, inhuman acts.

On the following day the master of the *Augusta* ordered his crew to unbend the cable, and at high tide the ship floated away from Block Island, carrying two passengers who had refused to leave their possessions. One of them was believed to be Mary Vanderline, who had much gold and silver plate in her cabin. The *Princess Augusta* was even then so close that several Block Islanders went out and rescued twenty chests and a considerable quantity of goods which they brought ashore and stored. Later many of these goods were given to their rightful owners.

The very next day the *Augusta* smashed ashore on the western side of the island and went to pieces. The two persons aboard her are not mentioned as having been saved, and their fate remains a mystery.

Food and supplies littered the beach, and "the Authority used their endeavor to secure the same for the Use of the proper Owners." Of course there was the usual salvaging which always accompanies a shipwreck, but the Block Islanders had proved their heroism that bitter December day when they rescued and took into their homes the stricken Palatines.

Only ninety of the 105 survivors from the *Augusta* were alive by January 19. I wonder if there are any known descendants of the shipwreck of 1738 alive today? If so, they should be interested to learn that of the 350 Palatine passengers, only sixty ever arrived at Philadelphia. The fate of the other thirty is unknown. The last item concerning the survivors comes from the pages of the *Boston Gazette*:

RHODE ISLAND MARCH 23 Last Tuesday Night sailed from hence 30 of the Palatines bound to Philadelphia and last night sailed 30 more.

And now, having given what is to the best of my knowledge the true account of the fate of the Palatines wrecked at Block Island, I should like to clear up some of those misconceptions mentioned earlier.

Probably John Greenleaf Whittier has done more to immortalize the tragedy than any one else, but some of the misunderstandings about it can be laid to the poem he wrote. When challenged as to the source of his poem, Whittier gave as his authority Mr. James Hazard of Newport, whom the poet called "a gentleman of character and veracity."

I quote from Whittier's *The Palatine*:

The ship that, a hundred years before,
Freighted deep with its goodly store,
In the gales of the equinox went ashore.

The eager Islanders one by one
Counted the shots of her signal-gun,
And heard the crash as she drove right on.

Into the teeth of death she sped;
May God forgive the hands that fed
The false lights over the Rocky Head.

Down swooped the wreckers, like birds of prey
Tearing the heart of the ship away,
And the dead had never a word to say.

And then, with ghastly shimmer and shine
Over the rocks and the seething brine,
They burned the wreck of the "Palatine."

In their cruel hearts, as they homeward sped,
"The sea and the rocks are dumb," they said:
"There'll be no reckoning with the dead."

But the year went round, and when once more
Along their foam-white curves of shore
They heard the line-storm rave and roar,

Behold! again, with shimmer and shine,
Over the rocks and the seething brine,
The flaming wreck of the "Palatine!"

When the Reverend Mr. Livermore wrote *Block Island,* he tried to solve the mystery of the Palatine passengers and crew. He claimed that there was much circumstantial evidence to indicate that a ship named "Palatine" was cast ashore at Block Island. In support of his theory, he mentioned Mr. Raymond Dickens, who frequently had heard his grandfather, Thomas Dickens, speak of the "Palatine." Thomas Dickens knew Simon

Ray, the warden of the island at the time of the wreck, and Ray had described the "Palatine" ship.

All well and good! But unfortunately for the Reverend Mr. Livermore's theory, evidence existed, even at that time, which would certainly have given the true name of the ship in question.

Mr. Livermore also introduced the evidence of Charles E. Perry of Block Island, who had done considerable research on the mysterious shipwreck. Perry had written in vain to both Amsterdam and Rotterdam for information. He was of the opinion that the vessel had sailed from some German port, laden with well-to-do emigrants bound for Philadelphia; that the captain died or was killed on the passage; that the officers and crew starved and plundered the helpless passengers, and finally abandoned the vessel. According to Perry, the deserted ship drifted ashore during the week between Christmas and New Year's. He further believed that the ship was burned, with one woman left aboard.

Mr. Benjamin Sprague, 88 years of age, gave his views on the subject in 1876. According to Mr. Sprague, his parents had said much concerning one Dutch Kattern, or Long Kattern, who married a Negro on the island. Their daughter, Cradle, was well-known. Dutch Kattern was feared by the natives and was said to be a witch. Livermore believed that she spread the story of the burning of the "Palatine" ship to get revenge on those who put her ashore on the island.

The Reverend Mr. Livermore believed essentially that a ship named "Palatine" was wrecked at Block Island, but was repaired, sailed away, and went down years later during a storm in the Bay of Bengal. Sheffield, writing in 1876, also believed that the ship was named Palatine and said that one woman passenger named Mary Vanderline, who had much silver and gold plate aboard the ship, refused to quit her, "and must have perished, as the ship was never heard from again."

Tradition tells of the "Palatine Light" which has appeared occasionally through the years. In the pages of the *Narragansett Historical Register* for February, 1886, I found Welcome A. Green's solution to the mystery of the blazing "Palatine" ship.

In common with most native born Rhode Islanders I had often heard the story of the Palatine Ghost Light of the Phantom Ship of Block Island. . . . All Rhode Island would know the story of the wreck of the *Palatine* and the murder of its ill-fated passengers and burning of the ship, and that, since then, the "Phantom Ship" is seen to sink in the sea, year after year, apparently in memorial of that terrible tragedy.

I went aboard the steamer *Leona* in September of the 80's engaged in the menhaden fishery, at that time cruising to the north-west of Block Island. The day had been warm. As night set in the air seemed clear but (was) excessively humid. At times we seemed to pass through little gatherings of fog, hanging in the atmosphere, scarcely perceptible as fog, only noticeable as a sensible dampening of the air when we passed through it, and of varying sizes and shapes.

Mr. Green goes on to tell of bringing up the subject of the "Palatine Light". The fishermen talked freely with him about it and described the light as flickering in the air, darting up in the form of flames at times. The mate remarked that it was a good night to see the light. Just as he spoke, Mr. Green saw what appeared to be the lights of a blazing ship, "thin, lambent, unsubstantial, but distinct and clear." The image suggested the masts and sails of a square-rigger, and he watched breathlessly as the sails seemed to catch fire one by one. The light was about two miles away, and the *Leona* sailed directly for it. They reached the location, set their nets and soon hauled out a remarkably large amount of menhaden.

After investigating the matter, Mr. Green stated that the menhaden was a very oily and phosphorescent fish and explained that, when in large schools and under certain atmospheric conditions, the fish gave off a considerable amount of light. When the air was clear, the light was not noticeable, but on nights when there were patches of fog or mist floating in it, those tiny particles of water in the air were just enough to catch and reflect the light from below. There was a particularly brilliant display on the night Mr. Green made the trip. The fishermen always choose such a night, for the light locates the menhaden for them and they usually come home with a good catch.

Green returned to the mainland rather disillusioned because he had solved, in that particular case, the mystery of the "Palatine Light". Of course, several scientists have lately announced that there are other elements, including electricity, which under certain conditions produce illumination at sea. These other sources may also have produced the illumination which many have seen in the vicinity of Block Island.

17. New Haven's Ship in the Sky

STORIES of phantom ships and deserted vessels have always appealed to the imagination of the human race. The people of Orr's Island in Maine have spoken of the spectre ship of Harpswell for many years; another phantom, the bark *Isidore*, has been seen several times off the Isles of Shoals since her wreck there in 1842. "The Flying Dutchman," the story of the Dutch mariner who is condemned to sail the high seas until the day of judgment, is known to almost every follower of the sea.

New Haven's ship in the sky is another type of story, however. We have three historians of the incident: James Pierpont, Cotton Mather, and John Winthrop. There is some discrepancy in the date, for although common belief places the episode in January, 1647, John Winthrop's *Journal* proves conclusively that it was January, 1646, when the New Haven colonists sent their ship to England.

In the early days, the New Haven settlement was considered one of the most prosperous on the entire Atlantic Coast. A goodly number of the settlers had been traders and merchants back in England and, of course, were desirous of continuing trade in the New World. For several weeks they studied the sheltered little harbor which the Indians called Quinnipiac before deciding that it was the ideal location for the town they were to name New Haven. The harbor was situated at the mouth of the Thames River, and had the advantages of being both deep and sheltered from storm by Morgan Point and Sandy Point.

The inhabitants planned for a great future when they laid out the town. They made arrangements for a large, central square with a public market where goods of all kinds could be bought and sold. And the town fathers passed a law that no sea captain should throw his ballast overboard in the harbor, lest it shallow the depth of their waterway to Long Island Sound. They excused expert carpenters from military service in order that they might build their sturdy vessels undisturbed. The tall spruce trees which served as masts were guarded carefully, and if any one wished to cut down a tree, the governor himself was the only one who could grant his wish. A long wharf was built out to the channel so that ships of deep draught could unload their cargoes. Indeed, the industrious settlers did everything in their power to make New Haven the leading seaport of Connecticut.

Captain Lamberton of New Haven soon began making voyages up the coast to Boston and Salem and down the coast as far as Delaware and Virginia. Having explored the mainland, the intrepid mariners of Connecticut then steered their vessels right out to sea and visited Bermuda, the Barbadoes, and many islands in the West Indies. They traded lumber, wheat, and furs for sugar, molasses and cotton. One might think that they would have established a prosperous commerce, but expenses ran high and mistakes proved costly. For example, a Milford miller who had ground his wheat improperly, sold it to the New Haven merchants for shipment to Virginia. A short time later poorly-seasoned lumber was transported to the West Indies, where it caused dissatisfaction. Because of these and other unfortunate incidents, the merchants of New Haven gradually lost their trade. They might have won it back through greater experience and better products if it had not been for the Delaware incident.

Captain Lamberton and several other men of New Haven

bought land in New Jersey, and sailed to their new possession to erect houses, arrange for a trading post, and organize the area for farming. But the Swedes and the Dutch who had settlements nearby claimed that the New Haven men were infringing on their rights. When Lamberton refused to move, the two groups organized against him, and in 1642 they landed at Delaware Bay, attacked the Connecticut settlement, and captured or drove into the woods every man there. Each prisoner had to pay a heavy fine before they would release him, and Captain Lamberton, who had been captured with the other prisoners, paid the largest fine of all. Then the Swedes and Dutch burned the buildings and confiscated the goods of the new colony. When Lamberton and his men returned to Connecticut, they were poorer by hundreds of pounds.

Time and again the men of New Haven tried to persuade the other New England colonies to help them get revenge, but they never received any encouragement. Captain Lamberton returned to the Swedish settlement on the Delaware and demanded satisfaction, but his former captors merely laughed at him. Later he again tried to colonize the New Jersey area and met with similar failure. It was many years before the people of New Haven gave up hope of establishing a settlement on the Delaware River.

Their next plan was to trade with England directly. For this purpose they purchased the *Fellowship*, a ship built in Rhode Island. When it arrived in New Haven Harbor, however, it did not please its new owners. Captain Lamberton said that it was a cranky vessel and might capsize in the middle of the ocean. John Winthrop, too, later called the ship "crank-sided."

Nevertheless the *Fellowship* was made ready for the long ocean journey to England. The ship was rigged with new masts and sails and the cargo began to come aboard. And what a cargo these enterprising merchants and farmers of Connecticut had gathered—beaver skins, wheat, peas, lumber, over two hundred West India hides and an amount of silver plate! The plate came from New Haven homes where householders believed that other things were more necessary than silver in Connecticut. In all, the cargo when fully loaded was worth six thousand pounds, which in those days represented a very substantial sum.

But the inhabitants were faced with another danger besides their "cranky" ship. John Winthrop tells us that "this was the earliest and sharpest winter we had since we arrived in the country and it was as vehement cold to the southward as here." That "vehement cold" froze the entire harbor of New Haven, trapping the *Fellowship* at the wharf. For three long miles the sea was frozen, and the men of New Haven were again in trouble, this time because of the forces of nature. Lamberton was equal to the occasion, however, and organized a large band of ice cutters to break a canal through to Long Island Sound.

In addition to the valuable cargo, some of the most influential people of Connecticut sailed aboard the ship. In all, about seventy persons left New Haven on the *Fellowship* with Captain Lamberton at the helm. Winthrop tells us that many of those who sailed "were of very precious account."

On the day of the sailing nearly every man, woman and child in New Haven went down on the ice and followed the progress of the vessel as she made her way through the canal. Conversation continued between the two groups until the final stretches of ice were reached. Then the Reverend Mr. John Davenport conducted a short service in which both those on board ship and those remaining at home participated. Raising his hand in prayer, Mr. Davenport spoke in a trembling, halting manner, and uttered some strangely prophetic words to the multitude: "Lord, if it be thy pleasure to bury these our friends in the bottom of the sea, they are thine; save them!"

Then the service ended; farewells were shouted from ice to ship; the sails filled with the breeze, and the *Fellowship* left New Haven Bay forever. Those whose loved ones were aboard climbed to the nearest headland and watched the progress of the vessel as she tacked back and forth on her way down Long Island Sound. Finally only a tiny flash of white sail could be seen as the sun caught and held it for a brief moment, but with the gathering darkness the ship vanished from sight.

With the coming of spring, word was expected of the *Fellowship*, but the weeks passed without news of any sort. Vessel after vessel came from England, but not one captain mentioned seeing or hearing from the New Haven ship. Summer arrived, and then fall, and still there was no news. By this time many people in New Haven had begun to worry, but the more hopeful ones felt that the ship had probably been delayed by a storm, or that it might have gone ashore on some island from which the passengers would later be rescued. One by one, however, as the weeks slipped by, the people lost their hope and gave in to blind despair. They recalled the words of Minister Davenport, and the entire colony went into mourning.

Winter came and still there was no word of the *Fellowship*. Long hours in prayer and meditation were spent by the pious men and women of New Haven. They entreated with God that He grant them some indication of what had happened to the ship. Finally when the sultry days of summer were at hand, their prayers were granted.

One hot June afternoon a terrific thunderstorm hit the Connecticut shores suddenly and unexpectedly. Lightning played up and down the skies for over an hour, and the rain came down in torrents all the while. The thunderstorm finally passed out to sea, but the sky was still alive with heavy masses of clouds slowly changing in shape.

And then a miracle was seen to occur. An hour before sunset the clouds unmistakably gave way to a strange image high in the firmament. It was the lost ship of New Haven, floating in toward them, sailing on a cloud through the sky. The news was relayed from house to house, and soon the people were all out in the streets, staring in astonishment at the miracle taking place before their eyes. The clouds came lower and lower, and then the ship sailed in so close that a man might have hurled a stone aboard her.

There was the *Fellowship,* just as she had left New Haven— her keel, masts, sails and rigging—all exactly as they had last seen her two winters before, with the tall, powerful form of Captain Lamberton himself, sword in hand, standing erect on his quarter deck.

Then, suddenly, without warning, the topmasts blew away, to hang tangled in the rigging. The masts soon went by the board, and within a few minutes the proud vessel was reduced to a battered hulk, with masses of rigging and sail in confusion all over her. A short time afterwards the *Fellowship* went over on her beams ends and sank slowly into the cloud. The populace at New Haven gazed in horror at this terrible sight. Soon there was nothing left of the ship in the sky, and the voice of the Reverend Mr. Davenport was heard as he spoke to his flock:

"God has condescended to send this account of His Sovereign disposal of those for whom so many prayers have been made."

The people, their prayers answered by the Divine demonstration in the heavens, returned to their homes, their worries and fears dispelled.

The loss of the *Fellowship* put an end to commercial enterprise in New Haven for many years and almost terminated the colony as well. Oliver Cromwell, then in power, offered the colonists the island of Jamaica, but they declined and turned to farming for the next few years.

Eventually they learned to forget much of the sorrow which had earlier beset them, but they never could forget that year of 1646 when the *Fellowship* left New Haven with all their hopes to return in such a strange fashion a year and a half later.

18. A Weird Tale of Mutiny

HIGH in the arm of the Statue of Liberty I stood and watched the great liners steaming in and out of New York Harbor. It was an inspiring sight, and it must have appeared even more inspiring when the famous clipper ships with their billowing sails were passing Bedloe's Island in the 1850's and 1860's. As I stood there, I recalled the story of another ship, the *Frank N. Thayer*, which had left New York on February 13, 1885, bound for Shanghai.

The *Thayer* arrived safely at Shanghai and discharged her cargo without incident. Then Captain Clark sailed her across to the Philippine Islands, where he loaded a cargo of sugar, jute and hemp consigned to Vernon H. Brown & Company in New York City. In Manila, he also took on two Filipino coolies to add to his crew.

Clark, a strict disciplinarian, had his wife and child on board with him, and was feeling particularly pleased with this voyage. He was extremely fond of the *Thayer*, and she was indeed a beautiful sailer.

On the night of Saturday, January 2, 1886, the *Thayer*, about six hundred miles southeast of the island of Saint Helena, off Africa, was sailing in easy fashion toward her destination. The weather was fine, and when the captain turned in at about ten o'clock nothing unusual had occurred. Aided by the steady southeast trade wind, the ship continued on her course. The port watch went below, and the starboard watch, coming up on deck in the moonlight, soon tucked themselves away where the moonbeams could not reach them and went to sleep. The two mates sat down on the booby hatch and began a conversation. It was a splendid night at sea with little work to be done.

Down below with the port watch were the two Filipino coolies who had been shipped aboard at Manila. Suddenly one of the coolies ran up the companion hatchway and disappeared from the sight of the men below. He called softly to his countryman, and the two men drew their long sheath knives and advanced on the unsuspecting mates sitting on the hatchway. They hid their knives as they spoke to the officers. One claimed that he was desperately ill. Then, without warning, the coolies fell upon the mates with their knives.

Maloney, the man at the wheel, was a short distance away when the coolies attacked the mates, and he watched with horror as the Filipinos stabbed again and again. But instead of arousing the watch below by shouting, he froze to the wheel in helpless terror.

The first mate staggered away from the booby hatch and was rescued by the sailors of the starboard watch, who were now wide awake and realized fully that they had two maniacs aboard ship. They fled with the first mate to the forecastle and barricaded the door. The coolies pursued them to the forecastle, leaving the second mate free to stagger to the cabin door, where he shouted, "Captain! Captain!" and then fell dead.

Already aroused by the screaming and shouting, Captain Clark slipped on his trousers. Only half awake, he thought that the *Thayer* must have collided with the ship she had been approaching at sundown. Hastily he threw open the door. The mate's body on the deck warned him at once that he was faced with mutiny, but he had no way of knowing how many men were against him. Of course, he should have returned for his revolver, but the mate's sudden death bewildered him, and he continued up the companion ladder. The moment his head appeared out of the companionway, one of the coolies laid his scalp bare with a knife. Then he was choked from behind. Drenched with his own blood, he swung around and landed a crushing blow which hit the coolie between the eyes. This staggered the Filipino for a moment. The captain then started to go to his cabin to get his revolver, but the coolie recovered in time to dig his knife into the master's side. The two men grappled with each other—Captain Clark's strong blows against the coolie's deep knife thrusts. Finally they both tumbled down the companionway. In the fall, Captain Clark's head struck the planking and he was knocked unconscious.

The coolie, thinking that the captain was dead, left him and scrambled up the ladder. But Clark was merely stunned, although bleeding from half a dozen knife thrusts, the worst of which had exposed the lobe of his left lung. He stumbled to his cabin door where his wife handed him his revolver. Then he crawled back to the foot of the ladder and sang out to Maloney, at the wheel, to shut the door at the top of the companionway.

"I can't, sir," replied the terrified man at the wheel. "There is someone there."

"Who is it?" Clark asked.

"I don't know, sir," came the answer. Actually, Maloney was so terrified he could not leave the wheel.

The bewildered captain had no way of telling which of his crew were the mutineers. He was too weak to shut the door at the top of the companionway, but he did barricade himself in the cabin, locking all doors leading forward and aft.

A short while later the captain heard a man coming down the ladder. Opening the door, he covered the intruder with a revolver. Seaman Hendricsen was standing there, obviously terrified.

"Save me, Captain. Hide me, hide me!" the sailor cried. Captain Clark, in his weakened condition, did not dare risk the chance that Hendricsen might be one of the mutineers. He shut the door and locked it, leaving the man in the entryway. Clark then returned to a corner of the cabin from which he could keep watch on both the portholes and the doors forward and aft. Without question, he believed himself a dying man, and he was indeed a ghastly sight. Mrs. Clark bandaged his wounds as best she could. While she was bandaging there was a terrific crash of splintering glass and the brown leg of a coolie could be seen coming through the porthole. The Filipino was attempting to enter the cabin.

Captain Clark, nearly unconscious from loss of blood, fired blindly at the leg. The shot, although it missed its mark, had the desired effect, and the coolie's leg was quickly withdrawn. The Filipinos had believed the captain dead, and it was quite a shock to them when Clark fired his revolver.

Meanwhile, down in the forecastle the first mate died. The other sailors armed themselves with capstan bars and went aft, only to meet a determined onslaught from the coolies. The mutineers wounded four of the sailors, causing all but one of the others to run in blind panic back toward the forecastle.

The one man who decided to remain, Robert Sonnberg, ran aft and climbed the mizzen rigging, where he took refuge on the crossjack yard. From this position he watched the coolies kill the man at the wheel, Maloney. (Luckily what wind there had been dropped away, and the ship drifted along in a dead calm without a helmsman.) The next to die was the carpenter, Booth by name, and his death was followed by the killing of Antonio Serrain, a man who had always been especially kind to the two Filipinos. Each man in turn, pleading for mercy, was killed without any show of emotion on the part of the stolid coolies.

After battening down the hatchway leading to the forecastle and spiking heavy timbers across the entrance to trap the crew below, the murderers turned their attention to Sonnberg. "Come down, Sonnberg, we will not harm you," one of them called up. But Sonnberg had no desire to test their veracity.

The Filipinos now dressed themselves in the dead carpenter's best clothes and paraded the deck in their finery.

Dawn finally came, and the morning passed without further activity. The afternoon wore on with Sonnberg in the rigging, the captain and his wife barricaded in the cabin, and the crew imprisoned in the forecastle. Then it was sunset and the last red rays disappeared from the western sky. Up on the mizzen yard, Sonnberg finally dozed off to sleep. But suddenly he awakened when he felt the rigging shake. Looking down, he saw the two coolies, knives in teeth, a few feet below. He quickly climbed farther up to the royal yard, where he remained until dawn.

Meanwhile Captain Clark gained strength, and by the next morning he had made up his mind to attempt to recapture the ship. He found Hendricsen concealed in his lavatory, and learned to his amazement that only two of his sailors had mutinied, that they had killed five of the crew and wounded four others. Shortly afterwards Clark discovered the Chinese steward hiding in one of the other cabins. He armed the two men, and at last was ready to take the initiative.

By now, the mutineers had decided to set the ship afire, leaving the crew in the sealed forecastle and the captain and his wife in their cabin, while they themselves fled in the ship's boat. Sonnberg, deciding that it was now or never, descended to the deck, grabbed an axe, and started to smash apart the barricade in front of the forecastle door. But the mutineers were too fast for him and came after the sailor with harpoon and knives. Sonnberg eluded them again and ran nimbly up into the rigging.

The coolies attempted a final onslaught against the cabin, armed with a harpoon and knives which they secured to sticks eight and ten feet long. As soon as they appeared, Captain Clark suddenly stood up near the smashed porthole, aimed at the breast of the nearest coolie and fired. The shot took effect, and the coolie staggered back.

Now the tide of events began to turn. Ah Say, the Chinese cook, managed to throw an axe in through the forecastle window to enable the trapped men to chop their way out.

By now the Filipinos realized that their plan to capture the ship was doomed. They pushed a heavy boom over the side, and the wounded coolie climbed down on it, but the other decided to set fire to the ship before joining his friend. He jumped down a ventilating hatch into the hold, where he ignited several piles of jute he had previously prepared. Clouds of smoke began to pour out through the hatch as the jute in the cargo burst into flames.

Dense pillars of smoke reached the forecastle. The imperiled crew chopped furiously to free themselves. Soon they had cut a hole through the barricade and burst out of their prison. Captain Clark gave two of them revolvers, and they went after the remaining coolie. Dodging back and forth the Filipino managed to elude them and rush to the side of the ship before one of the men shot him in the shoulder. But he still had the strength to gain the rail, where he shouted a terrible oath and leaped into the sea. He swam in painful fashion to the side of his fellow mutineer, still clinging to the boom. But the enraged sailors fired a fusillade of shots at them, and the two coolies, victims of a strange malady, sank to their death in the ocean.

They had done their work well, however, for the fire continued to gain in spite of all the captain and crew could do. It was a sad fate for Clark to lose his ship after having overcome as unusual a mutiny as ever befell an American sailing captain, but when at the end of four hours he knew that the ship was doomed, he ordered the boats made ready. The first boat capsized when launched, so that all seventeen survivors, some of them wounded, were placed in the remaining craft. The only provisions they had were the emergency rations in the second boat.

After pulling away, they stood by a short distance from the

Thayer hoping that the terrific blaze would attract the attention of some passing vessel. The men sewed desperately, converting several blankets into a serviceable sail which they soon hoisted. At dawn the next morning there was not another vessel in sight.

The captain declared that they should make an effort to reach the nearest land, Saint Helena. For nine long days they sailed toward their destination. Both food and water were dangerously low when the lifeboat finally reached Jamestown, Saint Helena, on the night of January 13, 1886.

Once safe in harbor, Captain Clark and the survivors of his ship's company were cared for by Mr. J. A. McKnight, the American Consul. All eventually returned to the United States.

Captain Clark later explained that he believed the two coolies planned to rifle the *Thayer* of all valuables and money and burn the ship to destroy the evidence of their crime. He thought that they expected to escape in a lifeboat, and when they were picked up later, claim to be the only survivors of a mutiny. It seems, however, that there was an added reason for their brutality. What it was we shall never know, but I have a strong suspicion that Captain Clark himself was more to blame than appears on the surface.

Later I searched the marine archives in New York for records of other ships under the command of Captain Clark.

Before the episode of the *Thayer*, he had sailed from Liverpool to San Francisco as master of the *Sunrise*, built by Robert E. Jackson of East Boston in 1860. When the *Sunrise* reached San Francisco in 1873, an investigation was held and it was found that Captain Clark had treated his men so brutally that he was prosecuted, convicted, and sentenced. Moreover, the first mate, Francis Harris,* had treated the sailors so viciously

---

* The mate was pardoned near the end of his sentence to accept a position on the San Francisco police under an assumed name.

under orders from the captain that he, too, was prosecuted and given four years in jail. The captain's sentence was only fourteen months, but he paid a fine of $1000 as well. For the rest of his life he was known as "Sunrise" Clark.

Just how much Captain Clark's treatment of his crew was responsible for the two Filipinos' wild adventure of murder, we shall never know, but certainly the evidence indicates that this must have been a factor in the bloody mutiny on the *Thayer*.

Part Four

SANDY HOOK TO CAPE HATTERAS

19. Shipwrecks and Adventures In New Jersey

Arriving at Sandy Hook, New Jersey, where I planned to begin my walk along the outer beach, I went at once to the old Sandy Hook Light which has guarded the approaches to New York City for so many years.

Sandy Hook's history began long before the days of American lighthouses. Henry Hudson sailed his *Half-Moon* toward the peninsula on the afternoon of Thursday, September 3, 1609, and the native Indians probably observed this large vessel with apprehension as it approached them from the ocean.

Henry Hudson went ashore at Sandy Hook and bartered for the Indians' beans, grapes and oysters, giving them knives and trinkets in return. His stay there was abruptly cut short two days later when one of his men was killed by an arrow as he was cruising along the shore in one of the small boats with four others. Hudson decided to sail away at once when he discovered the tragedy.

At the present time Sandy Hook has a military reservation known as Fort Hancock. I visited the giant muzzle-loading cannon there and marveled at its twenty-inch bore. The soldiers told me that the 115,000 pound monster was cast at the Fort Pitt foundry under the personal supervision of Captain Rodman, inventor of the gun which achieved such popularity during the Civil War. Designed in 1861, the Fort Hancock cannon was not finished until late in 1864.

The lighthouse at Sandy Hook, built in 1764, is one of the most interesting beacons of our coast. It is the oldest original lighthouse in America. There are others which were erected earlier, but all of them have been rebuilt at one time or another. Boston Light, for example, constructed in 1716, was damaged during the Revolution and rebuilt in 1783. The Sandy Hook Light has walls eight feet thick at the base, and the building itself is eighty-eight feet high. The beacon is a fixed white light with 45,000 candlepower. The day I called at the lighthouse the building had just been given its annual coat of paint and was resplendent as it shone in the sun.

The history of Sandy Hook light begins in the 1750's before the structure was actually built, when the merchants and ship-owners of New York began agitating for a beacon at Sandy Hook to guide shipping into the bay. It was not until 1761, however, that the New York Assembly voted to authorize a lottery for the express purpose of obtaining funds for the light-house. Twenty-six hundred pounds were realized by the lottery, and four acres of land at Sandy Hook were purchased for the establishment of the beacon and the keeper's dwelling. Unfortunately, the money raised was not enough to complete the building of the tower, so a second lottery was authorized by the Assembly in 1763. In addition, a tonnage tax was imposed on all shipping so that the current expenses of running the light-house would be met.

An examination of the deed for the lighthouse reveals that no public house for the "selling of strong liquors" can ever be erected on the grounds, and that the local farmers have the perpetual privilege of "keeping and pasturing two cows" on the property.

Sandy Hook Light was first illuminated on June 11, 1764. The merchants and seamen made of this an important occasion, and the event was duly reported in the New York *Mercury* the following Monday.

On Monday evening last the New York Light-house erected at Sandy Hook was lighted for the first time. The House is of an octagon Figure, having eight equal sides; the Diameter at the Base 29 Feet; and at the top of the Wall, 15 Feet. The Lanthorn is 7 feet high; the Circumference 33 feet. The whole Construction of the Lanthorn is Iron; the Top covered with Copper. There are 48 Oil Blazes. The Building from the surface is Nine Stories. The whole from Bottom to Top 103 Feet.

This structure was undertaken by Mr. Isaac Conro of this City, and was carried on with the Expedition that the Difficulty attending to and fro on the Occasion could possibly admit of; and is judged to be masterly finished.

During the Revolution, when the British fleet was sailing in and out by Sandy Hook, a group of American sailors landed at the lighthouse and dismantled it. The British fleet was discomfitted by the extinguishing of the beacon, and a party of British seamen landed and restored the lighthouse so that its glow would guide their navy. But on June 1, 1776, the lighthouse was again attacked by the Americans. Several small boats under the leadership of Captain John Conover bombarded the tower and damaged it. The Americans lost several men in the skirmish, but the damage to the tower was soon repaired.

After the war ended, the lighthouse figured in an interesting controversy between the State of New York and the State of New Jersey. In 1787 New York passed a law which required all vessels from other states to report at the local custom house. Here they were to be entered and cleared, after paying a substantial fee for the privilege. New Jersey retaliated by levying a thirty-pound monthly tax on Sandy Hook Light, still operated and owned by New York. The wrangle was settled in 1790 when the United States Government assumed control of the Sandy Hook beacon.

An interesting incident during the War of 1812 occurred just off Sandy Hook on July 5, 1813. The well-known Navy officer, Mad-Jack Percival, devised a scheme whereby he could capture the British guard sloop *Eagle*. While in port he hid thirty-two volunteers under the hatch of his fishing smack *Yankee*, put a load of vegetables on deck and turned a calf, a sheep and a goose free to roam over the deck.

Sailing out off Sandy Hook Light on Monday, July 5, Percival allowed the *Eagle* to draw close to inspect his vessel. The British captain ordered Percival to report to the Commodore's vessel five miles away. Just then Percival shouted the watchword, "Lawrence," and the thirty-two volunteers poured out of the hatchway and opened up with a terrific volley of shots against the British officers and men. After two officers had fallen dead on the deck, one of the others hauled down the colors in surrender, and a few hours later the *Eagle* was brought into New York Harbor amid the cheers of hundreds of New Yorkers who had gathered at the battery to witness the happy event.

The officers of the Coast Guard Station told me many stories of Sandy Hook, but the one which most attracted my curiosity concerned the cellar of the old lighthouse keeper's home.

A few years before the Civil War a new keeper, being of an inquisitive frame of mind, began to wonder what was under the first floor of the building. He found no door or window leading to what might be a cellar, and so he decided to investigate the underpinning of the building. He then discovered that there *was* a cellar after all. Loosening a few boards, he descended into the aperture and was horrified to find a skeleton sitting at a table facing a chimney and a rude fireplace. The mystery of the skeleton—whose it was or how it happened to be walled up inside the cellar—was never solved.

As the years went by two other towers, no longer in existence, were erected at Sandy Hook, one for the Western Union

Telegraph Company and the other for Postal Telegraph. The last old-time ship observer, Jim Gould, has passed on to his reward, but for thirty-five years he stood high in the Western Union tower with his telescope scanning the seas for sail and steam. His duty was to observe and report all vessels entering New York Harbor.

Jim Gould had often heard of the old days when the telegraph was the only communication from Sandy Hook to New York. The captain of an incoming ship from across the sea would watch for the arrival of a boatman who rowed out in a dory from Sandy Hook. When the ship passed the dory, the captain threw overboard a can containing important information in code. The boatman would remove the message and attach it to a carrier pigeon which would fly at once to the telegraph station at Sandy Hook. From there the message would be relayed to New York.

Down by the old right of way for the abandoned Sandy Hook railroad stands a memorial to thirteen young British officers and sailors who lost their lives over a century and a half ago. On December 31, 1783, a young lieutenant of the British Navy, Hamilton Douglass Haliburton, together with twelve other officers and sailors from the H.M.S. *Assistance*, went ashore at Sandy Hook to search for deserters from the Royal Navy. A quick storm and sudden drop in temperature caught them on the peninsula, and they all froze to death before help could reach them.

The young Britishers were buried in a common grave at Sandy Hook, and a monument was later erected by the mother of young Haliburton, Dowager Countess Katherine of Morton. Her inscription on the monument eulogized her son's bravery "in contempt of hardship and danger" and described him as "deserving of a better fate." The original inscription, I was told, had been destroyed by "barbarians from a French man-of-war" in the year 1808.

I climbed the old lighthouse tower with the present keeper, Richard Terhune, and we looked out at the liners and smaller craft as they passed Sandy Hook. It was a beautiful sight. But the sun was already getting close to the western horizon, and I wished to reach Long Branch before night.

For the next four days I spent most of my time hiking fifty-three sandy miles to reach Ship Bottom, New Jersey. But in the course of my journey I had learned the stories of seven shipwrecks.

The first disaster was that of a French vessel, the *Amerique*. On Sunday morning, January 11, 1877, the steamer *Amerique* went ashore more than a mile to the south of the Seabright Life Saving Station in New Jersey, and less than a mile to the north of Monmouth Beach Station.

The crews of both stations turned out for rescue work. When Keeper West of Seabright Station arrived on the scene, he saw the heavy southeast sea and ordered the lifesaving equipment brought to a position opposite the wreck. Meanwhile a light aboard the ship indicated that the crew was about to attempt to launch a lifeboat. Every member of the life saving crew ashore shouted to them not to try it, for the seas were far too high to allow a lifeboat to reach shore. But the cries went unheeded, and soon the outline of a large, white boat was seen against the background of the steamer.

Almost at once the boat was picked up by a tremendous wave, capsized and drawn on toward the beach. The twelve sailors it had carried were seen struggling in the water, their heads bobbing up and down between the cakes of ice floating in the sea. The lifesavers waded into the waves and rescued four of the sailors. Then they returned and were able to grasp four more. The eight survivors were utterly helpless, and the lifesavers had to lift them over the four or five-foot icy barrier on the beach.

A short time later Keeper West saw another sailor in the surf, and was able to grab hold of him, but as he did so the tide washed him out into deep water, and he and the sailor almost perished together. The next wave took West high on the shore against the wall of ice. He grasped a hummock of ice and held on desperately with one hand, clutching the sailor with the other. The two were pulled out of danger by other members of the crew. Three of the twelve sailors who attempted to reach shore were drowned, and later their bodies washed up at Sandy Hook.

By five o'clock that cold morning the lifesavers had set up the mortar which was to fire a line to the vessel. The first shot failed, but the second attempt carried a line over the steamer. Unfortunately the Frenchmen did not understand how to attach the line for the breeches buoy. When the waves went down a little, therefore, the lifesavers launched a surfboat and were successful in reaching the steamer. With skill and speed they attached the breeches buoy and brought fifty-four passengers and forty-six crew members in to safety. Later the breeches buoy was used to carry ashore two boxes of gold bullion, each weighing 275 pounds.

The three-masted schooner *David H. Tolck* was wrecked on Long Beach, New Jersey, at three o'clock in the morning of February 26, 1879. Aboard the schooner were Captain Irving Sawyer, his wife Ida, their eighteen months' old daughter, Geneva, and a crew of eight. The captain confused another light for Barnegat Light and subsequently wrecked his vessel.

The ship's boat was smashed to pieces, and the bottom soon crushed in under the feet of the crew.

At daylight Keeper B. F. Martin of the Harvey Cedars Station fired a mortar gun out to the ship, but the shot fell into the sea. The second attempt was successful, but by this time the vessel was breaking up, forcing the ship's company to take to the rigging. The seas came in with such fury and washed so high that the men were frequently carried from their feet and suspended almost horizontally while they clung for their lives to the rigging.

Suddenly, without warning, the line from ship to shore snapped. The ship had moved its position, and the strain was too great for the line to hold. There the *Tolck* lay, her stern to the sea, her hull under water except for the starboard waist, the masts and yards aslant, and the bowsprit and jibboom buried in the surf. The watchers from shore could observe ten persons clinging to the ratlines. One of the sailors, the second mate, held the baby, while her mother clung helplessly a few yards away.

Another line was shot out to the wreck, but when the sailors on the *Tolck* began to adjust it, one of them collapsed and fell to his death in the sea. The others managed to pull the breeches buoy out to the wreck and chose Second Mate Emanuel Clausen to go first so that he could save the child. Taking his seat in the buoy, which resembles a huge pair of shorts, Clausen held firmly to the baby while the others gave the signal to the men on the shore to haul away.

Then, halfway to shore, a terrible thing happened. The lines jammed, and the mate and baby were battered by each wave as it swept over them. The horrified lifesavers knew that there was only one thing to do. They took hold of the line which ran from shore to ship and pulled it until it snapped. If the break in the line came between the ship and the breeches buoy, they could haul the pair ashore, but if the break came between the shore and the breeches buoy, the mate and the baby would almost certainly drown.

The line snapped, and luckily the break separated the buoy from the schooner. The mate and baby were hauled to safety, hurried to a waiting team, and rushed off to the station half a mile away.

Now only the traveler rope still ran out to the ship, and there was no means of sending the breeches buoy out again. The life savers decided to choose a combination crew made up of the strongest oarsmen from the two stations, with Keeper Martin of the Harvey Cedars Station at the steering oar and Keeper Grimm of the Loveladies Station at the stroke oar.

The dangerous launching was accomplished successfully, but the terrific current swept the lifeboat by the schooner before contact could be made, and the attempt failed. Another launch was made. This time a tremendous wave knocked Keeper Martin overboard, and although his crew pulled him back at once, the accident caused the lifeboat to sweep by the schooner again, and the crew was forced to land on the beach a short time later.

Aboard the schooner, the captain and his wife, still lashed firmly to the ratlines, died of exposure. Another shot was fired into the rigging, but not one of the freezing sailors could reach it. Desperate in his anxiety to reach the vessel, Keeper Martin waded into the sea, and with difficulty attached a shot line to the rope which still stretched from the shore to the mizzen head. The rope was then slacked off, and the sailors out on the wreck were told to haul it in. Finally they were able to grasp the shot line, and in this fashion the breeches buoy was again sent out on the standing rope, ready to be worked back and forth.

Darkness was at hand, and it was raining before the first passengers reached shore on the new breeches buoy line. Four men landed in two trips, and they told the life savers that only two persons, Frank June and Richard Gordon, were still alive. They had been the most active men aboard the schooner and had agreed to wait until last. The breeches buoy was sent out for the last time, and the sailors' voices came in across the roaring seas signifying that they were ready. The lifesavers fell to with a will, but as they hauled, there was a sudden jerk and then the breeches buoy stopped completely. The frightened life-savers decided to try the same method which had saved the lives of the mate and the baby earlier that day. They ran down the beach with the line, trusting that the outer line would break and release the unfortunate sailors. But when the separation came, it was between the buoy and the shore, and the sailors fell into the raging sea. The next day their bodies came ashore three miles north of the wreck with that of the man who was lost from the lifeboat.

Later that same day Keeper Grimm visited the schooner and cut down the bodies of the unlucky captain and his wife, whose orphaned baby was still at the station, alive and well. The baby, Geneva, was cared for by Mrs. James Hazelton, wife of the proprietor of the Harvey Cedars Hotel. Later the baby's grandmother arranged for her return to New England. After the girl, Geneva, grew up she often returned to the scene of the tragic wreck of the *Tolck*.

On February 3, 1880 a mighty hurricane hit the New Jersey coast, the result of two storms coming together. The hurricane began with snow and sleet and ended with a heavy, lashing rain. At its height the schooner *Stephen Harding* collided with the schooner *Kate Newman*. One sailor, William Ray, managed to leap aboard the *Harding* before the *Newman* sank with all others aboard. The accident caused the *Harding* to go ashore two and a half miles south of Sandy Hook Light near the Spermaceti Cove Station.

On shore, Surfman Rex noticed the schooner's lights and hurried to the station. A beach cart with apparatus was quickly wheeled out along the sand. The going was very difficult, with the seas sweeping high into the dunes, but eventually the men reached the wreck. The first shot from the Lyle gun landed safely, and the breeches buoy was soon sent out. After three trips in which the buoy came in empty, a young German arrived ashore to report that the captain, his wife and the crew had decided to wait on board ship until morning.

Surfman Wilson was sent out to inform the ship's company that the *Harding* might break up at any moment since the storm was rapidly getting worse. Captain Harding's wife was finally persuaded to get into the breeches buoy and was the next to land ashore. Soon everyone including Wilson had reached safety.

At the approximate time that the *Harding* had gone ashore the brig *Castalia* of Bath, Maine, had hit hard on the sand at the Seabright Station, five miles to the south. Patrolman Disbrow discovered her while he was covering his beat, and soon six men were pulling and pushing the heavy mortar cart through the snowstorm. Reaching a point across from the wreck, Keeper West of the Seabright Station fired the Lyle gun, and the shot landed between the forestay and the foreyard. Two men came ashore in the breeches buoy to make certain it was in working order. Then Mrs. W. C. Seymour, the woman passenger, was sent in from the wreck. It was a terrifying experience for her. The *Castalia* rolled and jerked to such an extent that the breeches buoy was often fifty feet in the air! All eleven members of the ship's company were eventually brought to land and taken to the station.

During that same fierce gale, the schooner *E. C. Babcock* drove aground off Monmouth Beach and the station crew had terrible difficulty in getting their beach apparatus set up. Keeper Valentine, sick in bed at the time, got up to take charge. He fired the Lyle gun with accuracy, and the breeches buoy brought ashore all eight persons aboard the *Babcock*, including the captain's wife and his two daughters. By ten o'clock that morning there was nothing at all left of the schooner.

Just as the timbers of the *Babcock* began coming ashore, another vessel was sighted, making dead for the beach nearby. It was the Spanish brig *Augustina*, and the weather was now clear enough so that the crowds on shore could see the man at the wheel handling the vessel as if there were no danger at all.

By the time she struck, the beach apparatus was already set up and waiting. A moment later a shot was sent whizzing out over the brig. The breeches buoy was soon dispatched, but the Spaniards did not read the instructions on the tally-board attached, and soon the slack became entangled with the wreckage from the *Babcock*. To add to the confusion, one of the sailors began to come ashore hand over hand on the line. Halfway ashore, the surf caught him and he was trapped between the two lines, which held him fast and were strangling him as well.

Surfman Garret White rushed into the sea, holding on to the line. When he reached the choking sailor, White forced apart the two lines and brought the man ashore. Two more sailors began to use the line to get ashore by the hand over hand method. Surfman John Van Brunt started for the first, but a great block of driftwood knocked him down, and he was only rescued by the combined efforts of several fishermen nearby, who formed a human chain to bring him out of the ocean. Five Spaniards were eventually rescued after they had started out on the line. Each man was practically naked when he was saved.

Later it was learned that the captain and two sailors were still aboard the ship. Several surfmen went out and boarded the brig. They found that the captain had tried to commit suicide by shooting himself but had not hit a vital part of his body. All were taken ashore and the captain eventually recovered.

The final schooner in the vicinity to suffer from this terrific gale was the *George Taulane*, which hit the shore two miles from the head of Barnegat Bay. By the time she crashed against the beach she was afire and dragging two anchors in vain. She swung back and forth in the trough of the sea, the giant waves making clean breaches entirely over her hull. The crew was forced to take refuge in the rigging.

Life savers along the beach saw the ship wallowing in the

great seas, and began to follow the vessel as it dragged anchor, moving steadily southward. Soon the surfmen from the Green Island Life Saving Station sighted the dragging schooner, and joined those from the Swan Point Station in an attempt to rescue the sailors aboard the *Taulane*.

It was half past eight in the morning when Keeper Chadwick of the Green Island Station decided to make ready to fire the Lyle gun. The sea was still raging. Giant billows engulfed the schooner as they swept on toward shore and over the dunes to reach a greater distance than ever had been attained within the memory of the oldest inhabitant.

When the *Taulane* came close enough to shore for a shot to be fired, the life savers were ready. Mounting the gun on an unflooded hummock, they fired, but the shot failed to reach the ship. They fired again and again, unable to hit their objective.

To make matters worse, the *Taulane's* cargo of cordwood billets began to come ashore and kept striking the lifesavers as they worked the apparatus down the beach through the onrushing waves. The hardest task was to keep the shot line dry so that it could be fired properly. Suddenly the cannon toppled off the wagon and was lost in the surf and sand. The determined surfmen plunged after it, and in spite of its heavy weight, were able to lift it up on shore, where Keeper Chadwick carried it through the sand and seas on his shoulders.

The sixth attempt to reach the wreck was made shortly afterwards. The line flew out between the foremast and the jibstay. The current swept the bight of the line against the sides of the schooner, and the sailors were able to grab it and secure it to the rigging.

A short time later the wreck slued around broadside to the sea and began to roll frightfully. The hawser was sent out and the breeches buoy rigged on, but the roll of the schooner prevented a normal sand anchor's being set up on shore. Several men held on to the end of the hawser and moved back and forth with the rolling schooner, serving as a human anchor. The breeches buoy now traveled back and forth to rescue the five survivors.

Only two men from the *Taulane* were lost and they had drowned before the successful shot reached the schooner. One of the old-time seamen, veteran of a hundred shipwrecks, said that it was a miracle that anyone had been saved. Never in his career had he seen a wreck when the chance for rescue seemed so hopeless.

After a long but necessary detour around Barnegat Inlet, I finally reached Barnegat Light, its lower half painted white and its upper half red. The first beacon here was erected in 1834 and the new 161-foot tower was completed in 1856. The tower is no longer lighted, for the Barnegat Lightship was established in 1927, and vessels now are guided by this floating marine marker off the shores of Barnegat Beach. I recalled the occasion three years ago at Christmas when I landed in a helicopter with presents for the young people of Barnegat and the Coast Guard personnel.

On reaching Ship Bottom, I made my way to the summer home of Mrs. Henry Irving Oehler. Mrs. Oehler is the great-granddaughter of Dr. Charles Winslow, whose heart is buried on Nantucket Island, and whose story I told in my book *Mysteries and Adventures Along the Atlantic Coast*. In renewing my acquaintance with her, I learned the story of how Ship Bottom received its name.

Back in the early days of the nineteenth century Captain Stephen Willets, from nearby Tuckerton, was sailing along the coast shortly after a storm. Guided by what he always claimed was an inward spirit, he rowed ashore and looked for a vessel in distress. Just as he expected, he found a ship bottom-up pounding on the bar. He inspected the vessel carefully and was able to detect a faint knocking on the hull of the wrecked craft. Someone was inside, alive.

Twenty minutes later the captain was energetically chopping through the hull. When he had broken a hole through the bottom, he pulled out a young girl, the only survivor of the wreck. As soon as she was brought ashore, the girl kneeled and drew the figure of the cross in the wet sand with her finger. After her rescue the girl was taken to New York. She never returned, and no one today knows her name.

Another story fascinated me—that of the pirate treasure which had been uncovered at nearby Bond's Beach some three-quarters of a century ago.

One fine day two mariners rowed ashore from a schooner anchored offshore, and after getting their bearings from the members of the lifesaving crew at Little Egg Harbor, they struck out for a point between two old cedars and the site of the lighthouse station. The men from the station watched their progress through the spyglass. When the sailors began to dig furiously, the lifesavers decided to hike down the beach after them. Soon the diggers uncovered a large iron-bound chest, and removed bag after bag of coins from it.

When the sailors looked up and saw the lifesavers hiking toward them, they hastily thrust several bags into the rowboat and pushed off. They were out of hailing distance before the life savers arrived.

The lifesavers went up to the hummock where the sailors had been digging and found several dozen coins in an excavation in the sand. They also found a weatherbeaten map, a cutlass, and the chest itself. All gold coins, however, had been removed by the two men.

I don't vouch for this story because Commander Fred Griffin of the Bond's Beach Life Boat Station informs me that he has never heard of such a treasure. It is a fact, however, that Charles

Washington Beck of Philadelphia found a considerable number of coins around Beachhaven some years ago, and his granddaughter, Mrs. Nathan Eyer, told me that their dates range from 1682 to 1795.

The next day I visited the Ship Bottom beach, where I learned the story of another shipwreck. A singularly tragic episode in the history of New Jersey's outer beach was the unusual disaster which befell the Austrian *Bark Kraljevica*. At 1:30 a. m. February 11, 1886, the ship crashed under full sail on the south side of Barnegat Shoals. Foggy weather had prevented the lookout from sighting Barnegat Light. At the time the sea was moderate, but a short time later an easterly wind developed. The *Kraljevica* began to break up, and the crew of fourteen soon took to the lifeboat. For several hours they made no attempt to land, because they were not certain where they were. Finally when they attempted to ride their boat over the bar, it capsized and the eight men who tried to reach shore were drowned.

The bar was a mile below the Ship Bottom Station, and nine miles from the wreck itself. The six surviving sailors clung to the capsized boat, and eventually reached the shore. Here they found a well-stocked relief hut. After lighting a fire, they cooked food found in the hut, hung their clothes up to dry and fell asleep wrapped in the warm bedding the relief station afforded.

Unfortunately, a light from their vessel had been seen and even then the life savers were planning to launch a boat into the dangerous waves. At six o'clock that morning the launching took place, with Keeper Joel H. Ridgeway at the steering oar. The surf, which had been so calm a few hours before, was developing into an ugly, dangerous series of high, breaking waves. The surfboat reached the wreck safely. When the lifesavers saw that the vessel was abandoned, they turned the surfboat back toward the shore.

Suddenly, as they reached the dangerous breakers near the beach, a gigantic wave, with a mighty inner curve which no lifeboat could withstand, came rushing toward them. The men braced themselves, but the wave swept tons of foaming water into the boat and beyond, rolling the men under. One life saver, Samuel Perrine, was killed instantly by an oar; the others tried to climb back aboard the swamped craft, which kept turning over and over in the heavy seas. Two men, John Soper and Solomon Soper, died of exhaustion despite their cork life preservers. Keeper Ridgeway and Surfman Thompson reached the shore first, followed shortly afterwards by Surfman Reeves and Surfman Inman who crawled up on the beach some distance away.

While all of this was taking place, the survivors of the wreck were safe and sound inside the refuge hut, and their presence was not discovered until the following day.—The widows of the lost lifesavers were kept on the Government payrolls for the next two years, but after that, Government aid stopped.

After returning to the home of Mrs. Oehler and saying my farewells, I struck out for the mainland and the State of Maryland, the location of my next story.

20. A Forgotten American—
John Paul Jones

*A*FTER arriving at Annapolis, Maryland, I visited the Naval Academy, and made my way to the tomb of an illustrious admiral in the American Navy, John Paul Jones, whose brief lifetime of forty-five years included many remarkable adventures and several epochal battles. Most of us have studied his career in school. There are few who have not thrilled at reading of his appointment as an eager young sailor to the command of the American ship-of-war *Ranger*. The story of his capture of the British ship *Drake*, his invasion of Scotland, and his great battle with the *Serapis* are remarkable episodes in the career of an outstanding American Naval hero.

John Paul Jones had risen rapidly from a humble Master's apprentice to the eventual command of conquering squadrons. He was many-sided in his accomplishments. Although his brilliant victories in naval warfare were far more spectacular than his diplomatic conquests, he was an expert in both statecraft and diplomacy. In warfare he won his victories in spite of the condition of his ships, not because of them. No man-of-war on which he ever sailed was worthy of him.

When Jones was aboard the rotting, sinking hulk of the *Bonhomme Richard* at the very height of the battle with the Serapis, Captain Pearson of the English warship shouted across to him, "Have you struck your colors?"

"I have not yet begun to fight," was Jones' quick answer.

John Paul Jones went on to win that memorable battle fought off Flamborough Head, September 23, 1779, even though his ship went down under him and he was forced to transfer to the British vessel he had just conquered.

Upon another occasion, the English accused Jones of being a pirate. It all came about when Jones conceived the daring plan of going ashore in Scotland and capturing an important British subject, and holding him until the English released a goodly number of prisoners from that terrible hellhole at Brooklyn's Wale Bogt.*

This is how it happened: Jones, with a band of his sailors, slipped by the British Navy and went ashore at Saint Mary's Isle in Scotland to seize the Earl of Selkirk. Finding that the Earl was in London, the disappointed officers removed the silver plate from his mansion. Jones was embarrassed when the officers brought out the plate, although actually it was no worse than what the British had already done in the American colonies. However, Jones decided to purchase the plate at once from the officers and some years later sent it back to the Earl at a cost to himself of $2500. English historians, who for years have declared Jones a pirate for taking the silver, have always neglected to mention that Jones returned the plate!

He captured sixty vessels from the enemy, destroyed more than a million dollars' worth of enemy ships and supplies and took hundreds of English prisoners. The prisoners he captured to force the British to exchange them for unhappy Americans starving to death aboard the terrible prison hulks at Brooklyn.

John Paul Jones was generous and courageous at all times, and if he had a fault, it was his extreme hatred of a coward. He thought that there was scarcely a sin for which courage

---

* There were a number of old British prison ships anchored at Wale Bogt, in command of the infamous Britisher, David Sproats, who later boasted that he had killed more rebels by starving and freezing them than all the British armies in battle!

would not atone. His most famous remark on this subject was: "Bravery is that cheerful kind of spirit that makes a man unable to believe that there is any such word as Danger in the dictionary."

Admiral Jones was the first to hoist our present flag on an American man-of-war, the first to receive a salute to it from a foreign power and the first to raise it on a major foreign ship captured in battle. In life he was the most conspicuous personage on two continents, but after his death he was forgotten for over a century.

After his many notable victories, Jones returned to this country to await the building of a new ship worthy of his prowess. But when a French man-of-war was wrecked because of a Boston pilot's mistake, the *America*, the warship Jones had waited for, was given to France as compensation. Bitterly disappointed that he was not to command his own man-of-war, he sailed for Europe.

Later John Paul Jones traveled to Russia, where he made a brilliant impression on the Empress Catherine. But life in Russia eventually bored the former American captain, and he returned to Paris. Here he became ill in the spring of 1792 and the following summer died of a disease known at the time as a dropsical affection. He was buried in an obscure cemetery in Paris, and few Americans ever knew where he was interred.

The years passed. The second war with England was followed by a conflict with Mexico; then came the great Civil War. A period of national consciousness followed; honor and acclaim were given to all American heroes, and the days of the American Revolution were recalled and studied. When American Revolutionary heroes were brought into prominence, Admiral John Paul Jones' career was found to have been a remarkable one. This man, historians realized, was the first really great sailor America ever had. And what had happened to him? No one seemed to remember. It was very embarrassing that the subsequent career of this leading American should be unknown. Then it was discovered that he had gone to Europe, never to return, and had died obscurely in Paris around 1792. But no one really knew where John Paul Jones was buried!

General Horace Porter, Ambassador to France in the year 1899, was among those who felt a strong sense of shame that John Paul Jones, a national hero, was lying forgotten in some Paris cemetery. He decided to conduct a private investigation to discover where Jones had been buried. As he traced down the many clues and studied deeper and deeper into the life of the young naval hero, Porter realized that here was a man whose career read more like an ancient fable than like the story of an American sailor.

General Porter assumed the role of a detective in his efforts to find Jones' remains, and followed every fragment of information, no matter how improbable or insignificant it seemed. The search cost him many years of effort and thousands of dollars.

His first step toward finding Jones' tomb was to locate the burial papers. His search led him to the conclusion that the certificate of burial had been destroyed in a fire in 1871. Fortunately, however, he discovered that a Mr. Charles Read had obtained access to the certificate in 1859 and had recorded it at the time. The document settled a dispute as to the exact date of the admiral's death, which he found had occurred on July 18, 1792.

Porter then discovered a letter written by Colonel Samuel Blackden, who had attended the funeral. "His body was put in a leaden coffin on the 20th, that, in case the United States, which he had essentially served and with so much honor, should claim his remains they might be more easily moved," wrote Blackden in the latter days of the eighteenth century.

After being misled by the error of a copyist, Porter found that Jones had probably been buried in the Saint Louis Ceme-

tery, where foreign Protestants were usually interred. He uncovered papers which shed light on the circumstances of the
burial, and found to his chagrin that the United States Government did not even pay for the funeral expenses of their great
hero. A friend, Monsieur Simonneau, paid four hundred and
sixty-two francs for the purchase of a lead coffin, the alcohol
in which Jones was immersed, and the outer wooden coffin.
That a private French citizen should have to pay for the funeral
of an American naval hero seemed an outrage to General Porter,
and he tried to find a true descendant of the benevolent French-
man to whom he could pay back the debt. He could find no
one who even pretended to be descended from Simonneau.

Porter's next step was to locate the records of the graveyard.
When he finally obtained them, the four pages written at the
time of Jones' death were missing! Later, after an intensive
search which lasted several months, the pertinent pages were
found in a Paris library. They proved conclusively that the
admiral had been buried in Saint Louis Cemetery.

However, there were two other claims. The elder Dumas
had always insisted that Jones was buried in the Père Lachaise,
but Porter's research revealed that this cemetery did not even
exist until thirteen years after Jones' death. Furthermore, although there were five Joneses buried at Père Lachaise, John
Paul Jones was not among them. Another rumor placed him
in Lafayette's cemetery, but a search proved this, too, to be
false. After every other possible story or legend had been
tracked down and eliminated, Porter decided that he should
turn all his efforts to the Saint Louis Cemetery.

Now he discovered an amazingly strange story. The Saint
Louis Cemetery had been located at the corner of two streets
known today as the Rue des Ecluses Saint Martin and the Rue
Grange-aux-Belles. But in the year 1796 the Government sold
the cemetery to Monsieur Phalipeaux, a building contractor.
Shortly afterwards the graveyard was covered over, buildings

were erected on part of it, and later a public dumping ground (in which dead horses and dogs were thrown) was created over part of the old cemetery.

Such was the fate of the illustrious John Paul Jones, whose fame had once covered two continents! His body had lain for over a century in a forgotten cemetery in a squalid section of a foreign city.

Unfortunately, when General Porter went to the owners of the properties which had once been the cemetery, he found that he had been preceded by rumors that he would pay princely sums for the privilege of searching for the grave of John Paul Jones under the buildings and the dump pile. The owners demanded so much money that he was forced to abandon the project for a period of two years.

General Porter said later that the action of the French property owners was the most discouraging part of the entire proceedings. Two years later he quietly approached the owners and explained that he was paying for the work out of his own pocket. They agreed to let him tunnel under the buildings and yards, providing he replaced everything as he had found it, for a sum approaching $35,000.

Work began at once. The first shaft was opened at a depth of eighteen feet, and scores of bodies were found buried side by side, about a foot apart. During the long search of the entire graveyard, five lead caskets were uncovered. It was almost certain that Jones was in one of these caskets, and, as each was discovered, it was examined for identification. All but one of the five lead coffins was found to have a marker on it. It could be assumed, therefore, that the remains of John Paul Jones were in the unidentified casket. Every square foot of the cemetery was probed again with a steel rod, and it was definitely proved that no more lead caskets could be in the graveyard.

The remaining lead casket was taken out into the open air and opened in the presence of witnesses. The body it contained still showed signs of having been embalmed in alcohol. It was covered with a winding sheet and firmly padded with hay and straw. Once unwrapped, the corpse was found to be marvelously well-preserved, with the flesh still intact. By comparing the remains in the casket with a photograph of the Houdon bust, all present recognized the features which had been entombed for well over a century as those of John Paul Jones.

The American hero died at the height of the French Revolution when no engravers could be found to prepare an identification plate. Therefore he was buried without one.

The remains of the Admiral were sent at once to the School of Medicine in Paris, where experts held a post-mortem on the body of a man dead for 113 years. The body measured five feet seven inches in length, exactly Jones' height, and all other known characteristics agreed in minute detail. Even an attack of pneumonia in June, 1789, had left traces on his lungs which the Paris experts identified 113 years after his death! After an exhaustive study, the Paris medical men prepared a report which ended with the expected verdict: "the body examined is that of Admiral John Paul Jones."

The body was prepared for final entombment in the same leaden coffin, which was sealed in a new triple casket of pine, lead and oak. Finally all was in readiness for the long journey back to the United States. General Horace Porter, his mission a success, notified President Theodore Roosevelt that he had fulfilled his objective and that the body of Admiral John Paul Jones had been delivered to the American Church of the Holy Trinity.

The United States Government then officially recognized the body as that of John Paul Jones, and President Theodore Roosevelt announced that a squadron of war vessels, the *Brooklyn*, *Tacoma*, *Chattanooga*, and *Galveston*, be sent to transport the body back to the United States.

General Horace Porter declined Admiral Sigsbee's offer to

sail on board the flagship *Brooklyn*. He felt that his work was accomplished, and he wished to stay in the background. The squadron crossed the ocean with the remains of Admiral Jones, and memorial services were held at Annapolis, Maryland, which had been selected as the permanent burial place for the first hero of the American Navy.

At the commemorative services held on April 24, 1906, the 138th anniversary of Jones' capture of the British ship-of-war *Drake*, President Theodore Roosevelt fittingly eulogized the career of our great Naval hero when he concluded his remarks:

Remember that no courage can ever atone for the lack of preparedness which makes the courage valuable; and yet if the courage is there, its presence will sometimes make up for other shortcomings; while if with it are combined with other military qualities the fortunate owner becomes literally invincible.

21. Treasure and Hurricane
In Delaware

$\mathcal{A}$FTER leaving Annapolis, I finally reached Lewes, Delaware. Here I had two objectives. The first was to learn the story of a treasure ship, the sloop-of-war *De Braak*, believed to have gone down with a substantial hoard of money in 1798, and the second was to collect information about the terrible hurricane which swept the Delaware coast in 1888, ninety years later. There are still many persons in and near Lewes who recall the famous 1888 blizzard, and I was able to complete my research on the hurricane long before the last fragmentary report concerning the *De Braak* reached me.

The Cape Henlopen blizzard, as it is called at Lewes, is the same storm which suddenly submerged New York City under a record blanket of snow. In the Empire State the storm is still known as the *Great Snow of '88*.

The storm began suddenly just before midnight on March 11, when the wind without any warning suddenly veered from southeast to northwest. Snow, sleet, and rain hit the coast with hurricane force. The large number of vessels anchored behind Delaware Breakwater in expectation of an easterly were not prepared for this sudden turn of wind, and most of them were soon swamped at their moorings or driven ashore. The fleet was quickly thrown into the wildest disorder. The scenes which followed that sudden windshift were never forgotten by those out in the storm.

Where a moment before had been calmness, great, lashing waves swept through the fleet, pushing the schooners, steamers, barkentines, and sloops against each other in hopeless confusion. Chains snapped, and masts and spars came tumbling down. The wind soon developed to furious intensity with a wild, roaring whistle, and the frightened crews had barely time to scramble to temporary safety before it was too late.

Life savers attempted to leave their stations at Lewes and Cape Henlopen early in the storm to reach the shore, but one by one they were knocked down bodily by the force of the gale. Finally they fought their way through the cutting wind and sand by crawling on their hands and knees. During a lull in the storm they saw the schooner *Allie H. Belden* in the huge breakers a short distance away. The seas made a complete breach over her, and the men on shore could see the helpless crew clinging to the rigging.

The life saving crew from the Lewes station set up their apparatus on the beach and fired the Lyle gun into the rigging, but the master of the *Belden* saw the line blown away before he could secure it to the schooner. After two more attempts to get a line out, the life savers decided that the terrific wind was making the Lyle gun worthless. Only a surfboat would rescue the crew of the *Belden*, they agreed.

A line was run out to another stranded vessel, the pilot boat *Enoch Turley*, and the surfmen and volunteers carried the self-bailing lifeboat to a point on shore opposite the *Turley*. Their plan was to keep in the lee of the *Turley* as long as they could and then row with all their energy toward the *Belden*. But the moment the full force of the gale met the lifeboat, the wind pushed them from their goal, and they had to admit defeat. Another effort by five men in a smaller craft met with the same result.

A fresh crew of experienced pilots then rowed out to the *Dow*, also submerged offshore, and from that closer location attempted to reach the *Belden*, but within fifty yards of their goal, they hit a submerged bar and had to return to their starting point.

The station crew then left the shore in the lifeboat and carried out a plan which they had carefully prepared. They rowed one hundred yards, anchored, rested, hoisted anchor, rowed again, dropped anchor, rested, and by this method of alternately rowing and resting their goal was eventually attained nine hours after the *Belden* was first sighted. When they located the crew members, they learned that Moses H. Small of Dennis, Cape Cod, and the cook, name unknown, had already perished. Captain John Crowell, the mate, and two crew members were removed from the rigging where they had clung for twelve hours. They were quickly brought ashore, given medical treatment and put to bed.

While the crew from the Lewes station had been struggling to reach the *Belden*, the crew from the Cape Henlopen station were able to shoot a line aboard the pilot boat *Turley*, which had stranded fairly close to shore. All seven pilots aboard the *Turley* had been saved.

Now came the harder task of getting out to the *William G. Bartlett*, too far offshore to be reached by Lyle gun. The *Bartlett*, eight hundred yards from land, had grounded half an hour after the *Belden* hit.

As the life savers hurried toward the part of the beach where wreckage from the *Bartlett* was coming in, they saw three men struggling in the water close to shore. Rushing into the surf, they formed a human chain and succeeded after desperate efforts in saving all three. When the sailors explained that there were others still aboard the *Bartlett*, the life savers launched their life boat. With the help of the line already attached to the *Turley*, they battled their way first to the *Turley* and then across the terrific seas toward the *Bartlett*. When they reached the ship in a state of complete exhaustion, they managed to make fast to the weather chains and climb aboard. On the *Bartlett* they discovered two living and one dead man. All three were brought ashore.

Although three men drowned in the Cape Henlopen blizzard, it was indeed a miracle that the number was not much greater. The members of the Life Saving Service surely prevented the death of over two score. Many fine vessels went to the bottom in that gale to add their bones to the scores already in that particular Atlantic graveyard.

The fact that so many ships, upwards of one hundred, lie at the bottom of the sea off Lewes, Delaware, has made it increasingly hard for treasure seekers to search for the *De Braak* gold. Without question, the *De Braak* carried money when she sank beneath the waves on May 23, 1798, but whether or not it is worth another expedition is a matter for debate. Up to 1949, fourteen known expeditions have attempted to bring up the treasure.

When I was in London in 1942, I attempted to find definite evidence that there had been a great treasure aboard the former Dutch vessel when she foundered in 1798. All I could discover, however, was that the vessel had been captured from the French, who in turn acquired it from Holland. Built in the year 1787, the *De Braak* had been captured by the British in the Firth of Forth, August 20, 1795.

On May 23, 1798, after capturing the Spanish ship *Francis Xavier*, the *De Braak* sailed into an anchorage at Cape Henlopen. She was believed to be heavily overloaded with gold, silver, and a vast quantity of copper, which was piled on deck. The sloop sailed into her anchorage under reefed topsail and mainsail, and a boat stood by to take the captain and several members of the crew ashore at Lewes.

Suddenly there was a sharp, vigorous gust of wind, and the *De Braak* heeled over on her beam ends. Seventy tons of copper slid across the deck, the sloop filled and sank, and thirty-five men drowned. Another fifty-three floated free from the ship. When the sloop settled in eighty-four feet of water, the survivors clung to the upper rigging which protruded above the surface. Life savers from Lewes went out to the scene of the disaster, and one by one the British sailors were rescued and taken ashore. Later that week the body of Captain James Drew, master of the sloop *De Braak*, was recovered and brought ashore. He was buried with full honors at the old Lewes Cemetery.

Later, when the captain's wife heard of the disaster and her husband's death, she ordered a suitable gravestone memorial erected in the cemetery over the last resting place of her husband. The memorial reads:

HERE RESTS THE REMAINS OF

CAPTAIN JAMES DREW

WHO COMMANDED HIS BRITANNIC MAJESTY'S SLOOP OF WAR
DE BRAAK

In which he lost his life when she foundered
at the Capes of Delaware
the 10th of June, 1798

He was beloved for his virtues, and admired for his bravery
His affectionate relict has erected this monument to perpet-
uate his Memory.

A sum variously estimated as between $400,000 and $8,000,-000 is said to have gone down with the sloop *De Braak*, but salvagers have not as yet brought up any treasure. Although several expeditions have operated over the scene of the disaster in modern times, they have encountered so many vessels on the bottom that it has been almost impossible to locate the *De Braak*.

Over a century ago the British frigate *Assistance* conducted operations over the hull, without result. Later the frigate *Resolute* attempted in vain to pull the *De Braak* to the surface by means of attaching it to a half-submerged hulk and then towing it into shallow water.

Around the end of the last century, a number of salvage companies tried to locate the *De Braak* and its gold. Knowing that the sloop had been built of teakwood, the salvagers believed that they were on the right track when the divers brought up timbers of that variety. Suction dredges were employed to bring the gold to the surface, but they failed completely.

There are two sea captains of modern times who have made noteworthy efforts to find the *De Braak* treasure. Captain Jefferson Townsend of Somers Point, New Jersey, located what is believed to be the old salvaging chain used by the *Assistance* a century before. But he didn't find a penny in treasure, and he soon exhausted his funds and gave up the effort.

The other recent treasure seeker, a resident of Bayonne, New Jersey, succeeded several years ago in bringing to the surface one of the old cannons with teakwood fittings from the *De Braak*. When I discussed the matter with him in July, 1949, he expressed the feeling that he was on the verge of discoveries of a more important nature when the venture was discontinued.

"Only one other man and I know just where the *De Braak* lies at the bottom of the sea off Lewes," he told me. "She is in eighty-five feet of water. Now don't put my name in your book, for I don't want a lot of amateur treasure seekers pestering the life out of me. Remember, no names!"

This sea captain with a passion for anonymity told me later that there was a third member of the group who had known of the *De Braak's* location but that he was accidentally killed at the scene of the operations. Just what the circumstances were which led to his death I did not discover.

22. The Monitor and the Merrimac

On July 11, 1854, the keel for the first United States Navy steam frigate was laid in the Navy Yard at Charlestown, Massachusetts. At the launching June 14, 1855, the frigate was christened *Merrimac* in the presence of cheering thousands and given a thirty-one gun salute. American flags were flying everywhere, and the *Merrimac* was proudly carrying her share.

Almost eight years later, during her only brief period of combat, the *Merrimac* fired upon those same American flags under world-shaking circumstances.

On January 30, 1862, another battleship slid down the ways into the waters of New York Harbor, and barely a month later the ironclad *Monitor* steamed out of New York bound for a memorable battle at Hampton Roads.

All Americans have heard of the fight between the *Monitor* and the *Merrimac*, but few know the real story. For example, was this battle the first involving ironclads? Which of the two warships was in reality the most vulnerable? Was the North needlessly alarmed by the possibility that the *Merrimac* would steam into New York and Boston and damage the waterfronts? Was inventor John Ericsson's revolving turret the first of its kind? And which side actually won the naval engagement?

After the Civil War broke out, the *Merrimac* was trapped in the Norfolk Navy Yard and set fire by the Northerners to prevent her falling into Southern hands. A time bomb, set to destroy the Navy Yard, and the fire aboard the ship were extinguished by the invading Southerners, and the *Merrimac* was rushed into drydock for repairs.

Confederate Secretary of the Navy S. M. Mallory was anxious that the South build metal warships similar to those used in the Crimean War by Napoleon III. He began altering the *Merrimac* to make her into an ironclad. By July, 1861, he had 1500 men working on the project. Tests proved that double two-inch plates would best withstand enemy fire, and immediately the Tredegar Iron Works in Richmond began their manufacture. The *Merrimac* was remodeled with ten guns, six of which were nine-inch Dahlgrens, and a 1500-pound cast-iron ram was built out from her bow.

Captain Franklin Buchanan, who had resigned from the Northern Navy when he believed that his native Maryland was about to secede, became commander of the *Merrimac* on March 4, 1862.

The South was highly optimistic in believing that the *Merrimac* might alter the entire course of the War Between the States, and some of the claims for this strange battleship, then under construction at Norfolk, were fantastic in their scope. For example, Mallory himself thought the *Merrimac* could steam to New York and attack and burn the city. "Peace would inevitably follow," the hopeful Mallory said.

The *Merrimac* had many faults. Her engines were constantly breaking down; she could sail no faster than five knots; and she drew no less than twenty-two feet, making any expedition up the Potomac impossible. Furthermore, she was not capable of sailing out beyond Hampton Roads: the open sea would sink the three-hundred-foot battleship in a few hours. And the worst danger of all to Southern hopes was the Achilles Heel of the *Merrimac*. A single shot which hit just below her water line would sink her at once, for she carried iron only one-inch thick at this vital part of her hull. Even a small gun could have sent her to the bottom!

From the earliest stages of the war the North had been interested in ironclads, but the interest was greatly increased when reports began to reach the Union forces that the *Merrimac* was being remodeled and made ready to destroy the American Navy. As the weeks passed, Union spies reported the various stages in the conversion of the *Merrimac*.* On July 4, 1861, Secretary of the Navy Gideon Welles requested a special board to study the possibility of building ironclads, and on August 7 the Navy advertised for designs.

Cornelius S. Bushnell of Hartford, Connecticut, submitted plans for an ironclad which interested the Navy, but the battleship seemed too heavy, and he was advised to seek the help of Captain John Ericsson of New York.

Ericsson, born in Sweden, had already invented the screw propellor and the caloric engine. He had suffered loss of prestige in 1844 when his warship, the *Princeton*, was undergoing a test on her guns. One of the huge weapons exploded in the presence of leading men of the nation, killing United States Secretary of State Upshur, Secretary of the Navy Gilmer, and four others. Although Ericsson had no responsibility for the gun, the tragedy was unfairly blamed on him, and in his anger he had abandoned further plans for the construction of an ironclad he had invented.

When Bushnell called on Ericsson, the great inventor told him that he would examine his plans thoroughly at a later date. Ericsson then showed Bushnell his own 1844 design for an ironclad. Bushnell realized that it was vastly superior to the one he had just submitted. However, Ericsson had been so unjustly accused and humiliated by the *Princeton* tragedy that he had vowed never again to go to the Navy Department. Bushnell finally convinced Ericsson that he should forget his personal

---

* The *Merrimac* was renamed the *Virginia* but is rarely called by this name because of the alliteration when speaking of the *Monitor* and *Merrimac*.

quarrel with the Navy and make an effort to have his 1844 design approved.

Ericsson humbled his pride and went before the Navy board. Eventually he convinced them that the ironclad should be built. But he found to his dismay that the government was only willing to have his vessel built providing Ericsson paid for it himself if it should fail in battle. In other words, no victory, no pay! However, Ericsson secured the financial support of three other men, John F. Winslow, John A. Griswold, and Cornelius Bushnell. Each agreed, along with Ericsson, to bear one-quarter of the $275,000 it was estimated the ironclad would cost, although the Government would not reimburse him until a victory had been won! *

Ericsson was not one to delay. He laid out the keel of what was to be the *Monitor* at Greenpoint, Brooklyn, and worked a veritable army of men in three shifts, twenty-four hours a day, until the launching on January 30, 1862. The ironclad emerged with a smooth, rounded inner hull, 124 feet in length, and thirty-four feet in the beam. The outer hull was 172 feet long, and had a beam of forty-one feet under water. The vessel drew less than eleven feet. Although armed with only two guns, the *Monitor's* weapons were powerful eleven-inch smooth bores. Her smokstacks were designed so that they could be dismantled in action. Fifty-five feet forward of the turret, a structure which resembled a cheese box, was a pilot house constructed of heavy iron logs. Here the captain was to command the ironclad during battle. The pilot house was almost entirely hidden behind the visible part of the ship and rose less than four feet above the deck.

The turret was not the invention of Ericsson alone. In 1843 Theodore R. Timby had patented a revolving turret, and Erics-

---

* The United States Government didn't pay Ericsson in full until many years after the war ended. America can never be proud of this shabby treatment of a great inventor.

son agreed that Timby should receive $5000 on every turreted vessel built. As constructed on the *Monitor*, the turret was a cylindrical iron tower covered with plates eight inches thick, twenty feet in diameter and nine feet high, placed in the exact center of the ship. Its revolving nature made it especially suitable for navigation in shallow Southern waters. The guns could be loaded when turned away from the enemy and then turned and fired.

Ericsson announced that the ironclad was a "monitor to serve notice on England that all her wooden warships were useless," and his request that it be called the *Monitor* was granted.

John Lorimer Worden was chosen to command the new ship. At the outbreak of hostilities he had gone South with secret orders, and while trying to return was caught and imprisoned. Released in an exchange of officers, he had hardly recovered from his ordeal when he was commanded to report as captain of the *Monitor*. Commander Worden quickly won the respect and admiration of every man who served under him aboard the *Monitor*.

The Southern spy system, always more efficient than that of the North, soon reported that the Northern ironclad was nearly finished. As a result, extra construction crews were put aboard the *Merrimac*. A trial run was attempted on March 6, 1862, but because of the pilots' objections, the actual proving was delayed for two days. Even then, the guns had not been thoroughly tested; the officers and crew had been up all night; and the sailors were not as yet familiar with their ship. However, if all went well, Captain Franklin Buchanan planned to utilize the trial run for an actual attack on the enemy.

At eleven o'clock on the morning of March 8, the *Merrimac* steamed down the Elizabeth River, accompanied by two wooden warships, the *Raleigh* and the *Beaufort*. It was an ideal day for the *Merrimac*, for there was no wind, and the waters of Hampton Roads were calm and placid. Overhead the sun shone down out of a cloudless sky. Several miles away the Union Navy was enjoying wash-day, and a profusion of clothing hung in the sun on the decks of the *Congress* and the *Cumberland*. Also at anchor in the Roads were the steamer *Minnesota*, the disabled steamer *Roanoke* and the sailing vessel *Saint Lawrence*.

Shortly after one o'clock in the afternoon, the Federal lookouts observed a strange-looking craft far up the Elizabeth River maneuvering slowly in the direction of the Union fleet. One officer aboard the *Congress* fixed his spy glass on the object and announced not only that it was the *Merrimac* approaching but that she was coming out to do battle.

"Nonsense," shouted another officer. "Put that glass down and be quiet—I want to read my paper." But the sudden concussion of a shot from an alarm gun convinced even the most skeptical that at last the Southern monster was coming out to give them battle. Gunners rushed for their stations, and the decks were cleared for action. The *Minnesota* steamed for Newport News, and a tug began to tow the *Roanoke* out of danger. The *Saint Lawrence* was also towed toward Newport News, but in a short time Confederate batteries across Hampton Roads at Sewall's Point opened fire on the Union ships.

The *Merrimac* drew closer and closer at a speed of four knots. She resembled nothing more than the great roof of a building floating in the water, and no real trouble was expected of such a peculiar-looking craft. Expertly guided by Captain Buchanan, she steamed directly toward her first target, the fifty-gun battleship *Congress*. At three hundred yards' distance, she exchanged a broadside with the *Congress*, whose officers and men were certain that they would quickly end the battle and send the *Merrimac* to the bottom. Actually they could have achieved an easy victory if they had known enough to fire below the water line. Instead, the Union forces aimed for the *Merrimac*'s slanting sides, and their shells bounced ineffectually off the greased iron hull.

Even after witnessing the first exchange, officers on the nearby *Cumberland* were not seriously disturbed. They believed that the more powerful guns on *their* vessel would sink the *Merrimac* if those aboard the *Congress* failed. They soon had opportunity to test their belief. The *Merrimac*, instead of finishing off the *Congress*, continued on toward the *Cumberland*. Captain Morris of the *Cumberland* gave the order to fire, and the heaviest guns of the Northern Navy added their blasts to the din of the battle. But the best guns of the Union forces did little damage to the *Merrimac*, and she steamed closer and closer. Finally she opened up a terrific fire on the *Cumberland*. The damage was overwhelming.

Now the *Merrimac* was close enough to use her heavy battering ram. She drew off for a favorable angle and steamed in at full speed to smash the starboard vitals of the *Cumberland*. The terrible noise made by the impact could be heard even above the roar of the mighty guns.

When the *Cumberland* began to sink, the *Merrimac* was still in contact with her. If at that time the *Cumberland's* anchor had been thrown aboard the *Merrimac*, both ships would have gone to the bottom together. But a moment later the battering ram of the *Merrimac* snapped off and she floated free.

The sailors aboard the sinking *Cumberland* remained at their posts, firing their guns as long as they could. At the last moment, Captain Morris ordered every man to save himself. When the *Cumberland* finally struck bottom, it was in such shallow water that her flag still flew bravely above the submerged hull of the ship.

The *Cumberland* had succeeded, however, in damaging the *Merrimac*. The ironclad was now leaking, her smokestacks had been pierced and two of her guns silenced. But in spite of her damaged condition, she began a fresh attack on the *Congress*.

Captain Joseph Smith of the *Congress* ordered every man to his station, and the battle began. Within a short time, the captain was killed and by four-thirty in the afternoon the *Congress* was so damaged that Acting-Captain Austin Prendergast decided he would have to surrender. The interior of his ship was a shambles, and casualties had been very high.

A white flag was hoisted from the *Congress*, and the *Merrimac* immediately ceased fire. Lieutenant Parker of the *Beaufort* brought his ship in close to the *Congress*, leaped aboard, and accepted the surrender of the captain. But in the confusion, the Union batteries ashore kept up their fire, making it difficult to remove the prisoners from the defeated ship. Finally the Southerners gave up the attempt and returned to the *Merrimac* after having taken about thirty prisoners. There was no other course open to them but to resume firing at the surrendered *Congress*.

By now the *Merrimac* was substantially damaged. The prow, one anchor, the smokestacks, the steampipes, railings, stanchions, and davits—all had been seriously battered, and the ship was leaking. However, and this fact is indisputable, the victory of the *Merrimac* over the *Cumberland* and the *Congress* was unquestioned and overwhelming. The Confederate loss in killed and wounded was twenty-one, while there were a hundred and forty lost aboard the *Cumberland* and 136 on the *Congress*. It was a great victory for the South.

The *Merrimac* returned in triumph to Norfolk and there received hasty repairs before returning to finish her victory over the Northern Navy in the morning.

Meanwhile, in the North, the *Monitor* had made a trial run in a blinding snowstorm on February 27. Changes in the steering apparatus and adjustments in the engine proved necessary. By March third she was ready to be tested again. This time the trial was successful, and the vessel was prepared for the long trip to Virginia and Hampton Roads.

At eleven o'clock on the morning of March 6, the *Monitor*

sailed from Brooklyn for Hampton Roads in the company of the tug *Seth Low* and the steamers *Currituck* and *Sachem*. It was favorable weather when the journey southward began, and the *Monitor* made good progress until shortly after midnight on the morning of March 7, when the ocean became rough. By one o'clock in the afternoon a severe storm had developed, and the *Monitor* began to take in water through the hawse pipes and under the turret.

When the ventilator fans became wet and stopped operating, the engineers were overcome by smoke, and at six o'clock in the morning of March 8, Captain Worden ordered a distress signal displayed. Shortly afterwards the gale moderated, however, and the journey continued.

Then, around midnight, the storm increased and the seas became dangerous again. Just when it seemed the *Monitor* could not survive any longer, the gale subsided as suddenly as it had returned. Cape Henry Light was sighted at three in the afternoon, and the remainder of the voyage was completed in calm weather.

A short time later, Captain Worden and his men were amazed to see great clouds of smoke rising from the direction of Hampton Roads, and they soon heard the noise of battle coming to them from over the water. Although his crew of fifty-eight were tired from the long, dangerous journey from Brooklyn, Captain Worden ordered the decks made ready for action and the speed of the ship increased.

At seven o'clock that March night Pilot S. P. Howard was put aboard the *Monitor* to take her into Hampton Roads. He told the officers on the ironclad of the overwhelming disaster which had befallen the Northern Navy.

Just about the time that the *Merrimac* was returning to her anchorage at Craney Island in the Elizabeth River, the *Monitor* sailed into Hampton Roads. That evening Worden wrote his wife that he had anchored the *Monitor* near the *Minnesota*.

"The *Merrimac* has caused sad work amongst our vessels," his letter says. "She can never hurt us."

The *Merrimac*'s Captain Buchanan had been injured and was taken ashore the next day. The new commander was Lieutenant Thomas ap Catesby Jones.* He ordered the *Merrimac* to sail for Hampton Roads again at six o'clock that morning, in company with two wooden warships, the *Patrick Henry* and the *Jamestown*. Captain Thomas ap Catesby Jones had his first view of the new *Monitor* a short time later when he was summoned up on deck by Lieutenant Davidson.

"What are you going to do about her?" asked Davidson.

"Fight her, of course," came the quick answer. "But don't forget that she has many advantages over us. Our knuckle † is our greatest weakness. If she concentrates her fire on that, she will make short work of us." The *Merrimac*, indeed, was vulnerable. Added to her many other faults, her engines were causing much trouble, and at times the great ship barely moved through the water.

The *Merrimac* reached the vicinity of the *Minnesota* and, without further maneuvering, opened fire. This was the signal for Captain Worden to steam his little ironclad directly for the huge three-hundred foot *Merrimac*. The other Southern ships retired at once, and the *Monitor* and *Merrimac* began their epic encounter.

Captain Worden was naturally apprehensive about the ability of his narrow iron turret to withstand the direct fire of the *Merrimac*. His tiny *Monitor* with her two guns had challenged the mighty ten-gun Southern Goliath, and he and his men wondered at the result. But charge after charge from the giant guns of the *Merrimac* were unable to penetrate the thick iron plates

---

* The "ap" in Thomas ap Catesby Jones is not, as it appears, a typographical error. I was unable to discover its significance but it is definitely a part of the Southern hero's name.

† The place where the two surfaces of the vessel met at the water line.

of the *Monitor*. Hour after hour passed, with neither side gaining an advantage. All this time just one shot from the *Monitor* directed at the water line of the larger vessel would have sent her to the bottom.

At the end of three hours, the *Monitor* ran out of ammunition, and withdrew to reload her turret. The Southerners jubilantly believed that they had defeated the Northern ship, but the *Monitor* was back in action immediately after the necessary fifteen-minute loading pause. While the *Monitor* was reloading, the *Merrimac* had been firing at the *Minnesota,* but once again she attacked the *Monitor* as her worthy opponent.

At times the smoke of the guns completely enveloped the two combatants, and on several occasions Northern witnesses feared that when the smoke cleared they would find that the *Monitor* had been sunk. But each time she reappeared, and at last the Union forces along the banks began to take heart. The *Monitor,* they observed, could maneuver in and out because of her light construction, greater speed, and shallow draught, while the ponderous, unwieldy *Merrimac,* drawing more than twenty-two feet, became grounded time and again.

Finally, Captain Jones decided that if the *Merrimac's* fire could not penetrate the tough outer sheathing of the *Monitor,* he would try to ram the little vessel. But the superior speed of the *Monitor* enabled Captain Worden to slip out of the way and fire a devastating charge at the *Merrimac* from close range. At this very moment the *Merrimac's* guns were turned against the tiny wheel house of the *Monitor,* and a short time later a blinding explosion of powder and iron filled the pilot house and knocked Captain Worden unconscious. His face and eyes were filled with paint and slivers of iron; his face was blackened and torn. One eye was permanently blinded. As soon as he regained consciousness, the captain ordered young Lieutenant Greene to assume control of the *Monitor.*

"I kept the *Monitor* either moving around the circle or around the enemy," said Greene later. "We knew that she could not sink us, and I kept right on pounding her as long as she would stand it. Once we ran out of the circle to adjust a piece of machinery, and I learned that some of our friends feared that we were drawing out of the fight.

"The *Merrimac* took the opportunity to start for Norfolk. As soon as our machinery was adjusted we followed her and got close enough for a parting shot. But I was not familiar with the locality, and I did not wish to take any risk of losing our vessel, so I came back to the company of our friends. Except that we were, all of us, tired and hungry when we came back to the *Minnesota* at half past twelve p.m., the *Monitor* was just as well prepared to fight as she was at eight o'clock in the morning when she fired her first gun."

By the time she left the scene of battle, the *Merrimac* was leaking steadily. Neither her officers nor her crew wished to withdraw, but, in addition to the leaking, her engines were giving trouble, her smokestacks had been riddled by the *Monitor's* shells, and Engineer Ramsay reported that he "could hardly keep up steam." Shortly afterwards the carpenter and the chief engineer appeared on deck to notify Captain Jones that the *Merrimac* was taking in so much water that she would have to return to Norfolk at once. Captain Jones decided that he could make no further effort to continue the battle. He ordered a gunboat sent on ahead to prepare the Norfolk Navy Yard for the immediate drydocking of the now badly leaking *Merrimac*.

On the *Monitor*, Captain Worden had been taken to the cabin. There the surgeon removed the splinters from his eyes and face, and swabbed his blackened skin with oil. A short time later Captain H. A. Wise of the Ordnance Department went aboard the *Monitor* and told Worden that he had fought the most glorious battle in naval history.

"Have I saved that fine ship, the *Minnesota?*" asked the injured commander.

"Yes, and whipped the *Merrimac* to boot!" came the inspiring answer.

"Then I don't care what happens to me," replied Worden. A short time later he was taken ashore. He was the only one aboard who had been seriously wounded. Actually, the pilot house had not been badly damaged, and there were only twenty-one minor indentations of the turret and deck.

Thus ended the battle between the *Monitor* and the *Merrimac*. Neither side won the fight, and there wasn't a man killed on either ship. However, this drawn engagement which was fought that Sunday afternoon in March, 1862, was actually a Northern victory, for the *Monitor* accomplished her objective, and the *Merrimac* did not. The *Monitor* stopped the *Merrimac* from further depredations against the Northern Navy as was intended, but the *Merrimac* failed in her objective of sinking the *Monitor*.

The *Merrimac* was repaired, but it took more than a month of hard work to make her ready for duty again. Meanwhile a surprising order from Washington was delivered to the new captain of the *Monitor*. Under no conditions, it said, should the *Monitor* engage in combat again until Commodore L. M. Goldsborough arrived. When the Commodore reached the ironclad, he announced privately that Norfolk was even then being considered for capture, and nothing should be done to interfere with the plans of General George B. McClellan. The Northern ship was to stand by peacefully for the time being.

On April 11 the *Merrimac* was once more ready for combat. Commodore Joseph Tatnall steamed her out into Hampton Roads, but the Union Navy obeyed the orders of Commodore Goldsborough and offered no opposition at all. There was good logic in this refusal to fight, for the Northern Army was making steady advances on Norfolk itself.

The siege of Yorktown led to the capitulation of that stronghold on May 4, 1862. President Abraham Lincoln, informed of the impending climax, arrived at Hampton Roads on May 6 and went aboard the *Monitor* in company with Secretary Stanton and Secretary Chase.

On May 8 the Union Navy began a bombardment of Sewall's Point across the Roads, but when the *Merrimac* came out in answer, the Union fleet retired without attempting to do battle. As many officers and men aboard the *Monitor* and other Northern ships said later, Goldsborough's strategy was sensible, but at the time it was very humiliating to have to refuse to fight.

This policy of avoiding the *Merrimac* also annoyed President Lincoln, who, after witnessing the skirmish of May 8, decided to give Captain Jeffers of the *Monitor* his own personal instructions. He told Jeffers to sail out that morning against Sewall's Point, fire two shots, and await the *Merrimac*. If the *Merrimac* appeared, Captain Jeffers was to maneuver the *Monitor* toward two ocean liners which would attempt to ram and sink the Southern ironclad.

Promptly at ten on the morning of May 9 Captain Jeffers steamed across Hampton Roads under direct orders from President Lincoln. He fired two shots, and awaited the *Merrimac*. But the Southern ironclad did not appear, and the *Monitor* returned to her anchorage.

There was a very good reason why the *Merrimac* failed to answer the challenge of the Union ironclad. Norfolk was being evacuated, and the captain of the *Merrimac* had to choose between blowing up his ship or attempting to run for Richmond. Finally it was decided that the heavy ironclad could never negotiate the shallow channels which led to Richmond, and the decision was made to blow her up.

Commodore Joseph Tatnall was awakened at two o'clock on the morning of May 10 to learn that Norfolk was then being surrendered. Rushing out to Craney Island, he ordered his men to saturate the deck of the *Merrimac* with oil and turpentine, and a long fuse was prepared which led to the *Merrimac's* magazine.

At four o'clock in the morning of May 11th the ship was set afire and the fuse was lighted. The oil and turpentine on the deck blazed fiercely, and at four-thirty a terrific explosion shook the vicinity. Immediately there was a great cloud of smoke in the air, a cloud which soon gave way to bright, sparkling flames. Parts of the ship were seen flying in all directions as the powder and ammunition continued to blow up. The short, glorious career of the *Merrimac*, built to wrest supremacy of the seas from the North, was over. But every Southerner will always remember this ironclad battleship with pride, for the *Merrimac* covered herself with honor and glory in her brief dramatic career.

Two hours after the *Merrimac* had been destroyed, President Lincoln was told of the event. That same morning he went to Craney Island to visit the flaming, smoldering ruins before his return to Washington. The *Monitor* passed Craney Island at eight that same morning, and the crew saw many fragments of their late opponent floating in the water.

Less than two hours afterwards the *Monitor* anchored in Norfolk Harbor. It seemed to the men aboard that they were destined to enjoy a long glorious career aboard their invincible ship, but the David among battleships had an unhappy fate awaiting her.

On December 29, 1862, the *Monitor* left Hampton Roads in tow of the *Rhode Island*, headed for Beaufort, North Carolina. Also in the expedition were the *Passaic* and the *State of Georgia*. Her new captain, Commander John P. Bankhead, was worried about the weather and the ability of the *Monitor* to make the sea voyage. However, the ocean was calm when the ironclad rounded Cape Henry. Now the long trip southward began in earnest.

The following day, as she neared Cape Hatteras, the *Monitor* was hit by a wind which came in fresh from the southeast. A storm began by nightfall and increased to a bad gale in a few hours. The *Monitor* began to wallow helplessly in the terrific seas, and around midnight Captain Bankhead ordered a red lantern, the signal of distress, hoisted to the masthead. Shortly afterwards the violent pitching and rolling became so serious that he ordered the towing hawser cut, and the anchor let go. But this did not prevent tons and tons of water from pouring into the *Monitor*.

The *Rhode Island* immediately came about, and Captain Trenchard sent three lifeboats across to the sinking ironclad. The first lifeboat stove in her side against the hull of the battleship. In spite of this, several men were taken off, and the other two lifeboats removed a majority of the crew. Finally all but sixteen men had left the *Monitor*.

One old quartermaster was seen carrying his clothes bag under his arm and was reprimanded for trying to save his own belongings in an emergency. The quartermaster, without replying in his own defense, threw the bag into the lifeboat. Later, when the lifeboat returned to the safety of the *Rhode Island*, the bundle was passed up over the side, and a tiny messenger boy was discovered inside, petrified with fear but otherwise unharmed. The quartermaster, realizing that the boy was too afraid to jump into a lifeboat, had jammed him into the bag and carried him off the *Monitor*, thus saving his life.

When the three lifeboats and their occupants had reached the *Rhode Island* safely, another boat was despatched to pick up the remaining sixteen men still aboard the doomed ship. Having to row into the wind, the rescuers made slow progress. Finally the light from the *Monitor* disappeared from view, and the men in the lifeboat knew that the proud Northern warship had gone down with all sixteen aboard, four officers and twelve men, it was later discovered.

The lifeboat itself was in trouble and was unable to return to the *Rhode Island*. When morning came an impromptu flag of distress was rigged—a large black silk handkerchief. A few hours later a schooner hove in sight, and her captain noticed the black pennant. He fled the scene, evidently fearing an attack by pirates whose emblem was a black pennant. A few hours later, a second schooner sailed in close enough to recognize that the men from the Northern Navy and took them aboard. They were later landed at Beaufort, North Carolina.

Both the *Merrimac* and the *Monitor* had short careers, but naval history was made that day in 1862 when they battled off Fortress Monroe, Virginia. Although it was not the first engagement between ironclads, and although neither ship could have successfully sailed the open sea, it was only a question of time until better ironclads would be built which could steam across the ocean. The old sailing ships with their wooden hulls were no longer to participate in battle. The beautiful men-of-war with their splendid lines and billowing canvas sails gave way to the ironclads. Metal monsters had superseded the wooden sailing vessels in war as well in peace.

Although it is not common knowledge, the location of the wreck of the *Monitor* has been known for many years. At one time plans were made for salvaging her and towing her into Washington, D. C., to be placed on permanent exhibition. Unfortunately these plans were later abandoned.

It was my privilege recently to fly out to sea from the coast of North Carolina near Cape Hatteras and look down at the watery resting place of the Ericsson-built "cheese box on a raft," the ironclad which prevented Southern forces from gaining ascendency over the Northern fleet eighty-seven years before.

As we looked down through the clear water where the Northern battleship rested on the bottom, I wondered whether the government would ever raise the ironclad which saved the Union from defeat in 1862. Perhaps, after all, it is better that the *Monitor* should remain submerged in the Atlantic, an illustrious companion to the steamer *Portland* and thousands of other vessels claimed by the relentless sea.

23. Theodosia Burr's Strange Story

THEODOSIA BURR, the proud, brilliant daughter of Aaron Burr, once Vice-President of the United States, was one of the most talented women of her day. Sailing to New York in 1812, she and the ship on which she was traveling, vanished completely, and people have been discussing her fate ever since.

When I first pieced together her story it seemed too fantastic to be true, and I devoted much time and energy to finding any fallacies in my reconstruction. As I dug deeper into the records, I grew certain that every bit of my discovery was the truth. Not only did investigation prove the story accurate, but I was able to eliminate four other conflicting accounts as chronologically impossible.

Efforts to check the various clues led from state to state, and from lonely shores to the big cities of America. The story did not unfold itself suddenly, as have many others I have investigated. It resisted solution until the very end. Each part of the puzzle had to be literally struggled over day after day. The most unusual chase was from Nag's Head, North Carolina, to Elizabeth City and then to Amherst College and finally to New York City.

Theodosia Burr, the subject of our story, was born June 23, 1783, the daughter of the Revolutionary hero Aaron Burr and his wife Theodosia. Early in life, she was held high in the air by her proud father as they watched the British troops evacuating

New York. Although Theo, as her father called her, was only
five months old, she was even then considered a child of rare
beauty.

Colonel Aaron Burr planned that his daughter should be given
every possible opportunity to improve her mind. The descendant of two presidents of Princeton College should, if she could,
become a great woman. Burr was thoroughly disgusted with
the frivolous education for girls at that time. Although many
men of the day were well-educated, it was not thought essential
or even desirable that women should be their peers. There were
only two acknowledged alternatives for a girl: marriage, or
staying at home with her parents. Young women were prepared
for life by learning to embroider, play the piano-forte, sing de-
spondent love songs, and work samplers. All men had a chance
to become famous, but they had no desire for a woman to be
other than—just a woman. The wives of many renowned Revolutionary leaders were illiterate, and few of them were cultured
in any other way.

Aaron Burr, without neglecting Theo's feminine accomplishments, was determined that his daughter should be as well edu-
cated as any man of the period. He sat up one entire night
reading Mary Wollstonecraft's book, *A Vindication of the
Rights of Women*, and then determined that Theodosia should
be brought up on the precepts of mental and moral development
which the book emphasized. He told Theo of his plans early in
her childhood.

By the time she was ten, Theo could read Horace and Terence
in the original Latin and speak French with remarkable grace,
and she had studied Greek. She played the harp and the piano-
forte, rode, skated, and danced. At ten she was plump but very
pretty; she hated cats, was full of pranks, and fond of telling
fibs. She had a worshipful admiration for her illustrious father.

Theodosia's mother died the following year, in 1794, and
father and daughter were drawn even closer together. In spite

of the fact that, as a member of the United States Senate, he was away a great deal, Burr kept in touch with her constantly. Letters between the two became vital links, and this means of exchanging thoughts was kept up until Theodosia's death. One typical letter which precedes Mrs. Burr's death suffices to show the remarkably close relationship between father and daughter.

I rose up suddenly from the sofa, and rubbing my head— "What book shall I buy for her?" said I to myself. "She reads so much and so rapidly that it is not easy to find proper and amusing French books for her; and yet I am so flattered with her progress in that language, that I am resolved that she shall at all events, be gratified ... I went into one bookseller's after another. I found plenty of fairy tales and such nonsense, fit for the generality of children of nine or ten years old. "These," said I, "will never do. Her understanding begins to be above such things"; but I could see nothing that I would offer with pleasure to an *intelligent, well-informed girl of nine years old.* I began to be discouraged. The hour of dining was come. "But I will search a little longer," I persevered. At last I found it. I found the very thing I sought ... It was a work of fancy, but replete with instruction and amusement. I must present it with my own hand.

I am, my dear Theo,
Your affectionate papa,
A. Burr

At the age of fourteen Theodosia was rosy-cheeked, graceful, extremely self-assured and positive. With the death of her mother she gradually assumed the position of mistress of the household at Richmond Hill, Manhattan. In spite of her social duties and obligations, however, Theodosia was able to read two hundred lines daily from Homer, translate French comedies, and keep up with all the philosophical writers of her day. Her father's letters continued to mold her to his will, for her habits, her occupations, and even her features were under his guidance.

He told her to avoid alike the sneer of contempt and the smile which was really a simper.

Colonel Joseph Alston, who later became Governor of South Carolina, became deeply interested in Theodosia late in 1800, and in December asked for her hand in marriage. Theodosia promptly referred Mr. Alston to Aristotle, and told him that Aristotle had said a man should not marry before thirty-six. "Pray, Mr. Alston," she ended, "what arguments have you to oppose such authority?" After a long and involved answer from Alston, Theodosia capitulated, and they were married at Albany, February 2, 1801, when he was twenty-two and she was seventeen. Joseph Alston took his bride back to his plantation at the Oaks on Debordieu Island in the Waccamaw River, South Carolina. The following year their son was born, Aaron Burr Alston.

At the time of his daughter's marriage Colonel Aaron Burr was being considered for the highest office in the land. Both he and Thomas Jefferson had received seventy-three votes for the presidency. This tie of votes naturally created a deadlock, and there were thirty-five more attempts to elect a president before Alexander Hamilton assisted in an arrangement whereby Jefferson was elected to the presidency and Burr became Vice-President.

In July, 1804, Theodosia received the shocking news that her father had killed Alexander Hamilton in a duel. Soon afterwards he visited Blennerhasset's Island on the Ohio River in an effort to arrange with other conspirators to become Emperor Aaron I of Mexico. This plan met with opposition from the United States Government; Burr was accused of treason, and arrested on February 19, 1807. He was acquitted, however, at the trial. With the possibility of further charges to be brought against him, Burr fled to England, and remained there for four years.

Regardless of her marriage with Alston and the love she gave both her husband and her son, the most predominant factor in Theodosia Burr's life was her close relationship with her father.

Aaron Burr worshipped her, and that feeling was more than returned by his daughter. But what seems amazing in this close
relationship is the complete confidence between the two extending to matters which the average American father would hesitate
to discuss even with his son. Aaron Burr had sent Theodosia his
diaries for safe keeping, and often asked her to look up some
portion and copy it for him. The diaries contained some of the
most scandalous passages devotees of Eros have ever recorded.

Theodosia found her father's absence a very hard burden to
bear, though one which her husband was able to appreciate.
Finally Burr wrote that he was sailing home. He left aboard
the *Aurora*, disguised as a Mr. De Gamelli. Arriving in Boston,
he further disguised himself with a wig and false whiskers. The
government might be after him; he owed thousands of dollars to
various people; and there were many political enemies who
might still have grievances. Making his way to Mrs. Goodrich's
boarding house at Cornhill Square, he obtained lodgings for the
night. He had spent all his money and did not have the means
to engage passage to New York. But he did have a trunkful of
books acceptable at Harvard College. President Kirkland of
Harvard gave him forty dollars for several volumes, with the
assurance that Burr could redeem them at any time.

After several adventures on board the ship which carried him
to New York, he was finally taken ashore by "two vagabonds
in a skiff," who landed him in the city at half past eleven at
night.

The first night Burr was forced to sleep in a lodging house
garret with five other men, paying the sum of twelve cents for
his bed. He remained hidden in New York for three weeks
while his close friends attempted to sound out the government
and the more pressing of his creditors as to his setting up law
practice again. Finally it was believed safe to insert a small notice in the local paper announcing that Aaron Burr had set up
offices at 9 Nassau Street, New York, and was ready for active

practice. As a result of this notice, over five hundred friends and associates visited him before nightfall of the first day, and before a fortnight had passed Aaron Burr had earned two thousand dollars.

Unfortunately, a terrible blow was about to fall. He received a letter from Theodosia, dated July 12, 1812, shattering all his dreams for the future:

A few miserable days past, my dear father, and your late letters would have gladdened my soul; and even now I rejoice at their contents as much as it is possible for me to rejoice at anything. I have lost my boy. My child is gone forever. He expired on the 30th of June.

My head is not now sufficiently collected to say anything further. May Heaven, by other blessings, make you some amends for the noble grandson you have lost.

Theodosia.

Theodosia soon became desperately ill. The southern climate, combined with her sufferings at the death of her son and the fears she had for her father's welfare, finally prostrated her. Eventually it was arranged for her to go to New York, in the hope that the change of environment would benefit her. Burr sent his friend, Timothy Green, to South Carolina to accompany Theodosia back to New York by ship. Joseph Alston, now Governor of South Carolina, was offended that Burr should think it necessary to send a man from New York to assist his wife. He felt that if Mrs. Alston had needed someone to attend her, either he or one of his brothers could have accompanied her. Alston had planned to charter a vessel for Theodosia's journey northward, but, before this could be done, Green obtained passage on another ship.

The name of the vessel was *Patriot*. She was a small, fast pilot boat which had often been used as a privateer. Theodosia Alston and Timothy Green boarded her at Georgetown, South

Carolina, on December 30, 1812, and in so doing ventured into disaster, confused, tangled and obscure. The pilot boat never reached New York, and neither Theodosia Burr nor anyone else aboard the vessel was ever heard from again. The mystery was to remain with Governor Alston for the remaining three years of his life, and with Aaron Burr until his death in 1836.

As the weeks passed and no information regarding the *Patriot* came to them, the husband in South Carolina and the father in New York exchanged many apprehensive letters. Finally they decided to accept the inevitable conclusion that Theodosia had died either at the hand of pirates or by drowning. In February, 1813, Governor Alston wrote to Colonel Aaron Burr:

Your letter of the 10th, my friend, is received. This assurance of my fate was not wanting. Authentic accounts from Bermuda and Nassau, as late as January 30, connected with your letter from New York of the 28th, had already forced upon me the dreadful conviction that we had no more hope . . . My boy—my wife—gone, both! This, then, is the end of all the hope we had formed. You may well observe that you feel severed from the human race. She was the last tie that bound us to the species. What have we left? . . . You are the only person in the world with whom I can commune on this subject; for you are the only person whose feelings can have any community with mine. You knew those we loved. Here, none know them; none valued them as they deserved. The talents of my boy, his rare elevation of character, his already extensive reputation for so early an age, made his death regretted by the pride of my family; but though certain of the loss of my not less admirable wife, they seem to consider it like the loss of an ordinary woman. Alas! they knew nothing of my heart. They have never known anything of it. After all, he is a poor actor who cannot sustain his little hour upon the stage, be his part what it may. But the man who has been deemed worthy of the heart of *Theodosia Burr,* and who has felt what it was to be blessed with such a woman's, will never forget his elevation.

Joseph Alston

294

Governor Alston never recovered from the loss of both his only son and his devoted wife, and he died in the year 1816. Aaron Burr, made of stronger fiber, lived until September 14, 1836.

THEODOSIA'S FATE

AN INTERESTING comparison can be made between the voyage of the *Mary Celeste* and the *Patriot*. I told in detail in my book, *Mysteries and Adventures along the Atlantic Coast*, the strange story of the *Mary Celeste*, which sailed from New York in 1872, with ten persons aboard, none of whom were ever seen again. The brigantine itself was picked up a month later, abandoned at sea, with no indication of what had caused the ship's company to leave. The mystery of the *Mary Celeste* has never been fully explained. The case of Theodosia Burr and the *Patriot* rivals and in some respects even surpasses the gripping story of the *Mary Celeste*.

In analyzing events on the *Celeste*, I could only prove the solution I believe correct by circumstantial evidence. The mystery of the *Patriot* was at first even more difficult to solve, for there was no way of telling whether the schooner which washed ashore at Nag's Head was actually the *Patriot*. However, by the time all the evidence had been collected and evaluated and the story made ready for telling, there were many sworn statements and much tangible evidence to reinforce my theories. Although there have been several other versions of the fate of the *Patriot*, I believe I can prove none of them are accurate.

With all my information at hand, I made my way out to the great barrier beach on which the community of Nag's Head stands. The lonely stretches of beach grass, the curved hills and irregular valleys and hollows attracted me, and the long sweep of the outer shore, with the wild, thundering surf, drew me on. What an impressive geographical phenomenon this outer beach is, running all the way from the Little Life Boat Station south of Virginia Beach through False Cape, Kitty Hawk, Oregon Inlet, Rodanthe, past Cape Hatteras to reach Ocracoke Island and finally Cape Lookout, located out to sea from Beaufort, North Carolina! This 180-mile barrier reef protects Currituck Sound, Albemarle Sound, Pamlico Sound, and Core Sound from the furies of the ocean.

Countless shipwrecks had occurred along the beach, and many pirates and buccaneers sailed in the vicinity. Blackbeard himself considered the region his particular cruising ground, and he met his death at the hands of fearless Lieutenant Robert Maynard inside Ocracoke Inlet, not too far from where I was walking. The shipwrecks included such famous ones as the *Metropolis*, *Aaron Reppard*, *Henry P. Simmons*, *Carl Gerhard*, *Lizzie S. Haynes* and the *Elizabeth*. All of them took place many years after the *Patriot* had come ashore two miles below Nag's Head.

I had much to accomplish in my visit and hardly knew where to begin. My first two leads turned out to be hoaxes, but, for the elucidation of some reader who may know about them and believe them to be true, I include them here.

The first hoax concerns an alleged son of Aaron Burr, whose mother, he claimed, remarried after Burr's death in 1836. In 1902, at the age of 108, Charles Henry Burr Crosby, (he had adopted his "stepfather's" name), came forward with the claim that he was Aaron Burr's son. He also claimed to know something about the death of his "sister," Theodosia.

Crosby said that in 1813 he had shipped aboard the sloop *Independence* as a cook, and in the course of its voyage, the ship had picked up two men adrift on a raft. Their names were Gibbs and Wansley, and they claimed to be shipwrecked merchants. One night Crosby overheard them talking. Gibbs was telling Wansley that they never should have made Theodosia Burr

walk the plank after their pirate captain captured the *Patriot*.
Wansley agreed with his friend but added that their captain
would have killed them if they had disobeyed.

Realizing that these two men were pirates who had helped to
capture the *Patriot* that same year, Crosby notified his captain.
The two pirates were placed in irons for the rest of the voyage.
Then, according to Crosby, they were taken ashore in New
York and prosecuted by Aaron Burr. Burr won his alleged case,
and the pirates were convicted and hanged. Crosby's confused
story thus attempted to solve the mystery of what happened to
Theodosia. However, it is extremely doubtful that he actually
was Burr's son.

Moreover, Crosby chose the wrong pirates with which to im-
plement his yarn. Actually there were two such pirates (I mentioned them in my book, *Pirates and Buccaneers*), but that is
where the truth of Crosby's story ends. Charles Gibbs and
Thomas J. Wansley never met each other until the year 1830,
when they plotted the capture of the brig *Vineyard*. After
scuttling the ship off Coney Island, New York, they rowed
ashore at Pelican Island and here they were arrested. Later they
were tried for piracy, and both were hanged April 22, 1831.*
The brig they captured in 1830 could have no connection with
Theodosia Burr, who died in 1813, and Crosby's story can therefore be discarded as a hoax.

The second spurious tale concerns a mysterious grave in the
old Saint Paul's Episcopal Cemetery at Alexandria, Virginia.
The inscription on the stone reads:

To the memory of a female stranger whose mortal sufferings terminated on the 14th day of October, 1816, aged 23 years and 8
months.
This stone is placed here by her disconsolate husband, in whose

---

* Part of Gibb's body was preserved in a bottle and presented to the
Harvard College Medical School.

arms she sighed her last breath and who under God did his utmost to soothe the cold, dread fear of death.

Romantic tradition in Alexandria says that the woman buried with this inscription was Theodosia Burr. According to the adherents of this story, Theodosia left the *Patriot* with her lover, whom she secretly (and bigamously!) married. Many persons saw the two when they arrived in Alexandria. The woman, a creature of rare beauty, soon became very ill, and her frantic husband called a doctor. When the doctor opened the door of the sick room, he found that the husband of the beautiful lady had placed a brace of pistols on the table.

"Do not be too inquisitive," the husband said. "Ask her no questions about her family, but cure her if you can. If you ask her a single question about who she is, I'll blow your head off." Although the doctor was terribly frightened, he did his best to administer to the woman. She rapidly grew worse, however, and died the next day. The husband contracted for the strangely-worded tombstone and left Alexandria. Two years later he returned and paid a short visit to his wife's grave. For many years his visits continued, but he always refused to reveal either his identity or that of the woman.

The legend that he was the husband of Theodosia Burr quickly sprang up and has been repeated for more than one hundred and thirty years. But Theodosia had been dead for at least three years at the time of the young woman's death. Furthermore, the age given on the tombstone was twenty-three, and Theodosia would have been thirty-two when the lady of mystery died in the Alexandria hotel in 1816.

Now let us return to the actual circumstances which followed the embarkation of Theodosia Burr and her escort, Timothy Green, from Georgetown,* South Carolina, on December 30,

---

* Many mistakenly believe that the *Patriot* sailed from Charleston.

1813. When Captain Overstocks guided the pilot boat *Patriot* out to sea, her guns were stored below deck. The *Patriot* was a speedy sailer and the voyage was expected to take no more than five or six days. The captain carried a message from Governor Alston himself, asking that, because of her illness, his wife be allowed passage through the British blockade to New York. Two days later the British warships intercepted the pilot boat, the message was presented and honored, and the *Patriot* sailed through the blockade and continued until she was out of sight of the British men-of-war.

That very night a terrific gale lashed the Carolina coast, and the British officers believed that the little pilot boat must have foundered with all on board. Actually, the pilot boat did stay afloat, but she had been dismasted and damaged considerably by the gale.

On the morning after the storm, January 3, 1813, the battered *Patriot* was sighted by Captain Dominique You, former second mate for pirate Jean Lafitte. According to his later confession, he quickly bore down on the helpless vessel. There was no need for the firing of cannon, and the pirate captain and his crew soon took over the schooner. The captured men could not be allowed to live and provide the testimony which would hang the pirates later. Every one of them, including Captain Overstocks and Timothy Green, was hustled up on deck, lashed to the mast, and executed. According to eye witnesses, in ransacking the vessel, the buccaneers discovered Theodosia Burr in her cabin, seized her, and brought her up on deck to face the giant pirate captain.

"What is your name?" the ruffian asked.

"Theodosia Burr, the daughter of Aaron Burr, ex-Vice-President of the United States. I am the wife of Governor Joseph Alston of South Carolina."

"A grand conquest," exclaimed one of the pirates, "and we

shall have a jolly time with her." He began to advance toward Theodosia.

"Back, all of you," shouted Dominique You, and gave the speaker a tremendous blow with his huge fist. "Now you know that she must die. Death is the bond I signed, but never rape. Back, then, all of you." The men murmured at first, but the huge captain made another threatening gesture, and the pirate crew sullenly retired to their quarters.

Dominique You then told Theodosia Burr that he had no alternative but to execute her as he had all the others, and she agreed that it was better to have it done at once. She went over to the rail, where the plank had been tied across the center of the taffrail. A moment later, with two pirates to assist her, she walked up to the middle of the plank and paused, balancing the plank over the taffrail.

Then, with eyes uplifted, and with arms outstretched, Theodosia Burr walked calmly down the slanting plank into the sea.

The pirates spent the next few hours ransacking the pilot boat, gathering together their spoils, and preparing to return to the ship. A sail on the horizon hurried them, however, and their original plans to burn the *Patriot* had to be abandoned. Much of the material in Theodosia's cabin was left behind, including an oil painting of herself and a trunkful of dresses. At a roar from the captain the pirates transferred to their own ship, hoisted sail, and were soon far away.*

A short time later the pirates were practically wiped out when they attempted to capture another ship, and only three or four escaped.

The day after the pirates left the *Patriot*, she drifted within a few miles of Nag's Head, North Carolina, and wreckers from

---

* A surprising corroboration of my findings is a sworn statement made February 14, 1903, by Mrs. Harriette Sprague before Notary Freeman Atwell at Cass County, Michigan, of the confession in 1848 of Frank Burdick, who admitted that he was one of the pirates who murdered Theodosia Burr in 1813. The story agrees essentially with my account.

the area sailed out and boarded the abandoned vessel. She was in battered condition because of the storm and could only stay afloat a few hours, but the men removed whatever they could before she went to the bottom. While they were exploring the *Patriot,* the wreckers observed several things: the rudder was fastened; breakfast was set on the table in the cabin; and the berths were not made up. Although the cabins were all in disorder, there was no trace of blood or violence.

One wrecker named Mann, who had a sweetheart at Nag's Head, took as his share of the salvage a trunkful of dresses, some wax flowers, and a woman's portrait in oil which he had found resting on a locker. Everything in that particular cabin indicated that its occupant had been a lady of refinement and fortune. Apparently she had been the only woman passenger aboard the pilot boat.

When Mann went ashore that afternoon, he presented his sweetheart, Lovie Tillet, with his share of the spoils from the *Patriot.* Lovie lived in a shack made from the timbers of half a dozen shipwrecks, thatched with reeds and oakum. To brighten her surroundings, she hung the oil painting against the wall of her hut, where it remained for many years. Then she placed the wax flowers on the rude table and put away the dresses in a trunk.

Something went wrong with the romance between Lovie Tillet and young Mann, and Lovie married a rival suitor, John Wescott. Many years later when Lovie was an old woman and had gained a great deal in weight, she fell ill and required medical treatment. Dr. William Gaskins Pool of Elizabeth City was called to treat her. After he had finished with his patient, Dr. Pool glanced across the room at the portrait on the crude wall.

"Where did you get that?" he asked the old lady.

"My young man gave me that over fifty years ago," she answered, "but I married someone else after all."

Dr. Pool strode across the room and brushed aside the cobwebs which festooned the picture. In the semi-darkness he saw the striking face of an unusual woman. The incongruity of finding a portrait so well-executed hanging on the wall of this ramshackle hut impressed the doctor.

"Do you know who it is in the painting?" he asked Mrs. Wescott.

"All I know is that they went out to the wreck of a pilot boat and brought the painting back along with a lot of other things. The picture came from a woman's cabin on the vessel. The other things are in the trunk over there."

Dr. Pool showed such interest in the painting that old Mrs. Wescott ordered her family to open the trunk. They pulled out two soft black silk dresses and a lovely black lace shawl. The apparel was that of a petite gentlewoman. The dresses had very full skirts gathered at the waist, low-cut bodices, and short sleeves.

At the conclusion of his visit Dr. Pool invited Mrs. Wescott to come to his home when she recovered from her illness. Some time later she accepted his invitation, arriving in a tread cart which was none too big for her over-sized body. Lovie Wescott was a tall woman weighing over 250 pounds, but she had altered one of Theodosia's gowns for the occasion by ripping the garment apart in the back and inserting a homespun gore. The lace shawl held together over her shoulders with a long steel hair pin. In her hands she carried her most prized possession, the Theodosia Burr portrait, and she presented it to Dr. Pool in appreciation for his professional services.

Later a careful examination revealed that the portrait had been executed by an outstanding artist, John Vanderlyn. The color work was very good, executed with advantage to the pink cheeks, red lips, piercing black eyes, and hair tinged with auburn. The subject wore a white muslin gown of an empire cut. But it was the round full jaw which seemed to indicate beyond any reasonable doubt that it was indeed a painting of Theodosia

Burr, probably done in 1811 or early 1812 when she was twenty-eight or twenty-nine years old. In its emphasis on the vigorous jaw, the painting is quite similar to the earlier portrait by Vanderlyn.

The painting found on the *Patriot* and given to Dr. Pool by Mrs. Wescott has been exhibited for many years and copied many times, and no one has ever claimed that the subject was anyone other than Theodosia. A dozen members of her family have expressed the opinion that it *could* be no one else.

In July, 1888, Mrs. Stella E. P. Drake, fourth cousin of Theodosia Burr, visited Elizabeth City to examine the painting at the home of Dr. Pool, and a local writer interviewed her. He was amazed by the resemblance between Mrs. Drake and the subject of the painting. The two women had the same piercing black eyes, and the same brunette complexion. Mrs. Drake, in turn, thought that the painting was truly a likeness of Theodosia.

Dr. Pool kept the portrait for the remainder of his life, and when he died, his daughter, Mrs. Anna Overmann acquired it. According to Lovie Wescott's grandson, it was on exhibition in a museum around 1905. Some years later Mr. Herbert Lee Pratt of Glen Cove, New York, purchased the painting. At his death in 1945 his collection was broken up, and while Amherst College received the bulk of his art treasures, his immediate family kept the Theodosia Burr portrait, which is now officially listed in the Frick Art Reference Library as the Theodosia Burr portrait by John Vanderlyn.

The final episode in my visit to Nag's Head came three days after my first arrival there. I had walked all around the ancient settlement looking for the old shacks and huts which had been built out of the wrecks of ships. They had vanished, however, with the advance of Nag's Head as a flourishing summer resort.

Visiting the Coast Guard Station, I met Chief Boatswain's

Mate Nevin Wescott. I asked him if he had ever heard of the Theodosia Burr painting which had been found in a hut.

"I sure have," he replied, "and if you go over to Manteo, my father'll tell you the whole story."

An hour and a quarter later I had reached Manteo, and soon found the residence where John Wescott, a retired coastguardsman, lives on Water Street. I told him Theodosia's story in full, and he listened attentively until I had finished.

"Well, Mr. Snow, you sure have come to the right place. My own grandmother was the woman who gave Dr. Pool the painting. Her name was Lovie Tillet when she got the painting and the dresses. One of the young wreckers down the beach was mad about her and gave her the dresses, wax flowers, and the painting which he'd taken from the pilot boat. But it didn't do him any good. She married John Wescott later on, who, of course, was my grandfather."

Although the fate of Theodosia Burr is no longer a mystery, there remains one question which will always remain unanswered.

In the early part of January, 1813, there drifted ashore at Cape Charles, Virginia, the dead body of a young woman, whose clothes and general appearance gave every indication of refinement. She was buried on a farm a short distance away, and is still there, unidentified and undisturbed.

Was it the body of Theodosia Burr?

Index

Index

INDEX

INDEX

INDEX

INDEX

INDEX

INDEX

INDEX

INDEX

INDEX

INDEX

INDEX

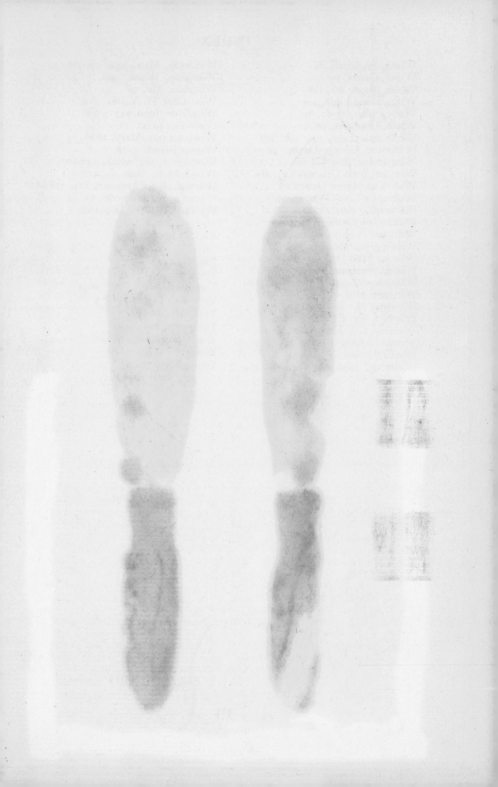

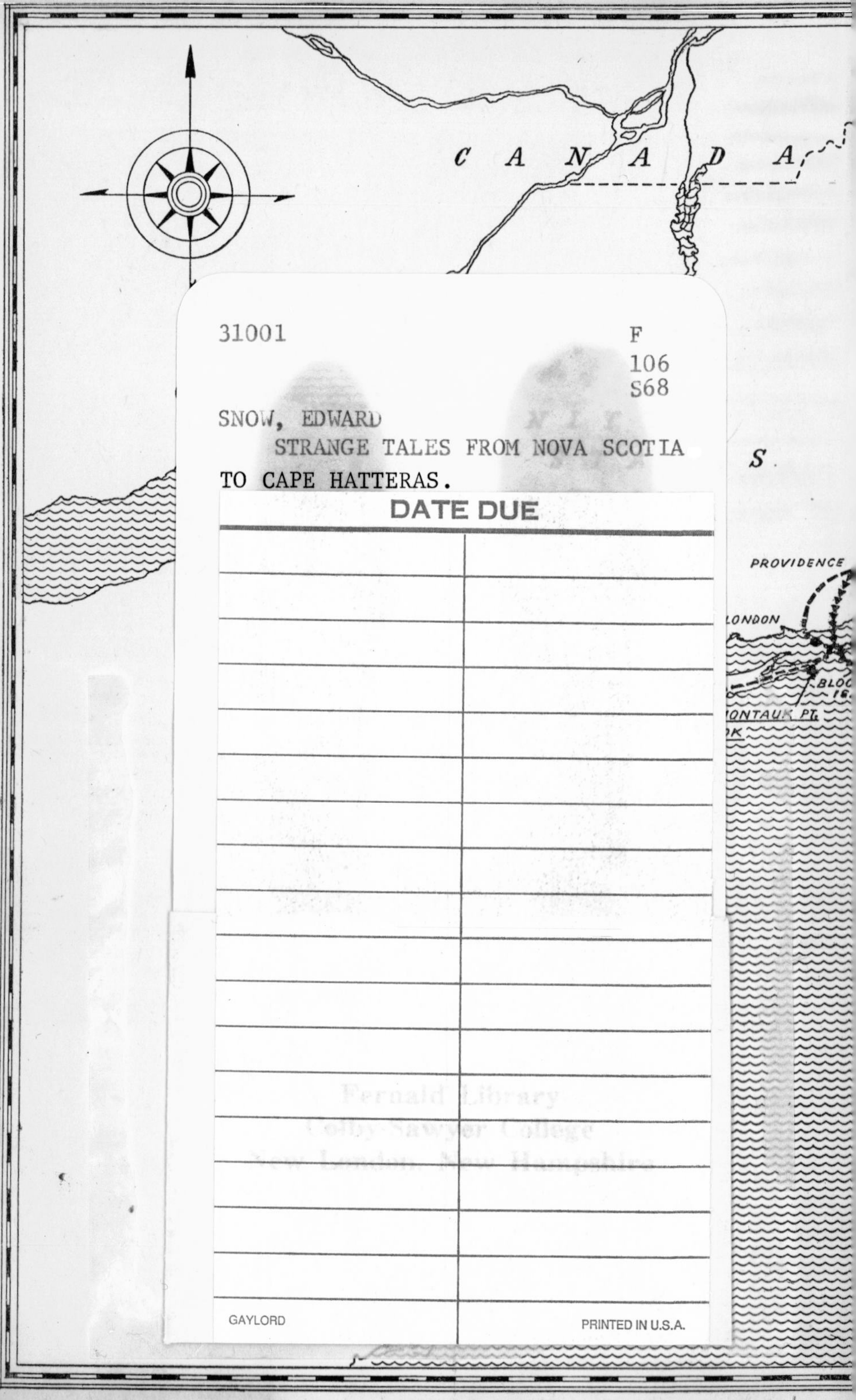
C A N A D A
PROVIDENCE